CHINA
THE EMERGING CHALLENGE:
A Christian Perspective

CHINA
THE EMERGING CHALLENGE:
A Christian Perspective

PAUL E. KAUFFMAN

foreword by
RUTH BELL GRAHAM

BAKER BOOK HOUSE
Grand Rapids, Michigan 49506

Some material in this book has been selected and adapted from a trilogy previously written by the author. Chapters 1-6 appeared in *China Yesterday*; Chapters 8-11 were taken from *China Today*; and chapters 15, 16, 18, and 19 appeared in *China Tomorrow*.

ISBN: 0-8010-5442-7

Printed in the United States of America

# Contents

Foreword   7
China's Major Dynasties   9

Part ONE

The Historical Challenge
From Confucius Through Communism

1 Before Christ   13
2 Silks and Gunpowder   30
3 The Opium Trigger   42
4 The Rape of China   51
5 The Sun Still Shines   62
6 Five Stars over China   73
7 The Waning of the Revolution   94

Part TWO

The Religious Challenge
The Impact of Christianity on China

8 Yesterday's Cross   115
9 The Church Takes Root   127
10 The Bold Ones   144
11 Through the Fire   159
12 The Church Becomes Visible   173
13 House Churches, Prisons, and Saints   206
14 Lessons from China's Church   223

63862

Part THREE

The Contemporary Challenge
An Indigenous Church

15 Conflict of Minds   239
16 Chinese Christianity   253
17 Through the Open Door   266
18 West Meets East Again   292
19 The Contemporary Challenge   306
   Spelling Guide   317

Foreword

It's a privilege to be asked to write a foreword to Paul Kauffman's portrayal of the land that we both call home.

We were both born of missionary parents who not only proved their love for China and its people but also passed on that love to us.

Having spent most of our early years there, we learned to appreciate the qualities we found in her people. My father, Dr. Nelson Bell, in his book *Foreign Devil in China,* told of those early years that for him involved life as a physician in a mission hospital.

It was my privilege to return in May of 1980 to our old home with my brother and my two sisters. We saw some of the changes that thirty years of political struggle had created, but we also experienced something of the changelessness of China's people.

Paul Kauffman, in this book, does us all a service by tracing, in interesting and highly readable form, the history of the Christian impact on China from the seventh century until today. He is known as a careful and accurate observer of the contemporary Chinese scene. That has not been an easy task. It required primarily a basic knowledge and understanding of the Chinese people, as well as their language. He has acquired this over forty years of close association with them, first in China for seventeen years, and then in Hong Kong. But he has had an additional advantage in that he has never lost sight of the sovereignty of God through all that has transpired. That triumphant conviction that God still loves and still rules in His world is echoed on almost every page.

It is not surprising that China has long been known as a land of mystery. The Chinese have created a unique and powerful culture that has enabled them, for the most part in isolation from the rest of the world, to survive a tempestuous history for more than fifty centuries. Today the Chinese make up a fourth of the earth's people, and they have extricated themselves from the demeaning submission of the past two centuries to become a powerful factor in international relations. Still, China holds an almost magical fascination.

The intensive, hectic, and, at times, disastrous social experiment presided over by Chairman Mao and The Gang of Four was attempted behind a deliberately constructed Bamboo Curtain. Even today, as tourists flood the Middle Kingdom, they are met by a well-oiled propaganda machine that makes the discovery of reality difficult. China still remains a land of mystery. So we are indebted to Paul Kauffman for his compelling insights. His etchings are clear enough for all to understand.

His greatest contribution, in my opinion, is in helping us to follow the progress of the church in China from its earliest days until now. It is a fascinating story, the last chapter of which is still to be written as God continues His quiet work in that great land.

Ruth Bell Graham

China's Major Dynasties

Shang (1766-1122 B.C.)

The Shang dynasty flourished in the Yellow River valley. Writing and wheeled chariots were in use in this brilliant but oft-times barbaric civilization.

Zhou (Chou) (1122-255 B.C.)

The declining years of the Zhou (Chou) dynasty fostered China's great sages—Confucius, Mencius, and Lao-tzu.

Qin (Ch'in) (255-206 B.C.)

China's first emperor extended the kingdom, unified the languages, constructed the Great Wall, and brought much reform during the Qin (Ch'in) dynasty.

Han (206 B.C.-A.D. 220)

Great expansion of the Chinese Empire. First contact with "foreigners," influx of Buddhism and the export of Chinese products to Europe marked the dynasty of which the Chinese are most proud. They are the proud "sons of Han," in tribute to the great Han dynasty which flourished during the time of Christ's life on earth.

Six Dynasties (A.D. 220-589)

These were troubled times for a greatly divided land. Invasions and migrations within did not stop amazing developments in mathematics, astronomy, and horticulture during the frequent government changes of the Six Dynasties.

Sui (590-618)

During the Sui dynasty the great Han empire was reborn. The country was linked by an efficient transportation network.

Tang (618-906)

The Tang dynasty concentrated upon military expansion throughout Asia. Japan adopted much of its culture from the Tangs. Tribute was brought to the Chinese court from near and far as her greatness was discovered.

Song (Sung) (960-1279)

First rebuilding a shattered empire, the Song then built China's great cities which surpassed anything in the world. Modern government made its appearance, and so did movable type during the Song dynasty.

Yüan (1279-1368)

This was the age of the Mongol rules of China and the visits of Marco Polo. The world began to take note of China during the Yüan dynasty.

Ming (1368-1644)

Long years of peace under Chinese rule brought prosperity and the craftsmanship so valued today. Architecture, furniture, paintings, as well as science and technology, flourished during the renowned Ming dynasty.

Qing (Ch'ing or Manchu) (1644-1911)

The alien Manchus from the north conquered and then expanded the empire only to fall before other foreigners—this time from the West. The Qing dynasty was the last of the dynasties, bringing to an end 3,600 years of continual dynastic rule.

Note: The Pinyin spelling of Chinese names is used throughout. Because readers may be more familiar with the older Wade-Giles system, that spelling appears in parentheses behind the new spelling. Example: Beijing (Peking).

Part One

The Historical Challenge

From Confucius
Through Communism

1

Before Christ

How far back shall we go to tell the absorbing and vital story of China and her peoples? Archaeologists say some 400,000 years; that's the date they have given to the discovery of a skull in a cave just outside of modern day Beijing (Peking). That's too far back for us to go. No one really knows where the Chinese people came from or even when they made their first appearance.

Chinese legend insists that a fellow by the name of Pan Gu (P'an Ku) created the universe with the help of a motley assortment of creatures. He spent eighteen thousand years chiseling the earth into its present shape. All this hard work apparently killed him. At death a metamorphosis occurred. His flesh became the soil, his blood formed the rivers, his sweat the rain, his hair the vegetation. His left eye became the sun, his right eye the moon, his breath the wind, his voice became the thunder. Where did people come from? "Oh," says the legend, "they were the parasites that fed on Pan Gu's (P'an Ku's) body."

One fact is clear. The Chinese did not ooze from the mud of the Yellow River valley or evolve from the parasites that

Note: The Pinyin spelling of Chinese names is used throughout. Because readers may be more familiar with the older Wade-Giles system, that spelling appears in parentheses behind the new spelling. Example: Beijing (Peking).

fed on Pan Gu's (P'an Ku's) overworked body. "In the beginning God created. . . ." Adam was the first man and from his union with Eve all of earth's peoples have come. It is interesting to note that the Chinese are an Oriental people and so were the children of Israel and present-day Israelis. There are real similarities between traditional Jewish customs and traditional Chinese customs.

We are, however, able to penetrate rather deeply into China's past because the Chinese had a written language over three thousand years ago. This foundation of Chinese culture was amazingly well developed fifteen hundred years before Christ, with as many as twenty-five hundred different distinct characters. Contrast this with the fact that some of the earth's languages have not yet been reduced to writing.

In the early eighteenth century, excavators probed the soil of North Central China in Henan (Honan) province. There they discovered indisputable evidence of an ancient, highly developed Chinese civilization. This was the Shang dynasty, extant almost two thousand years before Christ (1766-1122 B.C.). Writing and artifacts depicted a people who had achieved an astonishingly high level of technological skill and cultural development. The people wore furs and silks, produced as yet unequaled bronzes, fabulous paintings, pottery, and carvings. They rode to war on wheeled chariots and erected elaborate buildings. These developments in China coincide with the time of Moses. Obviously this was not a sudden civilization but one that had developed over a good many years—Chinese historians say five thousand years ago.

Without question China has the earth's oldest living civilization. This in itself should, but seldom does, produce some humility in the Western world. Evidence, of course, does indicate that there were civilizations in the valleys of the Euphrates, Nile, and Tigris rivers before the Shang dynasty of the Yellow River valley. Only the Chinese civilization, however, has had the durability to survive to the present day.

In trying to discover why this civilization has survived when others have perished we can only offer clues. Arthur Smith offers one exceptional clue: "The Chinese have the loftiest moral codes which the human mind unaided by divine revelation has ever produced, and its crystalline precepts have been the rich inheritance of every successive present from every successive past." Considerable evidence does exist that the philosophers of China did arrive at pinnacles of moral teachings unattained by others of their age. Whether they were aided by divine revelation or not no one knows. That these moral codes provided the backbone that enables them to survive is an interesting and probably largely accurate observation.

Two dynasties which ruled China before the time of Christ are extremely important to an understanding of China. These are the Zhou (Chou) dynasty (1122-255 B.C.) and the Qin (Ch'in) dynasty (255-206 B.C.). The Zhou (Chou) dynasty is important for two reasons, one traditional, the other philosophical. This dynasty began the Chinese governmental tradition, "the mandate of heaven," and gave birth to its greatest philosophers.

No nation on earth has been so completely circumscribed by tradition. Even the current leaders follow and benefit from the precedents of history. For example, the "mandate of heaven" concept helps to explain dynastic succession. How did the Shang dynasty become the Zhou (Chou) dynasty? Very simply. The Zhou (Chou) conquered the Shang. Why? Because after nearly three hundred years of rule the Shang had become morally and physically weak, corrupt, and self-centered. Therefore, claimed the Zhou (Chou), they had a "mandate of heaven" to conquer and replace the corrupt Shang. Thus a pattern and a precedent was established.

. From that time on, every change of government in China came about because of a "mandate of heaven." Here is the oft-repeated pattern. A dynastic ruler at first makes great contributions to the welfare of people and nation. Eventually he becomes corrupt and immoral and therefore loses his right to rule. Out of the chaos comes a new ruler with a divine right to destroy the corrupt ruler and get China back on the right track. This of course is precisely what Mao Zedong (Mao Tse-tung) claimed he was doing when he ousted Chiang Kai-shek. Dr. Sun Yi-xian (Sun Yat-sen) before him used it as his reason for overthrowing the Mongols. Obviously, if a rebellion against the ruling power failed, it was because the leaders did not have a "mandate of heaven."

Time was always on the side of the patient people. Tradition kept things moving over the passing centuries. Just wait a little while, so they reasoned, and the present despotic, corrupt regime will be replaced by one that, at least for a time, will have the welfare of the people at heart. Thus China was kept alive by frequent transfusions of new leadership. People never despaired, because "this too shall pass." Only the people, China's timeless, magnificent peasants, were eternal.

This helps to explain why the Chinese peasant, even today, is basically apolitical. He had no say in his country's government and therefore he was not particularly interested in what dynasty or what man ruled China. An ancient classical poem goes like this:

> I work when the sun rises,
> I rest when the sun sets,
> What is the emperor's power to me?

For the peasant nothing changed but the seasons.

The second major contribution of the Zhou (Chou) dynasty was the three great Chinese philosophers, Confucius, Mencius, and Lao-tzu. It is perhaps significant that these philosophers lived not during the period of Zhou (Chou) greatness but in the time of its decline. Their philosophies grew, at least to some degree, out of the disorder and despair of their times. So thoroughly infused are their ideas into the culture of China that every Chinese living today is a reflection of the teachings of these three great men. Let's try to get an inkling of what their teachings have meant to China for the past twenty-five hundred years, and what they mean to China today.

Some scholars declare that in order to understand modern China one must start as early as Confucius (551-479 B.C.). This may not be early enough because Confucius, too, borrowed from China's long past. In fact, the Duke of Zhou (Chou) who lived centuries before Confucius has been long honored in China as the founder of the Confucian tradition. He is the fellow who spelled out in detail the principle of the "mandate of heaven" so often attributed to Confucius. The "decree of heaven," as Zhou (Chou) called it, guaranteed that if a ruler did not serve the people well he would be replaced by divine authorization. The idea was twofold: (a) a ruler ruled by divine decree, (b) heaven rejected the ruler who did not treat the people well. Here, amazingly early in human history, was the concept that a ruler existed for the people rather than the opposite.

The tradition of filial piety is also falsely attributed to Confucius. A book written long before the time of Confucius stated that the worst form of criminal was "the son who does not serve his father respectfully; . . . the father who cannot cherish his son but hates him; and the younger brother who does not bear in mind the evident intention of heaven, and will not respect his elder brother; and the elder brother who forgets the tender regard in which he should hold his younger brother." Such criminals, it was declared, should be punished unmercifully. This is a time-honored Chinese tradition and one that proved a great asset, as well as a liability, to succeeding generations.

Confucius was without question one of a rare breed of men who by the force of their teaching have influenced the course of history. We of the Western world know the name of Confucius better than any other Chinese. There is just cause for this fame. To try and sketch some of his concepts in brief form is a formidable task for two reasons. First, he was a man of great intellectual gifts. Secondly, his philosophy is best understood in the context of the times in which he lived.

Born in what is now Shandong (Shantung) province, in humble circumstances, though it is probable there was nobility among his ancestors, his own life was not an easy one. He had little formal education and was largely self-taught. These experiences gave him a compassion for the common people. He bemoaned the sad lot of the average peasant. He felt that some drastic changes had to be made, especially in government. His pet peeve was the aristocrats who ruled the country by virtue of the simple fact that they were born into a certain ruling family and not by virtue of ability or concern for the people. He shocked his age by teaching that any man might become a gentleman and a scholar. He formed a school to develop not only knowledge but by mental and moral discipline to develop new leaders for China.

It is important from our point of view to point out that Confucius was not a religious prophet or teacher. Only long after his death did he become a religious factor. In fact, the first Confucian temple was not built in China until after the Nestorian Christians were forced out of China about A.D.

700. He did not speak of God as we know Him. He apparently had no concept of a personal God. He conceived of a moral force in the universe which he termed "heaven" or "god," a mysterious power that somehow somewhere stood beside the man who tried to do what was "right." The term he used for this great mysterious moral force is the same word used in today's Chinese Bibles to translate "God"— Shén.

He was not concerned about life after death, only about this life and how it should be lived. When asked about death by a student he replied, "You do not yet understand life, how can you understand death?" He made no claim to ultimate truth. He did not profess to be divine or to have come as a savior. He only admitted to be searching for the truth.

His concept of the nature of man is difficult to define, though very important. Apparently he did not conceive of man as being intrinsically good or bad. All men, he said, are essentially equal, thus pioneering what Abraham Lincoln was to declare centuries later in his Gettysburg address, "All men are created equal." He believed that all men wanted and deserved happiness. Confucius declared in negative form a principle which Christ was later to enunciate in positive form, namely, "not doing to others what one does not wish them to do to oneself." He taught that we cause other people a great deal of unhappiness because we act out of ignorance. Consequently, he promoted the revolutionary idea of universal education centuries before it was to become a reality anywhere in the world.

Perhaps his greatest contribution was what has been called his "intellectual democracy." He believed that man should be permitted to think for himself. His brilliant, uncluttered mind blazed new trails for human thought, yet when he died in 479 B.C. most of his contemporaries thought he had died a failure. Confucius was probably the greatest philosopher the world has ever known. His teachings created ruts for the Chinese mind to follow for untold centuries. So revolutionary were some of his ideas, in the context of his time, that at least one leading modern-day Maoist, Guo Mo-jo (Kuo Mo-jo), has depicted Confucius as a champion of the rights of the common people, the first revolutionary.

The second of China's great philosophers, Mencius, has been called the forerunner of Freud, at least in his educative precepts. Mencius, who lived from about 372 to 289 B.C., was born not far from the birthplace of Confucius and was a disciple of the great master. For our purposes Mencius differed in at least one vital respect from his predecessors. Mencius believed that all men were born with the same kind of human nature. He believed and taught that human nature is essentially good. Confucius would not have disagreed on that point.

When asked by a disciple about his concept of the essential goodness of human nature he replied, "Man's nature is endued with feelings which impel it towards the good; that's why I call it good. If men do what is not good, the reason does not lie in the basic stuff of which they are constituted. All men have the feelings of sympathy, shame, and dislike. These feelings give rise to the virtues of benevolence, righteousness, propriety, and wisdom. These virtues are not infused into one from without; they are part of the essential me." Here he is in direct conflict not only with Confucius but with the Bible teaching that man is "born in sin and shapen in iniquity." Perhaps he was searching for an explanation of conscience.

It is interesting that modern-day Maoists have basically the same concept as Mencius, at least in practice. Because man is essentially good there is no need for God. They proclaim that with proper education and training they can develop a perfect man, free from evil; again shades of Freud, and unfortunately too, much of our own modern-day educational philosophy—the problem-producing Dr. Spock approach.

Mencius, in discussing the question of why some men become good and others bad, employed a simile very close

The Great Wall stretches fifteen hundred miles along China's western border. It was built largely by convict laborers during the Qin (Ch'ln) dynasty.

to the one used by Jesus. He said that if one sows identical grains in different places, that which falls on rich soil and has plenty of moisture will field an abundant harvest, while that which grows in poor soil and gets too little rain will turn out badly. His application was totally different from Christ's. Men, he claimed, were shaped and molded by the environment in which they develop. A perfect environment will produce a perfect man.

Mencius taught that man was self-sufficient. "All things are complete within us." This led to his famous statement, "He who completely knows his own nature knows heaven.' What he meant by this has been the subject of eternal debate among China's philosophers. Certainly it was a relatively easy step from this postulate to the concept that man does not need God. He is complete within himself.

Another phase of the teaching of Mencius that has relevance in the understanding of today's China is his teaching on economics. This is a subject very rarely tackled by philosophers. Mencius, like many of the philosophers of his day, was an advisor to the ruling aristocracy. He was astute enough to observe that if a ruler was to rule his people well he must take practical steps to ensure their financial welfare.

Mencius advocated such advanced procedures as diversified farming and conservation of fisheries and forests. It has been pointed out that if China had heeded Mencius in this regard her present financial condition would be less difficult.

Whether the Communists have taken a page out of Mencius' book, or whether they arrived at the same conclusion independently, is not known. The result is the same; note the similarity. One of his favorite plans was to take a good-sized piece of land and divide it into nine equal parcels. Each of the eight parcels on the outside was to be given to, and farmed by, a single family. The ninth plot, the center plot, was to be farmed by all eight families collectively. The produce or income from the center square would constitute taxes and go to the government. The eight families would live as a closely integrated community. Mencius believed that hungry people cannot be expected to be moral; therefore, economics and ethics are interrelated. This is a basic postulate of Communism.

The fourth century in China was the golden age of philosophy. It is known as "the hundred schools," thus indicating the multiplicity of philosophical viewpoints. Mencius pursued his dogmatic viewpoint with little regard for the philosophical turmoil about him. His book called simply "Mencius" which he left to the world is one of the largest and most important philosophical works ever produced.

There is a little rebel in all of us. The Chinese philosophers were no exception. Up to this point we have seen real points of agreement between Confucius and Mencius. Both were basically traditionalists in that they emphasized the importance of respect for law and order, reverence for and obedience to father and mother. They proposed that man must learn to live within certain prescribed boundaries for his own good. They proceeded to set up their tight boundaries. It was to be expected, therefore, that in such a prescribed atmosphere a philosophical rebel would appear on the scene—at least a rebellious philosophical approach did.

Lao-tzu (old master) is credited with being the father of Taoism; the only problem is that there is really no evidence that such a man ever lived! Chinese tradition says he was an older contemporary of Confucius, a keeper of the imperial archives. Tradition also says Confucius came to him for counsel. Lao-tzu is said to have written a five-thousand-word masterpiece, containing basic Taoist teaching, and

then went straight to heaven without any further prelim-
inaries. If he lived, Lao-tzu was probably the world's first
flower child. He was the original free spirit whose basic
philosophy would fit into much of the sixties' culture.

Six hundred and sixty-six years before Christ a woman in
the Zhou (Chou) dynasty caught sight of a falling star and
became pregnant. There followed the longest pregnancy
ever. Sixty-two years later she gave birth to a strange child
with glowing white hair already capable of speech. This was
Lao-tzu, the old master or teacher. This mystical story fits a
mystical character.

The principle of Taoism cannot be defined, only illus-
trated. Taoism teaches harmony with nature rather than
competition with or against nature. Take the line of least
resistance. Why struggle with life when life itself may be
only an illusion? "Only fools know they are awake and just
what they are," says the book of Lao-tzu, who was probably
only a myth himself.

Taoism is the precise opposite of Communism. An absolute minimum of government was the ideal. Never try to
strive for an ideal society or attempt to live in harmony with
anything but nature. Taoists believed that the ideal society is
one in which the people of one village can hear the cock
crowing in a neighboring village but have no desire to make
any form of contact. The way of the universe is inaction.

Are you ready for some interesting Taoist philosophy?
"He who stands on tip-toe does not stand on firm ground."
Relax. "If you do not want to spill the wine do not fill the
glass." Take it easy! "Soft beats hard. The tongue outlasts
the teeth. Water is the ideal substance: it does not batter
itself against stone but oozes around it." Incidentally, this is
the principle behind Mao's guerrilla warfare, clearly spelled
out by Sun-tzu centuries before Christ. Sun-tzu's book
Thirty-six Deadly Tricks for Fighting is a classic. It's his

thirty-sixth trick that is the real classic: "If you can't win, run."

Taoism says nonaction is preferable to action. Nothing obviously existed before something. It is hard to dispute the kind of logic that declares, "The most important part of a bottle is the hollow in the middle." No hollow, no value. The whole universe, they say, moves in harmony except synthetically civilized man. Don't fight the universe, flow with it.

Taoism soon absorbed massive doses of ancient Chinese mythology, thus making it very popular with the uneducated Chinese peasants. Taoism became "way-ism" and degenerated into the worship of local gods, magic, and miracles. Later Taoism absorbed what it wanted from Indian Buddhism.

It might be said that the Chinese are schizophrenic. Their dualistic nature is a combination of the rigid restraints of Confucianism and the unfettered spirit of Taoism. The Chinese are tough and welded to tradition. They are also able to flow with the currents of life and survive when others become extinct. In hard times their Taoistic philosophy comes to the fore. In prosperous times, or when an individual tastes a measure of prosperity, it is his Confucian ethic that emerges. Thus Confucianism was the philosophy of the intellectual, Taoism the philosophy of the uneducated peasant. The delineation was, of course, not that precise. Both philosophies flowed into each other, mingling to produce the Chinese person of today.

The rich and progressive Zhou (Chou) dynasty finally faded and fell to the man who was to become the first supreme ruler of a unified China. Shi Huang Di (Shih Huang-ti) proclaimed himself the first emperor of China, as indeed he was, and launched an amazing career following the authoritarian legalized doctrines of Zhou (Chou)-dynasty philosophers. It is remarkable to see how closely Mao

Zedong (Mao Tse-tung) has borrowed from the policies of China's first emperor. This will become self-evident as we enumerate some of Shi's (Shih's) policies and accomplishments.

The Qin (Ch'in) dynasty (255-206 B.C.) gave us the modern name *China*. The Emperor created an empire that enjoyed an amazing degree of unity. Emperor Shi (Shih) demanded that all area commanders in the nation be subject only to him. Previous to this each area answered to a local king or feudal lord. These kings, who once controlled things, were brought to the capital where he could keep an eye on them. Shi (Shih) placed men loyal to him in all areas as his watchdog representatives.

He shipped off to the frontier anyone who disrupted or threatened to disrupt his rule. He moved people freely from one end of the country to the other to keep potential troublemakers off balance and achieve his ends. He greatly expanded the transportation system of the nation, both road and canal. He ordered a now famous book-burning spree, at which he rid the country of any writings that were at variance with his principles. Intellectuals who were foolish enough to protest were branded and sent out into the country to work in labor battalions. It appears that Mao was a good student of history, for he duplicated each of these policies.

Emperor Shi's (Shih's) most enduring act was the unification of the written language. Over the sprawling land so recently unified, myriads of different dialects were spoken. Shi (Shih) earned himself the undying gratitude of succeeding generations by unifying the written language. This probably contributed more to the continuity of Chinese civilization than anything else that he did. Similarly, Mao Zedong's (Tse-tung's) simplification of the written language, which until the twentieth century remained largely unchanged, may be his greatest contribution to China's future history.

A continual threat to the now unified Chinese empire was the nomadic barbarians who lived on the steppes of North Central Asia on the borders of China. The Emperor widely feared the Huns of Mongolia. We are to see that in later years these barbarians would become an important part of Chinese history. Being a northerner himself, Emperor Shi (Shih) decided that in order to meet the continual threat of these mobile horsemen, who were said to have over two hundred thousand archers, he would build a Great Wall to form a permanent barricade. Other feudal lords in the past had built walls for the same purpose in the same area. The Emperor set out to tie these all together in one continuous wall stretching some fifteen hundred miles along the western border of China. Built of stone, brick, and earth, it was constructed largely by convict laborers, thousands of whom paid with their lives. Twenty feet in height, with a roadway fifteen feet wide at the top, dotted every few hundred yards with a guard tower, it was manned by a quarter of a million soldiers.

We are told that the Great Wall is the last man-made edifice visible on the way to the moon. It was a monumental feat demonstrating what massive manpower can accomplish. Mao has since employed the same methods to build tremendous dikes, dams, canals, roads, and irrigation systems throughout China. One irrigation canal of which the Communists are justly proud runs over six hundred miles through rugged mountain areas. Millions of workers, without any mechanical equipment, literally tunneled through mountains and bridged huge chasms to bring water to a once arid region.

The success of Emperor Shi Huang Di (Shih Huang-ti) was that he united a divided people into a nation that commanded the world's fear and respect. This achievement has been the goal of every succeeding government right up until Mao Zedong (Mao Tse-tung). Who knows what might have happened had Shi (Shih) been granted a longer life. After his death, intrigue and regional revolt tore the Empire apart.

The mighty Qin (Ch'in) empire could not survive the death of its creator. The Qin (Ch'in) dynasty lasted for only fifteen years, the shortest of all China's dynasties. Perhaps there is a prophetic message here for modern day imitators.

The Qin (Ch'in) dynasty was quickly superseded by the dynasty of which the Chinese are most proud. The "Sons of Han" is what they prefer to call themselves to this day, because of the greatness of the Han dynasty. At no period in China's long history did the Chinese rule such a vast area as during the Han dynasty.

It is the Han dynasty that brings us up to the time of Christ. This, too, was the period of the great Roman Empire. A little-known fact of history is that the Roman Empire and the Han dynasty were strangely parallel, both in time and scope. Each controlled about the same amount of territory and ruled the same number of people. Chinese culture was just as advanced as the Roman and probably more so. The Roman Empire has long since disappeared; China's empire is undiminished.

One of the most obvious weaknesses of the traditional Chinese form of government is that no peaceful way of changing leaders had been found. In each dynastic change, from the Shang dynasty to the twentieth-century "Mao Zedong (Tse-tung) dynasty," blood has been the means through which the new leaders have struggled to power. So violent, for instance, was the struggle between the fading Shang and the aspiring Zhou (Chou) in about 220 B.C. that it was portrayed in terms that have since become a part of our language. One writer describing the conflict declared,

"Blood flowed like a river." This is a characteristic weakness of all totalitarian governments. No means of peaceful succession exists in such systems.

It is important to point out that, up to this point in time, little if any foreign influence had reached China. The main features of Chinese civilization, therefore, evolved without major outside influence. Her philosophy, social system, religious beliefs, as well as governmental tradition, were purely Chinese. This fact alone has made it difficult for both the Chinese to appreciate the non-Chinese world and for foreigners to understand and appreciate China. It does, however, point out the greatness of a people who, without outside influence had a national university in their nation's capital a thousand years before Christ, and were using a compass to chart their travels a thousand years before Europeans knew of the existence of such a device.

For more than fifteen hundred years the Chinese led the world in mathematics, astronomy, medicine, architecture, and construction engineering.

China was the center of the universe, the Middle Kingdom (Zhong Guo [Chung Kuo]). Its emperor was the "son of heaven." All the rest of earth's mortals, whatever area of the world they might come from, must bow before heaven's earthly representative. To be Chinese was to be part of the greatest people on earth. All others were merely barbarians.

2

Silks and Gunpowder

When Christ was born in Bethlehem of Judea, the message of the angel choir did not carry across the uncharted miles of Asia to the Middle Kingdom. China was still locked solidly behind the walls of the Han dynasty. Succeeding centuries were to see the nation of China skid from its heights of greatness to misery and defeat. The path it traveled in its decline is vital to our understanding of modern China.

About the time of Christ, an imperial relative of the ruling Han dynasty, Wang Mang, made a bold revolutionary move. Seeing the inequities of a system dominated by the landlord-scholar-officials, he led a peasant rebellion and created the world's first socialist state. Price control, land equalization, government monopolies, and state-owned enterprises were instituted, all in the year A.D. 8. This bold experiment collapsed in A.D. 23. The latter part of the Han dynasty regained some, but not all, of the prosperity known in the early years.

Aggressive expansion brought North Vietnam, Hainan Island, and parts of Korea into the empire. The fierce Mongolian Huns met the Chinese Han and were defeated and pushed back beyond the great forbidding Gobi Desert. This was the age when silk blazed a trail across central Asia into Asia Minor and on into Europe. The other world began to hear about China. Europe's leading families prized the fabulous silks from the fabled land of "Cathay."

30

Scholars in China became revered and then, like Confucius, immortalized. No Chinese then or for centuries thereafter would discard a piece of paper with writing on it. Like our reverence for the flag, that paper could only be burned in a special receptacle. Incidentally, it was a gentleman named Cai Lun (Chai Lun) in China's Henan (Honan) province that invented paper in A.D. 105. Made from mulberry bark, hemp, and rags, this paper gave great impetus to learning and scholarship. The first dictionary with precise meaning for ten thousand characters appeared. Philosophy and religion received great encouragement in this era.

The silk road proved to be a two-way street. Back along the road came Indian missionaries spreading Buddhism and promising salvation for the poor peasants. Already some five centuries had passed since the death of its founder, Siddhartha Gautama. Buddhism gained a foothold in China with surprising ease, partly because the form of Buddhism which arrived was not very different from early Taoist principles. Both sought escape from this life by right conduct and contemplation. The fact that the people suffered greatly further opened the door for this first foreign religion to penetrate China.

It was during this Han dynasty that the worst features of the Confucianist governmental system evolved. Three monumental changes were instituted. An imperial academy was established to train governmental officials. An examination system was created to select civil servants. Confucianism became the basis of all education. Those selected for government service were men with a high degree of scholarship based on moral concepts and artistic sensibilities. Who could ask for anything better? The trouble was that because of the emphasis of Confucianism and tradition there evolved a self-perpetuating bureaucracy. This was to prove a stagnating force which tied China to the past. Progress was virtually impossible. Soon China was to be left far behind by the civilizations of Europe which were unfettered by such conservatism.

Before we go any further we must stop and focus attention upon the lot of the peasant who did, and still makes up, the majority of China's vast population. Even though the Emperor who founded the great Han dynasty was himself a peasant, the lot of the peasant remained tragic. During the Han dynasty alone there were two peasant rebellions.

All of the many uprisings or rebellions in China's long history have taken one of two forms. They were led by either power-hungry generals or half-starved peasants. For countless centuries China's peasant population has had to endure unspeakable hardship. Today's Communist leadership would have us believe the landlord system was entirely at fault. This is not true.

Anyone who has lived or even traveled extensively in China knows it is not a kind, fertile land. Over seventy per cent of the land is unsuitable for farming. Only the lowlands close to major rivers or the sea coast offer a reasonable base for agriculture. Yet eighty per cent of the population of China is engaged in agriculture. To put it more realistically, they are engaged in the struggle to eke out an existence from a crowded, inhospitable land.

The Yellow River, along which much early Chinese agriculture was established, was a writhing, twisting demon. Called the "river of sorrows," it shifted its river bed drastically three times between 1 B.C. and A.D. 11, and repeatedly since. Peasants lost their crops and many times even their lands to the whim of the mighty river.

The flooding Yellow River sometimes drowned two to three million people at a time. Even today, China's agricultural productivity is markedly affected by the weather and the whims of nature. Famines and droughts have plagued the peasants, thus adding an unpredictable element to their struggle for existence. As late as forty years ago a famine in Sichuan (Szechuan) took over one million lives.

Since most of the land was not arable, vast irrigation systems had to be devised. Land ownership under those circumstances was not as important as water ownership or control. Calculating the amount of water to go to each farm was a complicated process. No illiterate peasant could cope with it. Therefore, the educated controlled the uneducated. Furthermore, these scholar-landlords often exempted their own land from taxation and wrung it out of others who soon became mere serfs unable to pay the heavy taxes. The peasants had one more problem to cope with.

Yet, the vast majority of China's population were, and are, peasant farmers. They have become masters at survival. By way of comparison, the United States farms three hundred and sixty million acres to support two hundred and twenty-five million people. China, with almost one billion people, farms only two hundred and eighty million acres. There are two acres of cultivated land in the United States per person, and only three-tenths of an acre per person in China. Many of the problems peasants faced in the Han dynasty during the first century of the Christian era are still largely unsolved.

Four hundred years old, the Han dynasty weakened and crumbled. In spite of the excellent governmental systems pioneered, or at least propounded by China's philosophers and scholars, no viable form of government emerged to take over from the Hans. During the next three hundred and sixty-eight years the government changed hands on the average of once every sixty-one years. Regional war lords carved up the empire into rugged chunks. No cohesive force remained to keep out the long-threatening nomadic barbarians.

For the first time in history, China's distinctive civilization, nurtured in isolation, was invaded by foreign influence. From the fourth century on, the Great Wall was breached repeatedly by the barbarians. Tibetan, Turkic, Altaic (more Caucasian than Mongoloid), and Tunguistic peoples poured into North and West China. The Chinese were driven south of the Yangtze River. Several interesting serendipities followed. First, the northern Chinese pouring into South China brought new life and vitality to the more passive southerner. This gave rise to a resurgence of culture, agriculture, and population. Meanwhile, in the north the Chinese intermarried with the invaders and not only absorbed them but benefited from this infusion of new blood. The barbarians often took Chinese wives.

This, too, was the golden age of Buddhism. Invasions, wars, and population dislocations drove the suffering people into the arms of a faith that offered help. Millions turned to Buddhism. Temples were built throughout the country. An enormous translation program brought the Indian Buddhist teachings to the scholarly Chinese. It is interesting to note that Buddhism at this time faced some of the problems which have confronted every religious invasion of China from Christianity to Communism.

So many philosophies burst on the scene in such a short time that there was considerable syncretism. One bled into the other. None was exclusivistic. A Chinese saying declared, "A wise man makes his own decisions; an ignorant man follows public opinion." This fondness for individualism was applied to the Chinese' religious world. He was quite prepared to accept what he wanted out of each faith, but also to reject what he didn't want. The result was an unbelievable mixture. He would add as many gods to his roster as he desired. None had an exclusive place.

They say that a Chinese is a Confucianist when he is in power or enjoying wealth because Confucianism does not call for change. In case you're not in power and not enjoying prosperity, Taoism fills the bill admirably because a Taoist sneers at both leadership and worldly possessions. When facing death Buddhism is the logical choice because it promises salvation. *Pragmatism* is the word. Above all the Chinese are a practical people.

Perched on top of all this is ancestor worship. Not only were respect and reverence for one's departed ancestors part of the Chinese culture long before even Confucianism or Taoism, but they have been incorporated into both faiths. Buddhism suffered the same fate. To the Chinese, ancestors are very much "alive" and active. Better be good to them or all sorts of tragedies might follow. They can be counted on to bring blessing if they are pleased with your worship as well as tragedy if displeased. No respectable Chinese will neglect his ancestors.

Before long, Buddhism, too, faced the opposition of China's native Taoist and Confucianist philosophies just as other foreign religions have done since. About this time Buddhists became targets of attack. Over forty-six thousand monasteries and shrines were destroyed. Thousands of Buddhist monks and nuns were forced to return to secular life. On one occasion three hundred Buddhist monks were executed.

Spurring opposition was an antiforeign element opposing this foreign religion. Adding further fuel to the fire was the fact that immense Buddhist monasteries had become tax-free holdings which more than once harbored fleeing criminals. A Confucian reported to the emperor that Buddhism was "one of the practices of barbarians." The persecution did not destroy Buddhism but did keep alive the Chinese resentment toward any foreign religious influence. Never again was Buddhism to gain such a strong position in China.

The religious invasion was not over. The barbarians of the North and West brought with them still another faith, Islam. No great Islamic revival swept China. Islam received a cool reception. Only in the North and West, where large sections of the population are ethnically non-Chinese, is Islam found in any strength.

It was not until the sixth century that China's enduring qualities brought order out of chaos. First the Sui dynasty and then the Tang dynasty brought three hundred years of unity. Once again the cycle was repeated. Land was redistributed to the peasants, taxes were levied in accordance with a person's ability to pay, and peasants from each prefecture were drafted into the army. The Tang dynasty devised a governmental system that was the finest China had ever seen.

Further progress in foreign policy extended the influence of China from Korea to Constantinople, from Manchuria to the Pescadores and Taiwan. Culture flourished at home. This was the golden age of Chinese poetry. It should be observed here that poetry has always been the most honored form of literature in China. The poets Li Bai (Li Po) and Du Fu (Tu Fu) of the Tang dynasty are still considered China's greatest poets. Of course, if you are a Maoist then the modern-day poet Mao Zedong (Mao Tse-tung) will hold the place of honor.

One of the truly great engineering feats of all times was completed about this time when the Grand Canal stretching some six hundred miles from the coastal province of Zhejiang (Chekiang) deep into central Henan (Honan) was completed. Ocean-going ships probed the heart of the nation. Her sailors called at ports throughout Southeast Asia.

The decline and fall of the Tang dynasty reads like an old story: palace intrigue, regional officers gaining riches, eunuchs manipulating monarchs. A peasant uprising in

Shandong (Shantung) spread rapidly. To save their skin, the Tang had to call on some of the nomadic barbarians to suppress the rebellion. From this point their empire declined rapidly. Mencius was again proved wrong. A good environment does not necessarily produce good people. Governments may and do change, but people don't except by divine regeneration.

The export of China's precious silk opened the back door to foreign influence. This influence would soon grow powerful enough to bring China to her knees.

Gunpowder was invented about this time. Its primary use was probably in the making of firecrackers. Their animistic concepts needed a loud noise to frighten off evil spirits. Gunpowder did the trick much better than traditional noise-makers. Interestingly enough, it is in a Taoist sacred writing that the first mention of gunpowder is found. Other uses were invented for this volatile mixture. The Chinese, who have recently mastered the intricacies of the atom bomb, produced the world's first grenades. Gunpowder, encased in sturdy, ever-present bamboo, created lethal grenades. About this time the crafty Chinese had produced crude but effective explosive bombs launched from catapults and flame throwers fed by naphtha gas and even crude cannon.

With all their genius, the fall of the Tang dynasty was to usher in the last dynasty before China was inundated by invading foreigners. From the standpoint of government and control of the country, the three-hundred-year Song (Sung) dynasty was probably the weakest in China's interminable history. The long-suffering people had not known anything like a lasting peace for three thousand years.

The Song (Sung) dynasty (A.D. 960-1279), though weak militarily, made very real contributions to China's cultural heritage. Perhaps, being unable to impose their will on others, they became introverted and concentrated on their own affairs. During this period there was apparently a real population explosion and cities of one million or more inhabitants began to appear. Kaifeng, Suzhou (Soochow), and Hangzhou (Hangchow) all exceeded a million in population.

A description of Hangzhou (Hangchow), then called Kinsai, capital of southern China, reveals the glory of that age. Incidentally, this is one of the cities visited by President Nixon nine hundred years later. Ancient Kinsai was an oriental Venice, built on lagoons and intersected by myriads of canals. The city was more than one hundred miles in circumference. Its main street, broken every four miles by large garden-like squares, was a massive two hundred feet wide and stretched the length of the city.

The greatest city in Europe at that time, Venice, would have fit into any one of Kinsai's twelve quarters and could not equal the magnificence of the Chinese metropolis. Later, Marco Polo visited this city and counted twelve thousand stone bridges, some high enough for full-masted ocean-going sailing vessels to pass beneath. He said that Kinsai's royal palace was larger and richer than anything a European king had ever known.

Glass, a Venetian specialty, had been in use in China for over a thousand years. Song (Sung) dynasty potters created works of art known for their vivid glazes and designs set in relief. Their landscape painters were the greatest in China's long history. On the practical level the Song (Sung) developed inoculation against smallpox and produced the first reference work on medicine. Drugs were investigated before being used on the public. Books were printed by the block-printing method. They even experimented with movable type.

It was in the Song (Sung) dynasty that neo-Confucianism was developed. This synchretistic philosophy was a mixture of the ethical teachings of Confucius and a strange religious application borrowed largely from Buddhism. These new interpretations of Confucianism became standard. What began as a mere ethical philosophy became a restrictive pseudoreligion that effectively shackles Chinese minds until today.

During this dynasty more and more was heard from the barbarians. The origins of most of these ethnic groups are lost in antiquity. Most of us have never heard of the Khitans, the Tangots, or the Ju-chens. About all even the anthropologists know is that they emanated from Manchuria and the vastness of Mongolia. Most were related to the Altaic people. This name is given to a group of Turkic people who inhabit the forested slopes of the Altaic range where they have been for long centuries. They are more Caucasian than Mongoloid. Today the Chinese Communists refer to them as "our minority nationalities."

While the Chinese attempted to settle their domestic problems during the Song (Sung) dynasty the fierce nomadic Northmen behind the Great Wall became stronger. Their population increased, good leadership emerged, the arts of war were honed in tribal conflict.

In 1235, one of these groups, the Mongols, swallowed up North China and forty-five years later conquered all of China. Three thousand years of Chinese history had never before known such a humiliating experience. China conquered by barbarians? Impossible—but true.

Under the leadership of Genghis Khan the rugged masses of mounted warriors wiped out all resistance in their path. This was destined to become the world's largest empire, stretching from the Pacific Ocean to the Danube River. China lay prostrate at the feet of the Mongols and so did much of the then known world.

Under Kublai Khan, the grandson of Genghis Khan, China became merely a part of the great Khan or Mongol empire.

In Chinese history it is known as the Yüan dynasty (1279-1368). Beijing (Peking) became the capital. Tremendous progress was made in civil projects. The Grand Canal was extended to Beijing (Peking). A massive postal system using sturdy Mongolian ponies was inaugurated.

The Mongols were determined not to be absorbed by the Chinese whom they ruled. Seeing the very real danger of such a possibility, they kept aloof from their subjects. The Chinese considered the Mongols a greedy, exploitative dynasty, but worst of all, a purely foreign one.

Without question the Khans built one of the greatest empires in history. It was to this great court in Beijing (Peking) that young Marco Polo came. Enthralled by what he saw, he stayed long enough to record its wonders and take his exclusive story back to an amazed Europe.

Given the extent of the Mongol empire and the fighting ability of their horsemen warriors, one would expect the Yüan dynasty to go on forever. As a matter of fact, it lasted only about ninety years. Corruption within, the rampaging Yellow River, and rebellion on the part of South China undermined the Mongols.

Victorious Chinese armies swept the Mongols from the face of China and established the proud Ming dynasty (1368-1644). Unfortunately, this dynasty's government was only a carbon copy of so many others that had gone before. Confucianism guaranteed that the most striking feature of Chinese government would be continuity. The Confucian state was reestablished. Landlord-scholar-officials started out with noble aspirations and degenerated to greedy, despotic tyrants.

The Mings failed to establish any lasting reforms, and saw that China remained committed to isolation and the status quo. The world came to China only to be treated with arrogance and insolence born of a conviction that all others were inferior to the "sons of heaven."

This was to be the last indigenous Chinese effort at effective government until the Republic was established in 1911.

From the mid-fourtheenth to the mid-seventeenth centuries the Ming lived in isolation, committed to traditionalism. Corrupt, insolent eunuchs held the de facto governmental power. Peasants suffered more than anyone else. Famines and natural disasters finally fanned the flames of latent rebellion. Two peasant armies marched on Beijing (Peking). A corrupt Chinese general, driven by a personal hatred, asked the Manchus to assist in quelling the rebellion. They complied willingly. In 1644 the Manchus conquered China.

At this time Europe was passing through a series of cataclysmic transitions. We know them as the Renaissance, the Reformation, and the Industrial Revolution. China was left hopelessly behind. Western traders appearing in China in the eighteenth and nineteenth centuries found not a nation whose progress amazed them but a backwardness that was wrongly mistaken for stupidity. The stage was set for tragedy.

3

The Opium Trigger

This is a chapter I wish I did not have to write. It's like looking in the mirror and seeing an ugly, greedy monster. The Opium War is a page of history that most Europeans are either totally ignorant of or have chosen to forget. In either case, the curtain must be pulled back so that we can see the part the West has played in forcing China into the hands of its present Communist masters.

The first European navigators to discover a sea passage to China were the Portuguese. In 1557 they obtained permission from the Mings to settle on a rather worthless piece of land off the coast of South China. This came to be known as Macau and gave the Portuguese a foothold on the mainland which they still hold today. Part of this book was written in this almost forgotten city of the past.

Portugal was flexing its naval power throughout the Pacific area. The Philippines, isolated islands, and parts of India tasted its might. There is no evidence, however, that the Chinese became alarmed. The emperors merely restricted the Portuguese to Macau and permitted them an occasional trip to Guangzhou (Canton), just eighty miles away. The Portuguese exploited to the full their tiny foothold which gave them a complete monopoly on the sale of Chinese goods in Europe.

The next to come were the Spaniards, who conquered the Philippines and used Macau as a trading point. In 1580 Portugal became part of Spain. The Dutch conquered Java in 1619 and from there made repeated but rather fruitless contact with a reluctant dragon throne. The Emperor was glad to receive their homage and worship, but assured the Dutch that China was a closed country and that was all there was to it. Understandably, the Dutch weren't very happy with this reception.

The English, who next arrived on the scene to exploit China's wealth, were a different breed of men. Fully able to match the insolent pride of the imperialist Chinese, the British were already masters of many seas, riding the rising tide of empire building and needing markets to sustain their rapidly expanding industrial revolution. They would not easily be denied a foothold in China.

British mercantile philosophy needs to be reviewed here, because it plays a key role in that which is to follow. A group of British merchants would band together and obtain from their government, in return for a substantial share of the profits, a complete monopoly on trade. The British Crown, to protect its share of the profits, was, therefore, quite willing to commit its military forces in support of its merchants.

Driven by the vastly increased productivity that followed the Industrial Revolution, Britain had to find markets around the world for its many products. Having gained more than a foothold in India, China became its next target. The monopoly that controlled the India-China trade was the British East India Company. Operating out of headquarters in India, this Company operated its own merchant fleet and commanded its own standing army in India. The massive profits channeled back enabled England to take full advantage of the Industrial Revolution. The Chinese, on the other hand, had little need for any of Britain's manufactured products.

By 1715 the East India Company, enjoying a hundred-year-old monopoly of all British trade with Asia, had established itself in Guangzhou (Canton), South China. In 1793 the Earl of Macartney headed a diplomatic mission to the Manchu Emperor. To say he received a cool reception was to put it mildly. The Emperor promptly sent a letter to King George III declaring, "As your ambassador can see for himself, we possess all things. I set no value on objects strange or ingenious, and have no use for your country's manufactures."

China didn't want to buy, but on the other hand China had much that the West wanted to buy. By the 1830s the Chinese had reluctantly authorized representatives of trading nations, without their families, to live under strict supervision at Guangzhou (Canton). The flags of Britain, France, the United States, and Holland flew over the warehouses at the port of Canton. How to pay for the goods purchased from China became a key issue. The U.S. decided on furs, silver dollars, and herbs. The British, on the other hand, opted for opium.

One Chinese word for opium can be literally translated "foreign mud." The use of opium in China up to this stage was restricted either to the very rich or for medicinal purposes. Chinese medical books as early as the thirteenth century claimed that it was beneficial in treating diarrhea and dysentery. Careless use of opium, it warned, was dangerous. It had the power to "kill like a knife." In 1829 an imperial decree forbade the use of "foreign mud" except for a medicinal purpose. The rich had learned that opium taken in a certain form had the ability to provide a false euphoria in hours of indolence.

The British quickly observed that the lot of the average Chinese was not too happy. Perhaps he would be willing to pay for a little chemical happiness. If an appetite for the stuff could be generated it would create a continuing demand that would solve Britain's China trade problem. What it would do to the Chinese the British authorities didn't seem to consider or perhaps didn't care.

Unscrupulous traders can always be found who will circumvent the law. It was illegal to import opium into China, but a few silver dollars in the right palms can work wonders. Cooperative Chinese merchants were not too hard to come by. Soon a booming illegal trade was under way. Britain established in Bengal, India, huge plantations for growing opium poppies. Calcutta was the location of the opium trading floor and the port from which it flowed to China. Special fleets carried opium in bales across the seas to Tsing Yi Island between Hong Kong and Macau. This became the base for a massive illegal smuggling operation with the blessing of the British Crown.

The extent and rapid growth of the opium traffic can be seen by the following statistics which total the number of pounds shipped into China by one British firm.

1800	30,000 lbs.
1825	1,443,150 lbs.
1830	2,814,000 lbs.
1836	3,902,700 lbs.

It is conceded that the cooperation of corrupt Chinese officials was a necessary ingredient in the opium trade. These dissolute officials were of every rank from boatmen to mandarins. The Chinese government became thoroughly alarmed. The governor of Canton wrote Queen Victoria a stinging letter: "When your Majesty receives this document let us have a speedy communication in reply. . . . Do not evade or procrastinate. . . . We have heard that in your honorable barbarian country the people are not permitted to inhale the drug. If it is admittedly so deleterious how can profiting by exposing others to its maleficent power be reconciled with the decree of Heaven?" Indeed how can it?

This was a tragic period when the conscience of Christendom had shamefully not been troubled by either slavery or the opium trade.

The appointment of Lin Zexu (Lin Tse-hsu) as Imperial Commissioner to Guangzhou (Canton) on December 31st, 1838 marked the beginning of China's get-tough policy against the importation of opium. Lin was a distinguished high-ranking official, a mandarin of the first rank, known for his honesty and toughness. He now faced not a small trickle but a raging river of raw hell as millions of pounds of opium were being almost literally forced down the throat of the reluctant dragon.

At this juncture I must point out that there were some British officials who decried the opium traffic. One of them was Captain Elliot, Chief Superintendent of British trade at Macau. Elliot was, however, powerless to do anything concrete about it. The British Crown obviously desired the trade to continue.

The British Crown did lose some sleep over one detail. England had developed a reputation for high-quality products using excellent materials. Her merchants were largely cautious and honest. Now, however, a full fifty per cent of the capital set aside for trade with China was tied up in opium. Adding to the tragedy was the fact that this was purely a smuggling racket. Britain concluded this had to be changed. In other words, Britain did not condemn the opium trade itself; merely the "smuggling" facet of it. Somehow it had to be legitimized.

What was needed, Britain felt, was a treaty with China guaranteeing free trade. This did not seem unreasonable to them. China had made it very clear, however, that she was not interested in such a proposition. Britain decided to force the issue.

Both sides were attempting to assess the military might of the other. It turned out that both were wrong in their assessment. The British concluded that China was so weak that with "the first vigorous and well-directed blow by a foreign power, it (China) will totter to its base." The Chinese, on the other hand, had little regard for the big bulky warships of the barbarians. "Good for high seas, maybe," they observed, "they do not know how to use fists and swords. Also, their legs are firmly bound with cloth and in consequence it is very inconvenient for them to stretch. Should they land, it is apparent they can do little harm. Therefore, what is called their power can be controlled without difficulty."

This mutual ignorance set the stage for an unequal collision of not only power but ideology. A Chinese revolutionary forest fire was to grow from the single spark thus generated. Adding to the explosiveness of the situation was the fact that in the course of its colonial expansion Britain had moved into Burma and Malaya. Quite evidently the British Crown was heading for further expansion in Asia.

Ten weeks after assuming control, Commissioner Lin showed that he really meant business by issuing the following edict. "Let the barbarians deliver to me every particle of opium on board their storeships. There must not be the smallest atom concealed. At the same time let the said barbarians enter into a bond never hereafter to bring opium in their ships and to submit, should any be brought, to the extreme penalty of the law against the parties involved." Three days were given for the British to comply with the order. Involved was an entire season's importation. Lin also called in all the Chinese import merchants. He warned them in severest tones that if they persisted in their perverted inclination to assist the British in illegal trade, he would "select for execution one or two of the most unworthy of you."

Entirely through the mediation of the aforementioned Captain Elliot, who had grave misgivings about the opium trade, a decision was made to comply with Lin's order. Over twenty thousand chests, valued at over one hundred pounds sterling each, were delivered to Lin. This was practically the entire 1838-39 opium crop. Lin chose to dispose of this lethal contraband by depositing it in trenches filled with water and sprinkling it with salt and lime. The area involved was closely guarded until the opium had decomposed and drained into a nearby creek.

Still Lin was not satisfied. He knew that as long as the British were cultivating huge areas of poppies in India, China was in danger of further opium trade. Consequently he wrote to Queen Victoria urging her to "have the plants plucked up by the roots. Cause the land there to be hoed afresh . . . and if any man dare again to plant a single poppy, visit his crime with condign punishment." This would have solved the problem and brought to an end a disreputable chapter in British history. Elliot himself had termed the opium trade "discreditable to the character of the Christian nations, under whose flag it is carried on." The British were not prepared to accept defeat at the hands of the "heathen Chinese." The Chinese had to be taught a lesson they would not soon forget. Proud Britain would not bow to the laws of a mere Chinese emperor.

In response to an urgent appeal by Captain Elliot, who sensed danger for British subjects, Britain diverted some of its vast naval power to Hong Kong. Tension was growing. A group of drunken British and American sailors on shore leave in Hong Kong got into a fight. After the melee one Chinese man lay dead. Lin called on the Chinese people living in Kowloon to cut off all supplies to the British on Hong Kong island just a mile off shore. Soon the blockade reduced the British to desperate circumstances.

Needing food and water, two British naval vessels crossed over to Kowloon to ask for these supplies. The Chinese met them with large war junks. Behind the junks on the shore there was a battery of cannon fully armed. After a fruitless day of negotiation the British lost patience. The H.M.S. Louisa and the H.M.S. Pearl opened fire on the armed junks and soundly defeated the Chinese. At nightfall the action was discontinued. The damage, however, had been done. These were the first shots in the Opium War. The effect was to be long-term and disastrous. The day was the eighth of September 1839. All the Chinese had done was to refuse to give the British the provisions, which, because of their own Government's orders, they were in no position to give.

There is little point in proceeding with the narrative of the next two-and-a-half years. Britain through a series of battles brought helpless China to her knees. August 14th, 1842 saw the final defenses leading to Nanjing (Nanking) crumble and fall. The Chinese, sensing that further resistance was useless, agreed to negotiate.

As a result of these negotiations the humiliated Chinese were forced to sign the infamous Treaty of Nanjing (Nanking). This was the price China had to pay for insisting that the British did not have the right to smuggle or sell opium to China. The key stipulations of the Treaty were these:

1. The island of Hong Kong was ceded to Britain in perpetuity.

2. Five ports, Guangzhou (Canton), Fuzhou (Foochow), Ningbo (Ningpo), Xiamen (Amoy), and Shanghai were opened to trade. Foreigners were given permission to live in these cities.

3. Chinese courts were denied jurisdiction over foreigners.

4. China was forced to pay Britain nearly six million dollars for the twenty thousand chests of opium surrendered four years earlier.

5. China had to reimburse the British about fifteen million dollars for Britain's cost of the Opium War.

6. The foundation was laid for legal commerce with China.

China's humiliation at the hands of the foreign devils was complete. From this point on, the opium traffic increased enormously.

To argue that the British merchants and not the British Crown must take the blame is to reveal an ignorance of the true picture. In the first place, monopoly trade was a British government policy. Without that policy Britain would not have backed with guns its merchants who were intent on trade with China. Secondly, Britain had a parliamentary form of government. The decisions of Parliament were the decisions of the government. The opium situation had repeatedly been debated in Parliament. In 1832, Parliament had been fully informed on the growth of opium in India for export. At the conclusion of the debates it was decided, "It does not seem advisable to abandon so important a source of revenue as the . . . monopoly of opium in Bengal." Gold was the goal.

In 1839 Jardine, who with his partner Matheson was a ringleader behind the opium trade, was honored by being made a Member of Parliament. At any point the House of Commons could have moved to forbid the export of opium from India—they did not. Matheson was elected to Parliament in 1843 at the death of Jardine. Their firm, the Jardine Matheson Company, is today one of the major economic factors in the British Crown Colony of Hong Kong—a colony built on the shattered lives of millions of opium addicts through the length and breadth of China.

It is a matter of record that Captain Elliot was removed from his post in 1841. The reason: "You have failed in obtaining . . . an additional opening for our trade to the Northwest." Elliot could not bring himself against his own conscience to do this.

4

The Rape of China

The tragic Opium War only marked the barest beginning. Now that a wedge had been driven into a weak, disorganized China, the West was determined to milk it for all it was worth. The story of a hapless China desecrated by a lustful West is by no means pretty.

In an earlier chapter, it was seen that China herself had contributed much to the tragic situation. To put the facts into clear focus, we must isolate them from the body of history. China was unconsciously guilty of creating its own problems on at least seven counts:

1. Long years of self-imposed isolation that had left them unprepared for a confrontation with the modern world;
2. The stultifying, stagnating effect of a Confucianism that was rooted solely in the past;
3. A scholar-landlord-ruler class that had far too little concern for its subjects;
4. A "theological" concept that made the emperor of China the "son of heaven" and therefore superior to all the rest of earth's rulers;
5. Failure to solve the traditional problems of the peasants who made up the majority of the population;
6. An educational system that was tied to the past and wholly unprepared to cope with the present;
7. Religion that was self-contemplative, producing not action but seclusion. Their religious concepts made no provision for a life-changing experience of regeneration.

In spite of a great and sometimes glorious past, China was totally unprepared to cope with the dynamic world of the West.

Exit Chinese leadership—enter the foreigners. Things would never be the same again. A brief digression to explain foreign intervention is in order. Soon after the Manchus came to power in the mid-seventeenth century an unforgivable indignity was forced upon all Chinese males. A symbol of subjection was devised lest the proud Chinese forget they were a conquered people. Every male was required to wear his hair long, braided down his back in a trailing pigtail. Salt was rubbed into the wound. I remember seeing those trailing queues as a boy in old China over two hundred years later. The indignity had persevered.

The Manchus, more sophisticated than the Mongols, had the intelligence to rule China with Chinese help. Though top positions of leadership remained in the hands of the Manchus, administrative offices were staffed by Chinese.

Two revolutionary changes occurred about midway through the Manchu rule that were to alter the course of history. First, the Manchus finally and thoroughly defeated the Mongol tribes of the north. They would never again pose a threat to China.

The second major event was not of Manchu or Chinese making. On the northern and western borders of China lived a nomadic people who at various times plagued India, China, and even distant Europe. These fierce nomads had produced Genghis Kahn and Attila the Hun. China was continuously aware of the threat posed by the aggressive Huns. Russia, too, recognized the danger. Russian armies marching across Siberia once and for all subdued the mighty Huns. China was now confronted with a European culture on its borders. Russia had become a factor to be reckoned with.

The mighty Manchus finally lost their grip on China, but not to a revived Chinese régime. One writer described what was to happen in these terms: "The Manchus were themselves to fall victim to a means and morality of exploitation far more efficient and ruthless than anything they could imagine—the exploitation of China by nations of the Western world." This cataclysmic collision had already produced the Opium War. More was to follow. The floodgates of foreign aggression were now open.

Numerous problems beside the foreign devils beset the Manchu lords of China. Faced for the first time with the fact that China's orthodox viewpoint was neither infallible nor even essential, the whole system was unstable. Added to this was a startling population increase that had decidedly upset the century-old balance of people and land. No industrial base had been established to meet the new challenge. Floods, famines, and frontier wars began to plague and weaken the dynasty.

Rebellions became a normal safety valve for the suffering peasants. The Manchus were getting it from all sides. They were discovering that it is easier to conquer China than to govern it. Paradoxically, the Chinese appeared to be weak as a nation but extremely tough as a race.

Lusting for further financial gain, the West took advantage of every incident to humiliate the Chinese. Fairly new on the increasingly crowded scene were the French, followed by the Americans, Germans, and Russians. In 1857 a union of French and British forces literally took over Guangzhou (Canton). Within a year they had moved far north and taken Tianjin (Tientsin) which was uncomfortably close to Beijing (Peking). The Chinese gave in and signed another "treaty."

The Treaty of Tianjin (Tientsin), was another slap in the face. More than that, it was a hard, cruel, humiliating blow that almost floored the government permanently. A look at the concessions the Chinese were forced to make will explain why this was true:

Under the treaty of Tianjin (Tientsin), the opium trading was legalized, Westerners were now free to travel to all parts of China, missionaries were sanctioned and given the right to practice their faith, and western diplomats were to reside in Beijing (Peking). Russia got her share of the booty. As China's newest neighbor, she was given all the Chinese territory north of the Yalu. As if that wasn't enough, a brief time later, as a result of a military confrontation which the Chinese again lost, the scope of the treaty was widened. The British picked up Kowloon, opposite the island of Hong Kong. Russia bit off another chunk of China including the present city of Vladivostok. The Yangtze River was opened to foreign navigation and commerce. America demanded and got equal trade opportunities along with everyone else.

As a response to all this pressure from without, the core of China erupted. Disgusted with their weak government, buffeted by natural disasters, humiliated by the incursion of the foreign devils, and dissatisfied with land policies, rebellion broke out in earnest. From its beginning in 1850 to its final defeat sixteen years later, the Taiping (T'ai P'ing) Rebellion, a true peasant uprising, blazed a bloody trail across the country. The Christian connotation of the Taiping (T'ai P'ing) Rebellion will be discussed in another chapter. Here we are concerned with other factors.

Much of the rebellion was aimed at the Manchus or "Tartars" as they were called then. One edict read in part, "We consider the world as China's, not the Tartars'; clothes and food as China's, not the Tartars'; sons, daughters, people as China's, not the Tartars'. It is regrettable that the Ming dynasty failed in their duties as rulers. The Manchus availed themselves of the chaos, defiled China, stole China's territory, raped and maltreated China's sons and daughters." The edict then calls for action. "Yet if China . . . calmly allows them to molest her without any reaction, can she be said to possess men worthy of the name?"

Another interesting feature of the Taiping (T'ai P'ing) Rebellion was its non-Marxist communism, that is, its application of communal living and socialistic programs. The Taiping (T'ai P'ing) were interested not only in overthrowing the Manchus but in establishing a peaceful, prosperous nation. The command was, "In the empire none shall have any private property . . . ." Their method was to divide the nation into groups containing twenty-five families apiece. Enough food was kept from the harvest for these twenty-five families; the rest was given to the public storehouse. The number of chickens and pigs was carefully determined. Each family was to have five hens and two sows. Every detail was regulated from patents to mines, from banks to boats, from insurance to newspapers.

Land, the core of peasant living, received special attention. First of all, land was categorized, that is, land was judged by its crop yield. There were nine separate categories of land. Every person over sixteen years of age was to receive land.

The "army" was a family affair. Every army was to consist of 13,156 families.

One more interesting regulation should be mentioned here because it, as well as other Taiping (T'ai P'ing) principles, would be duplicated by Mao a century later. "The rules of etiquette and education and upbringing should be fixed by law with an eye to uniformity so that the common people have something to rely on and need not go astray. As for those who have gone astray but are on the right path, education and law must be applied at the same time." At least an attempt was being made to develop a viable Chinese society. The Taiping (T'ai P'ing) were ahead of their time.

Within nine years the Taiping (T'ai P'ing), with half of China under their control, set up their capital in Nanjing (Nanking). Their army was like nothing ever seen in China before. There was no pilfering. The women were never ravaged; the Tiaping (T'ai P'ing) abolished opium smoking and foot binding and prohibited prostitution, slavery, witchcraft, alcohol and tobacco. Their women were elevated to equal status. Their land reform and government reform were urgently needed in China.

An American soldier of fortune, Frederick Ward of Massachusetts, was appointed to lead the fight against the Taiping (T'ai P'ing). When he was killed, the British gallantly loaned Captain (later General) Charles "Chinese" Gordon. None of the regal pomposity of nineteenth-century England was missing from Gordon, who marched fearlessly into battle unarmed. His "army" was a bastard mixture of Western soldiers of fortune and Chinese troops which he personally had trained. In addition, the Manchus still had crack troops which they put at his disposal. The military leadership of the Taiping (T'ai P'ing) was no match for this almost mythical General Gordon. The fall of the Taiping (T'ai P'ing) came in 1864 after a terrible massacre—few surrendered.

Much of the financing for the army came from the Chinese gentry, the landlord class, who opposed the agrarian reform policies of the Taiping (T'ai P'ing). One thing was certain: defeat of the Taiping (T'ai P'ing) would not quell forever the reservoir of revolutionary power latent in peasant discontent. The Manchus made little attempt to right the wrongs of government.

Chafing at the Manchu bit were some of the bright young

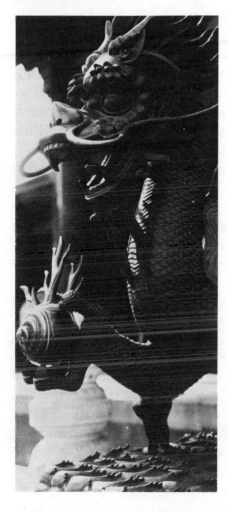

A ruler, one in a long line of proud, self-seeking Mandarins who plundered the wealth of China, erected this monument to himself. The Mandarins generally made little effort to serve the people.

intellectuals of China. Few succeeded in going abroad for study against the wishes of the Manchus. Their fear was rightly placed, for one of the young intellectuals would soon lead a rebellion that would overthrow the Manchus.

During this time, the West maintained its pressure. The Manchus now owed them for the defeat of the Taiping (T'ai P'ing). The British and French took over the maritime customs service. In the Western settlements of China, set up in coastal cities, Chinese law was not recognized. China was excluded from her own land.

The rape continued. Russia won the right to administer the railways through Manchuria. The cities of Port Arthur and Dairen were "leased" to Russia. Her troops seized large areas of Chinese Turkistan and then instigated the succession of Outer Mongolia from China. Russia made good use of its opportunities to plunder.

Germany moved in on mineral-rich Shandong (Shantung) province. France occupied areas of Guangdong (Kwangtung), Guangxi (Kwangsi), and Yunnan (Yunan). To the south, French troops took over what was to become French Indochina. Britain captured the Tibetan capital of Lhasa, took chunks of Burma, and negotiated a naval base in Shandong (Shantung).

Japan demanded her share of the loot. She wasn't going to let the Western powers get it all. First she went to war with China over Korea. China lost and Japan got Taiwan, the Pescadore islands, a portion of Manchuria, trading concessions, and a large chunk of cash. Since this is Japan's first appearance on the scene, it might be well to see what had been happening in Japan. No one was more surprised at the strength of the Japanese than the Chinese, who for centuries had called the Japanese "dwarf slaves" from an unimportant barbarian land. Japan, which derived much of her culture from China, had also lived for centuries in "splendid isolation." The visit of Commodore Perry's fleet in 1853-1854 more or less marked the beginning of forced Western influence on Japan.

Reaction in Japan differed from China's. Japan saw the superiority of Western mechanics, education, organization, and science. Being a tiny land, she could move with a greater degree of unity more rapidly than sprawling China. She set out to copy, borrow, beg, or, if necessary, steal everything from the West which she felt was useful. Her society was far more manageable than the Chinese.

Defeat of the Chinese armies in what has been called an "instant victory" was the result of her rapid modernization program. Japan has never looked back.

Russia and Japan's greed soon met head on in Manchuria. Mighty Russia went down in defeat to the upstart Japanese as its ships settled to the bottom of the China sea. Fearing further clashes between the big powers in China which might lead to world war, the cannibalization of China was temporarily halted by America's open-door policy.

This policy, advocated and negotiated by U.S. Secretary of State John Hay, has been variously interpreted. The U.S. claimed to desire the safeguarding of the territorial integrity of China. Other Western powers saw it as America's desire to share in the spoils. Chinese today will tell you that America was not acting in China's interest but purely from self-interest.

At the turn of the century a Manchu concubine, paramour of a former emperor, sat on China's imperial throno. She reached the throne by staging a coup d'etat in which she was said to have poisoned her own son on his throne, installed her infant nephew as emperor, killed his mother, and then ascended to the throne after throwing the young emperor into prison. She was an evil woman, hating the ground swell of public demand for government reform, and detesting the foreigners who plundered the land. Tied to the Confucian traditions, she turned China backward with an even more hopeless ultrareactionary regime. The depraved Empress Dowager, Ci Xi (Tzu Hsi), was backed by an equally depraved court eunuch, Li Lianying (Li Lien-ying). China had sunk to its lowest depths of despair.

Anti-Manchu outbreaks increased throughout the country. Behind most of the Chinese revolutions were the secret

societies, powerful, tightly knit, and overlaid with hatred for
the Manchus. One such was the Yi He Quan (I Ho Ch'uan),
who considered themselves undefeatable after performing
ritualized shadow boxing. Under the twin banners of
rebellion against the Manchus and later rebellion against the
foreigners, the "Boxers" soon controlled the countryside in
North China, threatening Beijing (Peking) and the Manchu
throne. The anti-Christian aspect of the Boxers will be examined later.

The wily old Empress, recognizing the threat to her
throne, decided to turn the wrath of the Boxers from herself
to the foreigners. This she did by siding with the Boxers and
issuing an edict commanding that all white people be killed.
Hatred for the foreign devil, long dormant, exploded all
across the country. The attack on Beijing (Peking) was successfully diverted from the Manchu throne to the foreign
legation in Beijing (Peking).

For two agonizing months the foreigners held out behind
the massive walls of the legation. Three thousand foreigners
and their friends endured repeated attacks. Alarmed Western powers around the world sent expeditionary forces to
the aid of the beleaguered legation. A mixed force of British,
French, Americans, Japanese, and Germans marched on
Beijing (Peking). The myth of the Boxer invincibility was
rapidly shattered. The rape of China took physical form as
the foreign troops went on an orgy of killing and destruction. One writer, a Frenchman, described the activities:
"Everything has been sacked, torn and destroyed . . . and
here and there, legs, hands, heads and bundles of hair. . . .
One should see the eagerness with which our soldiers fling
everything aside, hear their gay laughter!" The priceless
treasures of the imperial palace were looted and broken.

The tragic rape of China was not complete until the Western powers made the empire pay over three hundred and

thirty million dollars in reparations for the Boxer Rebellion damages. China was bleeding, broken, and handcuffed. The Western world had made an impact upon China—an impact the West would forever regret.

5

The Sun Still Shines

The dawning of the twentieth century saw an almost completely helpless China, pitifully prostrate from Western Imperialism and its own inability to meet the demands of the changing times. The stage was set for dramatic revolutionary change.

The foreign incursion of China created two disturbing factors which made transitory revolution inevitable. China's old order, though surviving longer than any other in history, could not survive the overpowering impact of the Western world. Sufficient for yesterday and workable in isolation, this extremely conservative Confucian order began to break down almost immediately. A new system had to be found to replace it. In addition, and to some extent for the same reason, China found it intensely difficult to handle the explosive impact of Western ideology, technology, or its overpowering economics. Doak Barnet classified the inevitable result as a "revolution of rising expectations."

Actually, neither the 1917 Bolshevik Revolution in Russia nor the inauguration of Dr. Sun Yi-xian (Sun Yat-sen) as the first President of the Republic of China in 1912 marked the real beginning of the revolution. Perhaps the most logical date was 1839. This was the year Britain fired the first shots in the Opium War, shots which triggered a series of deep and profound national revolutions, only the last of which was the Communist revolution.

In a little over one hundred years, China had changed more radically than any other nation. Profound changes were occurring in every phase of life from culture to ideology, from economics to the social system. In this process, I repeat, the Communists were only the last on the scene. Nor is the process yet complete.

Dr. Sun Yi-xian (Sun Yat-sen) occupies a unique role in modern China. Acknowledged as the first President of the Republic, he is honored by the Nationalists as the instigator of democracy, while at the same time the Communists honor him as the first revolutionary. So powerful were the winds of change in which he functioned that one is not always able to discern from whence they came or whither they were going. We do know that Sun Yi-xian (Sun Yat-sen) epitomizes the endeavor to create a new China.

Traveling widely in the United States, Japan, and later in Europe, Sun Yi-xian (Sun Yat-sen) observed that parliamentary democracy was the prevailing form of government in progressive Western countries. His restless, probing mind was also exposed to the socialistic writings of Karl Marx and others. He came into contact with a number of men who were talking of a new social order brought about by violent revolution. Thus democracy and socialism mingled hazily in his questing mind. Without training or expertise in government, Sun Yi-xian (Sun Yat-sen) proceeded to attempt first the overthrow of the Manchu dynasty in China and then the creation of a new China. Recognizing the obvious need for change in his beloved China, Sun Yi-xian (Sun Yat-sen) became an irrepressible activist.

His efforts to start the process of revolutionary change in China were certainly not crowned with immediate success. Despite a $750,000 price put on his head by the Beijing (Peking) government, and more than a dozen ill-conceived or ill-timed plots to overthrow the reigning dynasty, Sun relentlessly pursued his goal. A great deal of his time was spent traveling to the Chinese of the Diaspora around the world, attempting to interest them in the need for change in China. It was from these well-to-do Overseas Chinese that Dr. Sun obtained the all-important financial backing.

Meanwhile, back in China, the great debate was still on. It was generally agreed that China was in danger and therefore some kind of change was necessary—but what kind of change? Three distinct opinions emerged from the controversy. A reform group said that it was China's educational system which must be changed, in order to meet the challenge of the obviously more successful educational system of the foreigners. Their call was for slow, step-by-step reform. The Boxers represented those who claimed that the foreigners were responsible for all of China's troubles. The solution, therefore, was relatively simple: kill or expel all the foreigners from the sacred soil of China and all would be well. Dr. Sun and his followers claimed the Chinese rulers were corrupt and their government bad for the nation. They proposed an overthrow of the dynasty and the institution of a "democratic" government. Like most controversies, there was an element of truth in each position. Even though all three factions had suffered crushing defeats, all were still very much alive as the twentieth century dawned.

October 10, 1911 is celebrated by the People's Republic as the birthday of the Revolution. They call it the Double Tenth, that is, the tenth day of the tenth month. Actually there was almost a comic-opera sequence to the events of those days. Dr. Sun's revolutionary conspirators had established themselves in the Czarist Russian compound and were busily making bombs when one exploded on October 9th, thus prematurely disclosing Sun's plans. The next morning, an army unit in nearby Hankou (Hankow) revolted. The imperial palace was set afire and the once

mighty Manchu dynasty began to totter. Four months later
the Emperor abdicated his celestial throne. Dr. Sun had succeeded in his initial goal—the destruction of the corrupt
Manchu dynasty.

The man who sparked the revolution was in far-off
Denver, Colorado, on a fund-raising mission when news
reached him, via the morning paper, of the events in China.
In his absence, a provisional government was set up in Nanking and Dr. Sun Yi-xian (Sun Yat-sen) was elected the provisional President of China—but all was not well. A power
struggle still continued and would for years to come. Transition from China's ages-old dynastic rule to any form of
democracy was no flower-strewn pathway, nor indeed was
any change simple. Dr. Sun, now back in China, attempted
to strengthen the bond of his National People's Party, the
Guomindang (Kuomintang). His formal inauguration in
Nanjing (Nanking) on New Year's day 1912 did not significantly alter the difficult and extremely complex situation.

At this point we must examine the platform on which Dr.
Sun came to power. For years Dr. Sun had lectured on "The
Three Principles of the People." Abraham Lincoln was the
acknowledged inspiration for this concept with his unforgettable phrase, "government of the people, by the people,
and for the people." Dr. Sun translated this phrase "the people to have, the people to govern, the people to enjoy." He
listed the four aims of the revolution: (1) to drive away the
Manchus; (2) to restore China to the Chinese; (3) to establish
a republic; and (4) to equalize land-power. On the first two
aims he clearly wanted the elimination of the invading Manchus who had ruled China for 260 years. Points three and
four are open for interpretation. Dr. Sun himself wrote,
"The President will be elected by the mass of the people. A
parliament will be made up of men elected by the citizens."
Obviously, Dr. Sun's original plan has not been adhered to

by the present régime, which claims to wear his mantle. In point four Dr. Sun attempts to deal with China's most acute problem—land ownership. Socialism, he felt, offered the best answer to this recurring problem. "We shall establish a socialistic state that will ensure all citizens a decent living," wrote Dr. Sun.

Claims have not infrequently been made that Dr. Sun Yi-xian (Sun Yat-sen) was a Communist. This is, of course, the position of the People's Republic of China. Without doubt, he read and absorbed every socialistic book he could get his hands on. There is no doubt, either, that socialism seemed to offer solutions to some of the problems facing China as he saw them. Dr. Sun had reached these conclusions even before the Bolshevik Revolution of 1912. It is apparent his conclusions were not tied to communism but rather to the kind of equality which Abraham Lincoln was talking about. Dr. Sun Yi-xian (Sun Yat-sen) was profoundly influenced by his Christian faith. Dr. Henry Martin reports a 1912 speech which Dr. Sun gave in Boston to a crowded church audience. "Men say," he began, "that the revolution originated with me. I do not deny the charge. But where did the idea of revolution come from? It came because from my youth I had intercourse with foreign missionaries. Those from Europe and America, with whom I associated, put the ideals of freedom and liberty into my heart. Now I call upon the church to help in the establishment of the new government. The Republic cannot endure unless there is that virtue—the righteousness for which the Christian religion stands—it's the center of the nation's life."

In a letter to his old friends Dr. and Mrs. Cantile, Dr. Sun wrote from Hong Kong after his elevation to the Presidency: "I thank you for your earnest prayers on my behalf. I am glad to tell you that we are going to have religious toleration in China and I assure you that Christianity will flourish under the new régime." The records show that soon after his election he encouraged the destruction of heathen idols and temples. A considerable number of Dr. Sun's associates were Christians, including his private secretary, his son, at least three of his cabinet members, president and vice-president of the national assembly in Nanjing (Nanking), and twenty-five per cent of the members of the assembly. The impact of Christ upon China had reached the highest echelons of government.

As has been stated earlier in this chapter, there appears to have been no clear demarcation in Dr. Sun's mind between socialism and democracy. It is possible to isolate certain statements of his and "prove" he was a "communist." It is equally possible to "prove" he was not, by his own writings. One of his biographers, Lyon Sharman, puts it this way: "The more widely one ranges over Sun Yi-xian's (Sun Yat-sen's) writings the more evident it becomes that inconsistency is not a phenomenon of infrequent occurrence." His was not the ordered mind of a scientist, but rather the flaming mind of a man who wanted the best for his country.

Perhaps the single greatest mistake that Dr. Sun made was to assume that democracy, as he saw it in the West, could be instantly imposed upon the framework of China. The fact is, there was absolutely no foundation on which to build a democracy. Professor C. P. Fitzgerald points out that in the Chinese concept "there is no place for freedom as the West understands it, no place for salvation as the Christian understands it, and no place for individualism as the liberal would have it." In other words, there were none of the concepts that a true democracy requires. Someone has said that "democracy requires a Judaeo-Christian background." No such substructure exists in China. Hubert Humphrey is quoted as saying, "The whole moral justification for democracy is man and his relationship to his God."

Conversely, many Chinese concepts fitted conveniently into the order which evolved—humanism, a sense of obligation to a single sovereign, loyalty to a single doctrine (i.e. Confucianism), subordination of the individual to the decisions of others, and loyalty to the clan. Here was fertile soil for the concepts espoused by the Marxists, or alternatively another form of government which vested the bulk of the decision-making power in the hands of a sovereign ruler. I am not by any means suggesting, even faintly, that Marxism is the best form of government for China or for any country. What I am suggesting is that China, and many countries of Asia and Africa, find democracy as we know it attractive but unfeasible. Frequently, in the so-called developing countries of the world, the facade of democracy imposed upon them by their former colonial masters or, as in China's case, by revolutionary figures, disintegrates. The foundations have never been laid. The structure without foundations collapses.

Three years of brutal, rapacious, internal war and centuries of unconcerned Czarist rule preceded the coming of Communism to Russia. Thirty-eight years of civil war and centuries of rape by both the Western world and alien dynasties preceded the advent of Communism to China. In other words, the Communists only attained power when the structure of government and the entire fabric of society had been torn apart. Sun Yi-xian's (Sun Yat-sen's) attempt to impose a form of democracy on China failed. Mao Zedong (Mao Tse-tung) moved in on the almost totally collapsed governmental structure of the Guomindang (Kuomintang). What occurred in both instances was not the failure of democracy but rather the lack of democracy which paved the way for the Marxists. Never have the Marxists been able to dominate or subjugate a working democracy. This point is not in question. Communism is not an alternative to democracy but rather an alternative to chaos.

Sun Yi-xian (Sun Yat-sen) was now faced with an infinitely greater undertaking than bringing down the already tottering Manchu dynasty. Filling the vacuum left by the destruction of the dynasty was a Herculean task fraught with a myriad of unforeseen pitfalls. Time was to reveal that China had not fundamentally changed with the fall of the Manchus. It further disclosed that the government, which Dr. Sun headed, was totally unprepared to govern.

Politics, an unknown, untried element in China, soon gave way to the more familiar element of power. Just forty-three days after Dr. Sun's inauguration, he was dethroned and power was in the hands of Yuan Shi-kai (Yuan Shih-kai), a skillful northern warlord. China soon broke up into a cluster of self-contained dynasties headed by power-hungry warlords.

Not until ten years later was Sun Yi-xian (Sun Yat-sen) able to move back into the forefront of leadership, for a brief period. Much had happened in the intervening years causing the country to be racked and torn by internal dissensions. An attempt to reinstate the monarchy failed. The warlord Yuan died suddenly and another equally powerful warlord succeeded him. On the international front, the world was fully occupied with World War I.

Allied victory gave China hope that the Versailles Peace Conference would restore Chinese territory held by Germany. Instead, Germany's holdings in China were turned over to Japan. Woodrow Wilson's lofty principles and declarations of self-determination apparently were not meant to apply to China. Chinese disillusionment with the West was now complete. Paul S. Reinsch, then American Minister to China, described the situation: "Probably nowhere else in the world had expectations of America's leadership at Paris been raised so high as in China. The Chinese trusted America, they trusted the frequent declarations of principle uttered by President Wilson, whose words had reached China in its remotest parts. The more intense was their disappointment and disillusionment due to the decisions of the old men that controlled the Paris Conference. It sickened and disheartened me," wrote Reinsch, "to think how the Chinese people would receive this blow which meant the blasting of their hopes and destruction of their confidence in the equity of nations. . . ."

Militant nationalism was the immediate progeny, appearing for the first time in China's long history. The May 4th Movement of 1919 unleashed two powerful emancipation efforts. One was led by admirers of "American-type pragmatism and liberalism advocating democracy, science, and modern education." The cutting edges of this segment were attacks on the traditional culture and society, which they felt were a millstone prohibiting progress. The other group, almost insignificant at first, was inspired by the Bolshevik Revolution just two years earlier. They were convinced that Marxism, not democracy, was the cure-all for China.

Both groups now turned to Sun Yi-xian (Sun Yat-sen), who seemed to be the living polarization of both schools of thought and the only one capable of uniting a sadly divided nation. He called for a free and independent China. He urged democracy in which not just government but the people would have power. It was in his economic program that shades of Marxism appeared. He urged the State to move to the forefront in solving the massive problems of food, clothing, shelter, and land ownership. He believed that State capital should undergird industry.

It is important that we look carefully at Sun's proposals

for change. Ping-chia Kuo skillfully summarizes: "Sun believed that revolution and reconstruction should proceed by three stages: first, by military rule; second, by political tutelage; and last, by constitutional government." It is apparent the order was the only logical one as long as impatience didn't upset the order. Either too long a military rule, too short a period of political education, or too early a constitutional government could be disastrous. Traditional Chinese patience, however, had run out. No one was willing to wait for anything. Instant solutions were sought for complex long-term problems.

Events galloped. The rapidity of happenings show up clearly in this summarization:

1917 May 4th Movement launches militant nationalism and Sun Yi-xian (Sun Yat-sen) becomes the leader.
1921 Communist Party formed in China by twelve Marxists.
1922 Chiang Kai-shek appears as a promising military leader in Sun's Guomindang (Kuomintang).
1922 Soviet Union establishes itself as only nation willing to extend Sun a hand to rebuild China.
1925 Dr. Sun Yi-xian (Sun Yat-sen) dies; Chiang Kai-shek gradually assumes leadership.

The death of Dr. Sun did not basically alter China's direction. The Guomindang (Kuomintang) proclaimed him a national hero and attempted to adopt his program. By 1928 China was well on its way to solving many of its problems. Observers felt that at last meaningful steps were being taken to harmonize with the realities of the modern world. No less a historian than Kenneth Scott Latourette summarizes the situation in these words, "Observers . . . saw indication that China's long agony and weakness were passing. . . . Here and there were inefficiency and corruption, but they were no more pronounced than in some of the greatest periods in

China's history or than in many strong Western governments. Education was being improved and extended to a
growing proportion of the population, cities were being
modernized, automobiles and airplanes were improving
communications, railroads were being repaired after the
years of domestic war, banditry was being reduced, and
progress was being made in regaining the nation's full
autonomy." Hopes were riding high. Then catastrophe
struck!

In September of 1931, Japan began its long, devastating
war to capture Chinese raw materials, offset the incursions
of the Russians, and gain added territory for its population
expansion. The Japanese invasion of China eventually resulted in the collapse of Chiang Kai-shek's armies and the re-
sultant Communist takeover. Again Latourette summarizes,
"Many observers held that had Japan not intruded into the
domestic scene the Guomindang (Kuomintang) would have
succeeded in effecting an orderly transition to a China
which would have had much of what the Anglo-Saxon
world called democracy. That, however, was not to be."

Republican China, birthed by Sun Yi-xian (Sun Yat-sen),
turned now to the threat of Japan and the cancer that would
eventually drive it into exile. To this day, Dr. Sun continues
to hold the respect of Chinese peoples the world over. As he
lay dying on the 11th of March, 1925, his family and intimate friends gathered at his bedside. His long, hard struggle was almost over. His mind had been exposed to many
conflicting ideologies, each offering promise for the future.
None succeeded in robbing him of his faith in Christ. His
deathbed message was, "I am a disciple of Jesus Christ, commissioned by God to declare war against evil. Even when I
die, I want people to know I am a Christian." Sun still
shines!

6

Five Stars over China

To describe the period before and after the death of Dr. Sun Yi-xian (Sun Yat-sen) as "transitional" would be an understatement. History will use the radical, acrid term, "revolution!"

There are grounds for believing that the Guomindang (Kuomintang) party founded by Dr. Sun, and inherited by Chiang Kai-shek, might have been able to cope with mere transition. I am well aware of the fact that the favorite sport of many observers of modern Chinese history is to paint the Guomindang (Kuomintang) with the darkest colors on their pallets. Incompetence, bribery, and corruption are the favorite smears. Any fair judge, however, would take into consideration the mitigating circumstances. Take, for instance, China's population explosion. In a single century China's population had more than doubled. China was administratively unprepared to cope with the situation. The ramifications were complex and profuse—often taking the form of chain reaction.

As a by-product of the exploding populace there was an abundance of cheap labor. This deterred China from entering the era of the Industrial Revolution with other nations. Entering the manufacturing era, China would have been forced to train its youth in both leadership and the sciences. She would have thus been better prepared economically and militarily. As it was, China was chained to the primitive past while the West made dramatic progress.

Foreign intrusion produced additional unlimited problems for government and created revolutionary tendencies.
Consider the several million square miles of China's most
vital areas usurped by foreigners after World War I. Consider the jarring clash of cultures, the rapid assimilation of
some of the worst features of Western civilization, the
haughty air so often displayed by the sophisticated, but
often less cultured, foreigners, and the acrid taste left by the
non-Chinese emperors that had ruled China for so long.

No country in history was more ripe for revolution—any
revolution. The revolution began to take shape in "The New
Cultural Movement" that soon was ensconced in the National Beijing (Peking) University. Originating as an all-out
attack on Chinese tradition, especially Confucianism, it was
basically pro-Western. Hardly a trace of socialism could be
found. This was a call for the destruction of the old and the
adoption of Western culture with emphasis on science and
democracy. Soon many of the best young minds in China
were reading, and being greatly influenced by, the movement's influential magazine, "The New Youth." A bright
new day appeared to be dawning.

Two significant events altered the course of this well-
meaning revolution and spawned the anarchic Communist
movement in China. The first event had little impact upon
China, strangely enough, until after the second had
occurred.

The Russian "October Revolution" of 1917 had not attracted much attention in China, even among the intellectuals. China had entered World War I on the side of the
Allies. The end of the war in 1918 caused jubilation in
China. Right had conquered might; democracy was obviously superior to any form of imperialism. Hopes were high
that the Versailles Peace Conference of 1919 would restore
Chinese territory held by Germany. Surely the democratic

nations of the world acting on Woodrow Wilson's "Four-teen Points" would right this wrong.

Instead, that territory within China was awarded to Japan who had seized it from the Germans during the war. All of China's hopes were dashed. The West was to pay dearly for this unjustifiable decision. On May 4, 1919 China exploded into what was virtually the first mass expression of popular political action in its entire history. Now known as "The May 4th Movement," it demonstrated for the first time, to the Chinese, the power of nationwide political organization. Strikes and boycotts on Japanese goods began to take effect. Those who desired change found a means to an end.

Faith in democracy was shattered and virtually des-troyed. The West had let them down completely. China could never trust them again. The Chinese began to look elsewhere for guidance and assistance in solving China's multitudinous problems. It was at this time that Chinese in-tellectuals began to take a second look at the Bolshevik Revo-lution. Russia seized this opportune moment to move in on the vacuum left behind by the Versailles Peace Conference. She declared her friendship for the great Chinese people, promising to support them in their struggle for complete freedom and to return land seized by their former czarist rulers. The Russians were soon in a privileged position.

The disillusioned intellectuals of The Democratic League began to read, with great interest, the writings of Com-munism. The Communist Manifesto was first published in China in 1920. The Soviets began a well-planned campaign to export this ideology to China. As a result of these efforts the Chinese Communist Party was formed in 1921, made up primarily of members of the New Democratic League, who only so recently were convinced that democracy held the answer.

It has been pointed out, and I think correctly, that the initial attraction to Marxism was not because of any inherent value the Chinese may have seen in Marxist theory, but simply because Marxism rose triumphant out of the Russian revolution. In the early days of the Revolution in China, very little was known about Marxism. A few Chinese intellectuals studying abroad in France, Japan, and England had come face to face with this ideology. Chinese intellectuals in China did not pay much attention to Marxism until their hopes for democracy were shattered by the Versailles Peace Conference.

Certain facets of Marxism undoubtedly forcefully appealed to the revolutionary Chinese mind. The emphasis upon science, the systematic methods, the call for the destruction of the past, and the emphasis upon the material world all held strong attraction. Anything that could possibly help to generate change was appreciated. It is very doubtful that Marxism's atheism was really understood at this time by many who were seriously considering Marxism as the cure-all for China's ills.

A rapid swing toward Marxism now occurred among some intellectuals throughout the country. Confusion was prevalent as each faction attempted to extract what they could out of Marxism. Even Dr. Sun Yi-xian (Sun Yat-sen) and, later, Chiang Kai-shek were involved. The great need was for change. Willingness was demonstrated to forget one's differences and unite for a common goal—a New China. Strange bedfellows developed during that period.

It is not the aim of this chapter to discuss in detail the origins of Chinese Communism or even how they finally succeeded in gaining control of China. We shall, however, have to make some observations before we look at China under the Five Stars.

From 1919 onward, Moscow begain to train Comintern ([Com]munist [Intern]ational) agents in the art of inciting rebellion against capitalistic or imperialistic governments and to form Communist parties. Very soon many of these agents were operating within China. Among the best known were Voitinsky and, later, Joffe. As a result, the Chinese Communist Party (C.C.P.) was established with direct guidance from the Comintern and acted initally under direct orders from the Soviet Union. The C.C.P. rapidly matured and expanded under this experienced guidance.

Mao Zedong (Mao Tse-tung), although one of the founding fathers, did not come into immediate prominence. His genius lay in the fact that he was not willing to follow the Soviet example. He saw China as a different situation demanding different tactics. Mao was not a follower—he was a leader. During the internal struggles of the next few years these leadership qualities were duly recognized as he evolved a distinctive Chinese branch of socialism.

Mao's success lay largely in the fact that he was able to make indigenous what was a foreign import, Marxism-Leninism. "In the past," Mao wrote, "China has suffered greatly by accepting foreign ideas simply because they were foreign. Chinese Communists must effect a genuine synthesis between the universal truth of Marxism and the concrete practice of the Chinese revolution. Only after we have found our own form of Marxism will it prove useful."

He realized that China, to a degree unknown by other nations, was primarily a peasant nation tied to tradition. For instance, China traditionally held that every man had "three bonds": those between prince and subject, father and son, and husband and wife. These were the heart of the Confucian ethic. Mao rejected all this and more when he wrote, "Our country's three bonds must go; [they], constituted with religion, capitalists, and autocracy, are the four evil demons of the empire." There is no question as to whom he considered his greatest enemies.

Mao's study of the "Communist Manifesto" and other standard socialistic works blinded him to the revolutionary potential of the peasants until 1925. From that point on, Mao never swerved in his emphasis on the peasants.

The "Long March" of 1934-36 was the turning point in his life. Called "one of the great triumphs of men against odds and man against nature," it was a personal triumph for Mao. Though it was actually a six-thousand-mile forced retreat on foot from the armies of the Guomindang (Kuomintang), it proved his leadership ability. Up until that time, Mao was ridiculed by the Communist leadership for his "countryside policy" and his "banditry doctrine." In January of 1935 he assumed the chairmanship of the Politburo fully fifteen years after his open espousal of Marxism.

The road to victory for Mao and his followers was long and intensely difficult. It was a cold February morning in 1949 when General Lin Biao's (Lin Piao's) divisions finally marched into Beijing (Peking). Eight months later Tiananmen (Tien An Men) square was throbbing with the now characteristic masses when Chairman Mao proclaimed the birth of The People's Republic of China on the first day of October.

The five-starred crimson flag now waved, at least symbolically, over all of China. The large star represented the Communist Party. The smaller stars represented the workers, the peasants, the intellectuals, and the small "capitalists." All fit neatly on the upper left-hand corner of the new flag. Whether they could coexist in China was still to be tested. Twenty-eight years after the founding of the C.C.P. the nation was held in its tightfisted grip. The "Mandate of Heaven" had been transferred to a new kind of emperor, Mao Zedong (Mao Tse-tung).

Liu Shaoqi (Liu Shao-chi), president of the new state, sounded the theme of the next few years of China's history when he declared, "The cause of Communism is a long, bitter, and arduous—but ultimately victorious—process of struggle. Without such struggle there can be no Communism." He himself was later to taste, along with millions of his countrymen, the bitterness of the struggle when he was toppled and completely humiliated during the Cultural Revolution. Still in disgrace he died, probably of cancer, early in 1973. No official explanation of his death has ever been given.

All revolutions are by nature bloody. Mao's was certainly no exception. Changes in China have always required bloodshed. The war in China from 1946 till 1949 probably took more lives than any war of modern times. Mao came to power at a time when only a small minority of the masses cared who ruled China. All they wanted was peace. The road to "Peace" had been so very long and bloody.

From the very beginning of his reign Chairman Mao began to appeal to the Chinese sense of pride. Many centuries had slipped by since there had been occasion for national pride—but pride in the Han race (Han Zu [Han-tzu]) was perpetual. It was to this pride that Mao appealed in his now famous speech delivered on September 21, 1949. "It was only in modern times that [the Han people] have fallen behind, and this was due solely to the oppression and exploitation of foreign imperialism and the domestic revolutionary government." Mao went on to declare, "Our nation will never again be an insulted nation. We have stood up." Mark carefully these words, "We have stood up."

All Chinese believed it was time for this to happen. There was indeed considerable difference of opinion on how this could be achieved. Mao believed that socialism held all the keys. In another 1949 speech he declared that the goal of "The People's Democratic Dictatorship" was to advance China "from an agricultural to an industrial country, from a new democratic to a socialist and Communist society, to abolish classes and to achieve world Communism." In this single speech Mao delineated the two most important factors in the successes of the future: the appeal to national, or more correctly, racial pride, and his policy of aggressive revolution under a new social system.

In his goal of a "People's Democratic Dictatorship" Mao picked up three separate concepts of government and attempted to mold them into a single, cohesive unit. Borrowing from China's past, from its contact with the West, and from the Soviet Union, he proceeded to work out his own form of government.

In analyzing Mao's governmental plan, it breaks down into three steps epitomized by the three words "People's Democratic Dictatorship." Each describes a phase of government. "People's," of course, is mentioned first to appeal to the masses who have never had a voice in government. It is a kind of smokescreen behind which the government can do what it wishes with the people. Actually the people come last in the chain of command.

At the top of the chain of command is the Central Committee, which dictates desired policies. The Central Committee is dominated by the Chairman. All policies find their genesis at that point. Never do the people initiate policy.

Second in the chain is the Party. This organization permeates all levels of society—national, provincial, city, country, village. This is at once the all-seeing eye of the Central Committee, the agency to carry out its orders, and the executor-executioner that sees that proper punishment is administered where necessary. The Party exists to carry out the orders of the Chairman. This is the day-to-day government, governing according to the mandate of the Central Committee.

Last on the list are the people. Mao gave to them the great

and glorious honor of participating in the government of the country. Actually they have no voice in real government. All they can do is what the Chairman decides they can do. This is, in fact, a dictatorship that uses pseudodemocratic means to govern the people. In practice, Mao's form of government had become a military dictatorship, in the sense that the army was frequently called on to enforce government policy and quell dissent and rebellion.

Mao reversed the age-old relationship of the intellectuals to government. The intellectuals now became the target of the people's hatred, rather than being aloof from the people's hardship. It is true that certain classes of people in China have been enlisted to participate in the government of the country at a local level. This is a step forward, but a far cry from the government by the people.

Mao believed that violence is a vital ingredient in revolution. "A revolution," he wrote, "is an act of violence whereby one class overthrows the authority of another. Revolution is not a dinner party." Never has he been known to shrink from violence.

No price was too great to pay for these objectives. This explains the immediate readiness of many Chinese to accept Mao's policies, and also the frequent disputes, conflicts, and purges that were to follow. Mao was convinced that much had to be destroyed before anything new could be built. He saw it as a sort of "urban renewal" project on a national level. Never did he wince as the old came crashing to the ground. In his eyes he saw the glorious new society that would rise out of the rubble of the old.

Mao and his leaders were forced to make a rather rapid transition from mere opposition to a ruling régime to being the régime that ruled. The peasants constitute four-fifths of China's total population. They farm the country's ten per cent of arable land for food for survival. The first order of business thus became the "reorganization of the peasants and land reform." This entailed a campaign against the landlords and moneylenders. Owners of as few as three acres were considered landlords. China herself estimated that between 1950 and 1952 800,000 persons were killed in the campaign to wipe out the landlord class. At first the land was divided among the peasants, then when Mao's position became more secure it was taken away from them and transferred into state-owned cooperatives or communes.

Systematically all opposition to the régime was eliminated. A succession of "anti" campaigns purged the bourgeois class. Thought reform or "brain washing" was refined and intensified. Friends were turned against friends, children against parents. Everyone became a suspect—one even suspected oneself. It has been suggested that a sense of "sin" was now introduced into the Chinese mind for possibly the first time as confession meetings were frequently held. Written confessions were encouraged and often demanded. A calculated attempt was being made to mold the minds of earth's largest nation and in the process destroy all forms of opposition. The traditions of Confucianism, filial piety, and reverence for the old were supposed to coming crashing to the ground as unworthy survivors of another era.

By 1956 Mao thought that sufficient progress had been made in eliminating the bourgeois mentality to permit a slackening of pressure upon the intellectuals. The "Hundred Flowers Movement" was launched, encouraging intellectuals to criticize the policies and actions of the government. The barrage of criticism which started slowly but soon gained alarming momentum shocked the government into reactionary reprisals. A large number of China's vocal intellectuals were shipped off to China's "Siberia" for either liquidation or thought reform. A few were executed publicly. Criticism of government became from then on a crime of high treason. The gist of the criticism was that Communist officials were the new "privileged class" of China.

The ever-optimistic, but not too realistic, Chairman concluded by late 1957 that the time had come to institute instantaneous socialism culturally, socially, and economically. He called it "The Great Leap Forward." In an earlier paper Mao had written, "In a few decades, why can't 600 million paupers by their own efforts create a socialist country, rich and strong?" Now he proposed to leap those decades. The Great Leap Forward began in 1958.

Utilizing what was possibly history's most massive use of manpower, Mao hoped in one fell swoop to destroy the past and overnight turn China into an industrial-agricultural nation equal to any Western nation. 60 million peasants built and operated backyard blast furnaces; 100 million peasants with baskets and shovels set to work on miles of irrigation canals. Other millions of peasants were urged to produce greater harvest. To generate maximum labor power and strike a deathblow at the Chinese family unit, communes were established. Men and women were separated and the entire nation turned into a state farm.

Initial reports spoke of great success. Soon it became apparent that both the attempt to destroy the family unit and the attempt to leap the centuries failed. To compound the problem, severe drought and then severe flooding hit the nation for two successive years. The Great Leap became a debacle. Communist China hit its lowest ebb during the winter of 1960-61. Mao himself became the target of strong criticism within his own party.

To get the country back on its feet more realistic policies were inaugurated. The commune system was drastically revised. Private plots of land were granted to the peasants and incentives were established. Liu Shaoqi (Liu Shao-chi) became the head of the government, though Mao retained his Chairmanship.

During the next few years policies of moderation became the norm. China made dramatic progress in industrialization and agriculture—even education seemed to get a new lease of life. Mao bided his time. Somehow the country must be saved from revisionism. He, the great revolutionist, must act. This he did in what is now known as The Cultural Revolution.

Attempting to understand, much less appraise, the Cultural Revolution during the turbulent years 1966-1969 was virtually impossible. Chinese Communists maintain it was a great success. Most observers would disagree with this appraisal. It has been claimed that the Cultural Revolution was "the most important and momentous movement in Communist China during her twenty years of existence." If indeed it was, then we must look closely at one of the most violent periods in China's immediate past. Perhaps at this distance we can make a more realistic appraisal.

Chairman Mao Zedong (Mao Tse-tung) had been forced into semiretirement mainly because of his ill-fated Hundred Flowers Movement and The Great Leap Forward. The image of infallibility had been completely shattered. There were strong elements in China that now felt that they could get along better without Mao. He was too much of a revolutionary idealist—not pragmatic enough.

Putting the country back on its feet following the fiasco of The Great Leap Forward was no easy task. The man who did the job was President Liu Shaoqi (Liu Shao-chi). President Liu had been hand-selected by Mao as his successor. They were both old hands in the Chinese Communist Party, having traveled a long hard road together.

It seems apparent that Liu Shaoqi (Liu Shao-chi) felt that

the physical and financial well-being, rather than the ideological climate of the nation, was the most important issue of the time. New policies and attitudes began to emerge. Incentive plans spurred the people on to greater production both in farming and industry. Peasants were given private plots of land for their own use. Heavy industry was downgraded to provide the light manufacturing items needed by the average person. The complexion of the communes was completely changed. A new governmental policy began to emerge that had all the appearances of moderation and restraint.

There is evidence that at this time both Mao and Lin Biao (Lin Piao) had quietly withdrawn from Beijing (Peking) to an area where they felt safer from a possible coup. In fact, for several years Mao disappeared almost completely from the political scene. This is not to say that he was inactive, though he did complain that he was never consulted. One can only imagine how dismayed he must have been as he surveyed the situation.

The great savior of the Chinese people now felt despised and rejected. He found his revolution was dying in the wake of policies over which he had no control. Something had to be done to save China from revisionism. China must be put back on the right road—the road called revolution. Mao believed that perpetual revolution was the only way to maintain socialism. Any degree of moderation or liberalization would destroy the great Marxist society he dreamed of. The situation obviously called for action—drastic action.

Mao carefully laid his plans for a comeback. The magic word to him has always been "REVOLUTION." The Chinese phrase translated "cultural revolution" literally means "great revolution of civilization." Obviously that would take a lot of prearrangement.

Soon he had gathered a team he considered loyal to himself and the revolution. Marshall Lin Biao (Lin Piao), hero of many battles against the nationalists and during the Korean War, became his right-hand man. What Chairman Mao did not know at the time was that Lin Biao (Lin Piao) aspired to the chairmanship himself.

Marshall Lin Biao (Lin Piao) was a little man with a high-pitched squeaky voice and very little personal magnetism. He was, however, a brilliant military man destined to become one of the main heroes of The Cultural Revolution. His position in the Communist hierarchy also was secure because he had been a close confidant of the Chairman since the earliest days of the revolution.

> The most devastating and destructive of all the "rectification campaigns" was the so-called Great Proletarian Cultural Revolution. This turned into a real donnybrook. It was a dog-eat-dog, no-holds-barred period for settling personal and Party scores.

As the Minister of Defense, Lin Biao (Lin Piao) began his attempt to mold China's massive army into a political machine. This was no easy task. Loyalty to Mao was stressed by the study and application of Mao's thoughts. Though Chen Boda (Chen Po-ta) is credited with being the creator of the Mao cult, it was Lin Biao (Lin Piao) that really got things moving. Chen originally put together "The Selected Writings of Mao Zedong (Mao Tse-Tung)" but it was Lin that assembled the now world-famous *Thoughts of Mao Zedong (Mao Tse-tung)*—The Little Red Book.

As the Mao cult intensified Mao was described to be "the greatest genius of our time." His thoughts were declared to be "the greatest truth ever known since time immemorial." It was announced that in a period of five months in 1967 the mobilized printing industry of China printed 35,000,000 copies of Mao's selected works. In a two-year period over two billion copies of Mao's writings rolled off the presses. Unquestionably this was the greatest short-term explosion of one man's writings in print that the world has ever seen.

There are clear indications that Mao was genuinely concerned about Chinese young people in 1965. What direction would the young people take? On toward complete socialism, or back to a revival of the Guomindang (Kuomintang) and capitalism? He could see no middle road. During the period of Liu Shaoqi's (Liu Shao-chi's) revisionism the youth were showing evidence of losing their revolutionary fervor. If the young could not be kept in a revolutionary frame of mind then all was lost.

The Peoples Liberation Army, though led by his loyal supporter Lin Biao (Lin Piao), was sadly divided. The generals were jockeying for power and position. They could not be counted on to do exactly what Mao wanted. In fact, Mao only had three people he could completely rely on: his wife,

Marshall Lin Biao (Lin Piao), and his political secretary Chen Boda (Chen Po-ta).

In one master stroke Mao bypassed both the doubtful army and the party machinery which was firmly under the control of President Liu. He took his revolution directly to the class of citizens who react most readily to a call for revolution—the youth. In order to give the youth an added impetus Mao ordered all schools to be closed. Soon he had orchestrated a massive revolution, with the youth as the cutting edge.

The Red Guards (literally "soldiers who protect the red") blossomed after the students of Beijing (Peking) University were encouraged to purge their revisionist president. That accomplished, Mao asked them to travel throughout the entire nation and destroy the four olds—old ideas, old culture, old customs, and old habits. No school, free travel passes, and a total absence of discipline for the first time in their lives were weighty liberties for Chinese youth.

Response to Chairman Mao's call was overwhelming. On August 18th Mao reviewed one million youth gathered in Beijing's (Peking's) Tiananmen (Tien An Men) square. During the three-month summer period in 1966 Mao is said to have reviewed over eleven million Red Guards in Peking.

The keynote of the revolution was to "struggle against and crush those persons in authority who are taking the capitalist road . . . and all other exploiting classes . . . to transform education, literature and art, and all other parts of the superstructure that do not correspond to the socialist economic base."

As could be expected, young revolutionaries are easier to start than to stop, easier to inspire than to control. The Great Proletarian Revolution soon became a carnage. Everything from Western dress to Western hair cuts, from cosmetics to perfume, was purged. Houses were looted and old people insulted. The demonstrations became increasingly violent.

Demonstrations against religion began on August 23rd when all Protestant and Roman Catholic churches in Beijing (Peking) were closed. Religious pictures and symbols were destroyed and replaced with Red flags and portraits of Chairman Mao. In Guangzhou (Canton) all churches were closed four days later. Even in remote Lhasa (Tibet's capital) Red Guards sacked the principal temple of Lhamaism and destroyed all religious effigies. Confucianist temples, images of Buddha, and all the religious literature they could find were destroyed throughout the country.

The ruthless, undisciplined action of the young Red Guards soon aroused considerable popular resentment and enmity. Armed clashes between the Red Guards and the populace began to occur with increasing frequency. Rival groups sprang up within the Red Guard movement. Pitched battles occurred as disorder and anarchy spread, splitting the country into hundreds of disjointed pieces.

There is no point in cataloguing the excesses of the Cultural Revolution. As could be expected, all this anarchic behavior soon brought China's economy to the brink of disaster. Farming was neglected and food was soon in short supply. Conflict spilled over China's borders and her relations with foreign countries generally deteriorated. Since one of the goals of the revolution was a destruction of "Soviet Revisionism," relations with Russia became strained almost to the breaking point. The damage may never be repaired.

Finally, in June 1968, Mao officially admitted that the Red Guards had sadly disappointed him—and they certainly had. All the high ideals and moral virtues that Mao had tried to instill in them were forgotten or completely ignored. Obviously, he had not succeeded in changing human nature. The true nature of man quickly surfaced once restraint was removed. It was reported, for instance, that one million illegitimate children were born to these meandering young

Red Guards. The ground swell of opposition throughout
China to the Red Guards became so intense that a counter-
revolution seemed a distinct possibility.

Mao and Lin had to act. There was only one thing they
could do—turn to the army to restore order. The army, in
essence, agreed to do it for a price. They demanded and got
a much stronger voice in the leadership of the nation. Part of
the price Mao paid was the naming of Lin Biao (Lin Piao) as
his heir apparent. Soon the military was in control of most
of the nation's revolutionary committees from the provincial to the municipal level. Chairman Mao was forced to
share his throne with the army. This may well have been a
carefully calculated move by Lin Biao (Lin Piao). Subsequent events seem to indicate this.

President Liu Shaoqi (Liu Shao-chi) meanwhile was
humiliated, abused and abased by the Red Guards. He was
branded a "renegade, traitor and scab," a "lackey of imperialism and the Guomindang (Kuomintang)." He was dis-
missed from the Communist Party and all his posts. He died
in disgrace some four years later. Liu Shaoqi (Liu Shao-chi)
had been a close companion of Mao through all the bitter
years of struggle only to come to such an ignominious end.

Not long after the end of The Cultural Revolution two of
Mao's closest companions disappeared mysteriously. Two
of the three people considered closest to Chairman Mao
were, suddenly, nowhere to be found. Chen Boda (Chen
Po-ta), his political secretary, amidst veiled accusations and
rumors, seemed to evaporate.

Then in September of 1971 news leaked out of a Chinese
military plane crashing in Mongolia. At first Beijing (Peking)
withheld details then announced that Marshall Lin Biao (Lin
Piao) had died in an air crash trying to flee to the Soviet
Union after an abortive attempt to assassinate Mao.

Was the Great Proletarian Cultural Revolution a success
or a failure? Arguments for either postulate are not difficult

to find. For instance, if you are a confirmed Marxist, you would conclude that no price is too great to pay for the destruction of tendencies toward capitalism. Therefore, the revolution must have been a success.

Chairman Mao used the revolution to reaffirm his leadership. However, it is debatable whether he really came out as the winner. One of the functions of the Red Guards was to build Mao's image. They placed his portrait and his statues in every conceivable nook and corner of the nation. As they humiliated, looted, and generally made a nuisance of themselves they waved the Little Red Book and chanted Mao thoughts. In the minds of many in China, it is Mao's name that is linked with the boorish, bombastic actions of the Red Guards. In addition, the man responsible for popularizing the Little Red Book, Lin Biao (Lin Piao), was now labeled as a great enemy of the state.

Soon, throughout China, a damper was put on the cult of Mao. His pictures slowly began to disappear and so did his statues. The silk looms of China began turning out more portraits of Zhou Enlai (Chou En-lai) than Mao. The Little Red Book was now marked for elimination. In fact, those found reading the Little Red Book today are suspected of being followers of the traitor Lin Biao (Lin Piao). Fewer titles were attached to the Chairman's name. The day-to-day government of the nation slipped from Mao's grasp. Possibly time alone will tell whether Mao won or lost in The Cultural Revolution. It appears that he did come out of the shadows but was slowly eased out of the responsibilities of real leadership.

We must also consider the traumatic effect this revolution must have had on the Chinese Communist Party. Never before in any Communist country had a purge by a section of the Communist leadership been directed against the party bureaucracy. This was real infighting. The party had to yield the reins to the military. This was a total reversal of

Mao's stated policies. He had always insisted that the military must be subject to the party.

The dominant figure in immediate post-Cultural Revolution China was Premier Zhou Enlai (Chou En-lai). This fact alone is worthy of a book. At the helm was a man who survived fifty years of the kind of political storms that shipwrecked such stalwarts as Lin Biao (Lin Piao) and Liu Shaoqi (Liu Shao-chi). Zhou (Chou) had never been far from the top post during all those years, yet he successfully avoided fatal confrontations. Five civil wars, two world wars, and a dozen years of Japanese aggression all flowed past this amazing man.

He demonstrated the traditional Chinese capacity to bend with the wind and remain standing. Others who resisted the wind were broken. Few men in history weathered as many political storms and earned as much respect from friend and foe alike as Zhou Enlai (Chou En-lai). A biographer called him "China's Gray Eminence." Readers' Digest described him as "Beijing's (Peking's) man for all seasons."

Zhou Enlai's (Chou En-lai's) capacity for survival must be linked to his intellectual brilliance and his abhorrence of extremism. The French philosopher Voltaire stated, "It is the triumph of reason to live well with those who have none." Zhou (Chou) was a realist among dreamers, a moderate among radicals, one of those rare breed of men, the born diplomat.

Putting all these factors together you begin to get a picture of the direction in which Zhou Enlai (Chou En-lai) guided China.

The policies of Zhou Enlai (Chou En-lai) unquestionably began to change the entire world scene. Though a Communist since his student days in France, Zhou (Chou) was a pragmatist, a realist. He obviously faced up to the realities of his own still primitive and poor nation. Within China the atmosphere became more relaxed, calm, and normal. Zhou (Chou) was the technocrat—the technician who bordered on genius, who knew how to run a country. Balance was restored. Priorities became more realistic. At long last China began to open its doors to the outside world. Belatedly there was recognition that no nation is an island.

On the international scene Premier Zhou Enlai (Chou Enlai) slowly but surely made his mark. Perhaps he, more than any other man, was responsible for the winding-down of the Vietnam conflict. Appeals to China by the North Vietnamese and the Vietcong met with little real response. The red-carpet treatment accorded President Nixon and the lightning-fast diplomatic recognition of Japan have changed the course of history. China's entry into the United Nations and the rush of nations to recognize the People's Republic of China all bear his distinctive signature. At last an able internationalist was at the controls of China.

7

The Waning of the
Revolution

The towering figures of the great helmsman Mao Zedong (Mao Tse-tung) and the beloved Zhou Enlai (Chou En-lai) were soon to be toppled by death. But just before his death Zhou (Chou) accomplished two significant tasks that would shape China's destiny long after his demise. In September 1971, largely due to the efforts of Zhou (Chou), China was admitted to the United Nations. This event immeasurably cheered the dispirited people of post-Cultural Revolution China. The fact that the Peoples' Republic of China had displaced the Republic of China, with its base in Taiwan, pleased only the political leaders. The people were cheered by something of far greater significance. They felt that by rugged self-determination they had picked themselves up from the rubble of colonial domination, shaken off the dust of lingering humiliation, and now stood as an equal to the great powers of the world. It was, for them, a triumphant and long-overdue moment.

The China of those days was filled with corrosive political intrigue, even more so than usual. The people lived in fear and uncertainty, never knowing which was the correct political line at the moment. Behind the scenes a struggle for power was underway. Chairman Mao, tottering in old age, had already lost most of his luster. He launched a campaign the very name of which pinpointed the fundamental struggle underway. The "Movement to criticize Lin Biao (Lin

94

Piao) and Confucius" dominated the political scene for three years. It was, in reality, a closed-door combat between the rock-hard ideologies of Maoism and the more pragmatic policies of Zhou Enlai (Chou En-lai). During this critical time Zhou (Chou), demonstrating his enormous skill, succeeded in having one of his own disciples, schooled in pragmatism, made Vice Premier. That was in January of 1975. The road ahead for Vice Premier Deng Xiaoping (Teng Hsiao-ping) was not to be an easy one, but it was his leadership that proved to be the most steadying influence in the years immediately ahead.

Zhou Enlai (Chou En-lai) died in January of 1976, Chairman Mao nine months later. The deaths of these pillars of the revolution were omens of impending change. But the changes did not come easily. Even before Mao's death, a cold wind swept across the country. The Party was completely out of step with the people, and the people were in no mood to be browbeaten any longer. Confrontation was inevitable.

This occurred just three months after Zhou's (Chou's) death as the people gathered in Beijing's (Peking's) massive Tiananmen (Tien An Men) Square on the traditional day to honor the dead. Their object was to pay respect to Zhou (Chou). This they did by heaping floral tributes to their hero. The next morning all the thousands of tributes left the day before in commemoration of Zhou (Chou) had been removed. Within hours Tiananmen (Tien An Men) Square was a battleground. The people were angry that the government had removed the tributes to Zhou (Chou). Security forces attempted to keep the massive crowds which had quickly gathered out of the Great Hall of the People and silence the angry anti-Mao speeches being made on the steps of the Martyrs' Monument. The square, often the scene of triumphant Mao demonstrations, now saw the people rebel

against him. Several hundreds, or was it thousands, of
demonstrators were arrested and reports of people being
beaten to death by the security forces persist to this day. The
message of the riots was that the people were sick and tired
of the constant political bickering. They were far more interested in the long-promised, and patiently anticipated, better-
ing of their standard of living. They felt that Deng Xiaoping
(Teng Hsiao-ping), Zhou's (Chou's) best pupil, was the man
who would most likely achieve this for them.

The Party reacted by dismissing Deng (Teng). They saw
him as a threat to Mao's policies. Meanwhile Mao's health
visibly deteriorated. It became obvious that his awesome
presence would soon be a thing of the past. Preparations
were made for someone to take over Mao's duties. Hua
Guofeng became Acting Premier. Then on September 9 the
father of the revolution, "the Great Helmsman," Chairman
Mao Zedong (Mao Tse-tung), died.

Earlier we commented that Zhou (Chou) accomplished
two important tasks just before his death. It is not possible to
give the feeble Mao the same credit. True, during his lifetime he had been China's Marx and Lenin, as well as its
Stalin. But he lived too long. If he had died some twenty-five
years earlier he would most certainly have gone down in
Chinese history as one of the greatest Chinese reformers. As
it was, he lived long enough to thoroughly destroy his own
hard-won reputation. He did this by three disastrous decisions and one failure to make a decision. The Hundred
Flowers Movement, the first of his miscalculations, soured
the people on his leadership and taught them that Mao
could not be trusted. The Great Leap Forward demonstrated
clearly his ideologically caused blindness. Mao was out of
touch with reality. The Cultural Revolution, his third disastrous decision, soured almost the entire nation on the revolutionary policies of Mao. Communism, as a system, had

earned the hatred of the people. These three decisions had a catastrophic effect on Mao's image. Even the father of the revolution would have a hard time living these down.

It was Mao's failure to make a decision when it needed to be made that was the most unforgivable. Perhaps he can be excused because of his old age; however, the Chinese people were not willing to forgive his failure to control, if not eliminate, the Gang of Four. This was unpardonable partly because Mao's wife, Jiang Qing (Chiang Ch'ing), was the ringleader of the Gang and the Chinese believed a man should be able to control his wife. As Simon Leys put it, "Without Mao there would have been no Madame Mao." Given Mao's frequently demonstrated ruthless political power to crush any individual or group that he wanted to, one can only conclude that the Gang of Four had Mao's backing. No amount of subsequent Party double talk could wipe the blood off Mao's hands. He must have been guilty either of the sin of commission or the sin of omission. Thus all the torment the Gang of Four caused the Chinese people over several difficult years was blamed on Mao.

Mao did make one decision, virtually on his deathbed, that was to prove at least a temporary stabilizing influence. That was his appointment of Hua Guofeng as his successor. It is true that he was only attempting to perpetuate his own political policies. But, as it turned out, Hua Guofeng actually completely undermined Mao's reputation. Whether intentionally or not is a matter of conjecture. But this is how it happened.

On October 6, 1976, barely four weeks after Mao's death, the new Chairman of the Communist Party, Hua Guofeng, called a meeting of the Politburo. They were facing a brand new situation; Communist China without Chairman Mao. There was much to discuss. Far-reaching decisions had to be made. It soon became evident that there was a "Grand

Canyon" separating various factions of the Communist Party present that night. What occurred was the biggest open split in the fifty-five years of the history of the C.C.P. At that meeting, held in the home of the Defense Minister, Madame Mao made her bid to become the next Empress of China. She had been preparing for this moment for several years. Three men that she could count on, and an unknown number of other supporters in the Party, gathered around her ambitious plans.

Jiang Qing (Chiang Ch'ing) wanted to take over her late husband's job as Chairman of the Communist Party. She wanted to displace Hua, who had a slip of paper supposedly given to him by Mao saying, "With you in charge I have no worries." Madame Mao contested the legitimacy of the piece of paper. She had one of her own, probably counterfeit, legitimating her bid. In addition, she wanted one of her Gang appointed Premier and another head of the National Peoples' Congress. The few reports that have leaked out of that post-Mao gathering of the Politburo indicated that Jiang Qing (Chiang Ch'ing) made a do-or-die bid to succeed her husband.

That same night the four ambitious power seekers were arrested on orders of Chairman Hua Guofeng and put behind bars in southwest Beijing (Peking). This courageous act by Hua Guofeng put Mao's image in great difficulty. The Gang had been working for several years to set the stage for a leftist takeover upon Mao's death. They had even developed a paramilitary force to oppose the Peoples' Liberation Army in the event of a coup d'etat. They had controlled the media for several years and, by this means, caused much of the political instability that rocked the country. This instability suited their purposes. Mao's wife, as Minister of Culture, imposed her own will in an attempt to become virtually the next Empress of China. After her arrest she was characterized as being vain, extravagant, immoral, self-indulgent, and a power seeker. At the subsequent highly publicized trial of the Gang of Four she amply demonstrated her arrogance and vanity to a watching world. When the Chinese people spoke in derision of the Gang of Four they held up five fingers, thus inescapably linking Mao with the notorious Gang of Four.

Deng Xiaoping (Teng Hsiao-ping) returned the second time in five years from disgrace to a position of enormous power. Ostensibly he was the number three man in the Party. However, the following years were to demonstrate that his influence far exceeded his position. Eventually he succeeded in ousting the innocuous but Mao-branded Chairman Hua and placing his own man in the top spot. Deng (Teng), like his mentor Zhou (Chou), preferred the second or third spot as a base for his considerable management skills. Let someone else kiss the babies and greet the dignitaries. He had great hopes for China and recognized that much still had to be done. But Deng's (Teng's) troubles were not over by any means.

Almost immediately Deng (Teng) began to impose his will on the country. He began to turn the country in a totally different direction. The disillusioned people of China began to see an effective demonstration of the Chinese proverb *Shun xi wan bian (Shun hsi wan pian)*—"Ten thousand changes in a moment." It was all very confusing, both to the Chinese people and to the world at large. China seemed to suddenly turn its back on the revolution. Freedom, an almost forgotten experience, became more meaningful as people began to move about their own country more freely, and openly express their opinions. Colorful clothing began to gradually replace the drab Mao blues. This new "revolution" seemed to be coming from the top leaders who had seen the paralysis caused by Mao's policies. Most of them, like Deng Xiaoping (Teng Hsiao-ping), had been rejected by the leftists, and now they were rejecting the policies created by the instigator of the revolution, Mao himself. The fact is Mao had taught them revolution and now they were in open revolt against his once revered policies. "Chickens come home to roost" is a time-proven axiom.

The Bamboo Curtain suddenly all but disappeared as travel both ways dramatically escalated. Young Chinese were now able to travel abroad for study and research. "Foreign guests" became a familiar sight on the streets of China's major cities. Despite orders to the contrary, Chinese and foreigners were soon able to mix quite freely. The dreaded ogre of capitalism seemed to spring up overnight and proved to be just as natural to the Chinese as eating rice. Shanghai, as usual, led the way and the rest of the nation followed. So dramatic were the changes that the period was being dubbed "The Second Liberation," as the often brutally restraining straightjacket of ideological coercion was loosened in the pursuit of more pragmatic goals.

Deng Xiaoping (Teng Hsiao-ping) had launched a new drive dubbed "The Four Modernization Movement." Its stated aim was to modernize four aspects of Chinese life: agriculture, industry, defense and technology-science. This became the driving force in the country. To achieve "modernization" seemed to suit almost everyone. At last the people were to see some material progress. But unaccustomed and dangerous degrees of freedom had to be granted. This gave birth to a massive poster campaign, known as *Daziboa* (Big Character Posters).

These uniquely Chinese expressions were penned by courageous souls and posted in the shadow of Chairman Mao's mausoleum. Thousands of Chinese marched through the streets of Beijing (Peking) chanting, "Chinese democracy! Long live democracy!" Other thousands gathered in

63862

Tiananmen (Tien An Men) Square, which, it seems, only yesterday echoed to the march of militant Red Guards, to hear and applaud speakers calling for democracy. These speakers and poster-proclaimers specifically stated that they were thoroughly sick and tired of Mao's brand of pseudo-democracy. They wanted the real thing.

A nondescript wall in Beijing (Peking) suddenly became world-famous as the "Democracy Wall." It was plastered with *Daziboa* and became the focal point of world attention. Posters on the Democracy Wall were read by the world. The Big Character Posters, which ranged from pages torn out of school notebooks to one-hundred-foot scrolls, provided some deep insights into the real thinking of the people. Perhaps even more significant was the revelation that Mao's revolution had done little to change the thinking of China's people. One massive, beautifully executed *Daziboa*, signed by eight young men, labeled the techniques of Mao's rule "even more fearful than those of feudal society." This was also an indirect attack against certain unpopular aspects of the present régime. The poster said, "America is a capitalist country, only two hundred years old, but it developed because it had no idols or superstitions." This no doubt was a direct attack on the deification of Mao. Another poster asked, "Why can't the national economy catch up with the one in Taiwan controlled by the Chiang Kai-shek clique?" The inference was obvious. One must read between the lines of a *Daziboa* to get the primary message.

Deng Xiaoping (Teng Hsiao-ping) apparently initiated the Big Character Posters, partly because he knew that a degree of freedom must accompany a modernization drive. He also knew how the people felt about some of the radical policies of the past. It is probable that he was merely using the people as his allies against remaining Party radicals who were opposed to his pragmatism. Deng (Teng) used these Posters

The family has been important in many cultures, but it is doubtful that it has been anywhere more important for a longer time than in China.

to great effect against his opponents and, at the same time, won enormous popular support. The Big Character Poster, in Deng's (Teng's) skillful hands, became powerful political weapons. However, freedom is a heady brew, especially for people to whom it has long been denied. The posters went much further than the Vice Premier intended. The important message of the posters was that the Chinese people were longing for true freedom. For instance, in early January 1979, a Beijing (Peking) wall poster called for direct elections of state and local leaders; for state bodies to hold their discussions in public; for patronage and corruption to be stamped out; for the abolishment of the secret police; for living standards to be improved; and for freedom of speech, thought, reading and the written word.

One of the early surprises of the pragmatic stage was the joint announcement by President Carter and Chairman Hua that full diplomatic relations had been reestablished between China and the United States. It was surprising because of the thirty-year anti-America propaganda war China had sustained. This dramatic announcement had been preceded by the even more startling Nixon-Kissinger thaw of 1971-72 which marked the high point in Mr. Nixon's presidency and appeared to be a significant factor in the relaxation that was to follow. Chairman Mao and President Nixon, drinking tea together in Beijing (Peking), triggered a fusion of friendship. Subsequent to the Carter-Hua announcement Americans rolled out the Red Carpet for a nine-day state visit to their country of the architect of normalization, Deng Xiaoping (Teng Hsiao-ping). During his energetic visit to America this diminutive dynamo almost single-handedly erased what animosity there remained in America towards China.

Shortly after Deng Xiaoping's (Teng Hsiao-ping's) return from Washington he launched a military invasion of Vietnam. This was a dangerous move because of the obvious risk of Soviet involvement in order to defend their client state, Vietnam. Perhaps the Chinese saw a Vietnamese-Soviet pincers movement. The world feared a Sino-Soviet land war that might lead to a nuclear war. The Vietnamese, emboldened by Soviet backing, had been making repeated incursions into Chinese territory. Historically the Chinese have strongly resented such intrusions and demonstrated their willingness, if not their ability, to defend at all costs. However, what will be debated for a long time is whether Deng Xiaoping (Teng Hsiao-ping) made a wrong move in invading Vietnam at a time when China was seeking to normalize the political situation and modernize the country. Subsequently Chinese troops were withdrawn from Vietnam with a great loss of life and at substantial economic cost to the government. War is costly! The short-lived Vietnam conflict substantially dimmed Deng's (Teng's) hard-earned luster.

By February 1980 Deng Xiaoping (Teng Hsiao-ping) concluded the wall posters had done their job. At the Third Plenum and the Fifth Plenum Deng (Teng) got rid of his most powerful political enemies, including the Chairman of the Communist Party. His next move was to turn against the now world-renowned "Democracy Wall," calling it "anarchic, counterrevolutionary and reactionary." This was because the whole Communist system was now coming under open attack by both peasants and intellectuals. Deng (Teng) could see the genesis of a popular revolt. This simply could not be permitted. Placing a poster on the Democracy Wall suddenly became illegal.

Early in 1980 the Party called for a revocation of the "Four Freedoms." Feeling that the Democracy Movement had gone far enough and the security of the country was at stake, the movement toward freedom received a severe setback. It now became illegal to "speak out freely, air [one's] views fully, hold great debates or write Big Character Posters." These four freedoms had only recently been granted. A champion of freedom, Wei Jingsheng, was condemned to jail. Even this small degree of freedom that had been granted apparently was a threat to China's political system. The voice of freedom was once again silenced, thus enabling the Communist leadership to sleep better at night. Either imprisonment or the threat of imprisonment, or worse, muffled the calls for freedom but, more significantly, it was an attempt to silence the widespread open criticism of the Party.

Meanwhile forces released by the death of Mao became increasingly evident as the country attempted to achieve the "Four Modernizations." The image of Chairman Mao took a severe beating. His "mistakes" were openly publicized. Especially hard hit was the Cultural Revolution, Mao's brainchild. Once lauded by the Communist Party, it was now labeled a serious mistake. In fact, it was officially judged by China's leadership to be a "wholly negative experience." Journalist Simon Leys called it "a bankruptcy so enormous, extreme and evident that there could be no room for discussion." He concluded "the alternative after Mao was either to change course or risk destruction."

China appeared ready to change course. They proceeded to attempt the intensely difficult transition from revolution —Communist revolution at that—to normalcy. Starting a revolution was relatively simple, given the circumstances. But continual revolution had proved counterproductive. For two years the Deng- (Teng-) induced policy of liberalism held sway. Efforts were made on many fronts to dismantle the machinery of revolution.

Looking back, it seemed as if the actual demolition of the thirty-year-old New China was under way. Every aspect of this New China came under scrutiny if not direct attack. The Four Modernizations seemed to repudiate the entire economic system of the past thirty years. Fear was openly expressed in the *People's Daily* as to whether the Party would "live or die, persist or perish." Nothing like this had occurred previously in the writhings of the great giant. Questions were raised as to the value of socialism itself. The all-powerful Party came under attack. Faith in Marxism itself was at an all-time low ebb. It must be stressed that these doubts were now being expressed in official publications and by Party leaders. The general public had become disenchanted with the system much earlier.

On July 1, 1981 the Communist Party of China was a venerable sixty years old. Mao was dead. His appointed heir had been demoted and a new Chairman appointed. Hu Yaobang made his debut by delivering a fiery ninety-minute speech in the Great Hall of the People. He proclaimed, "Beyond a shadow of doubt this is the most radical social change in Chinese history. It is a leap," he shouted, "of the most far-reaching significance." If words have any meaning at all in the mouth of a politician he was certainly downplaying the Liberation of 1949.

His speech, all things considered, was understandable if not predictable. Born in Mao's home province, Hu Yaobang has been a Communist Party member since he was eighteen years of age. Shorter even in stature than the five-foot Deng Xiaoping (Teng Hsiao-ping), Chairman Hu has had very little formal education but is said to be well-read and self-educated. Visitors have been impressed by his intelligence. He is considered to be the most liberal of the top echelon of the C.C.P., which may explain why he was hand-picked by Deng (Teng) to lead China into "the most radical social changes in China's history." He is reported to be "contemptuous of theory for its own sake, and always ready to challenge useless dogma." Achieving his goals will prove to be extremely difficult, given the smothering effect of China's massive bureaucracy. But he's young enough to have a chance at success eventually.

Deng's (Teng's) and Hu's criticism of Mao, while brave and pleasing to the ears of the younger generation and those who had suffered as a result of those policies, had a boomerang effect. The military is top-heavy with men who owe their position to Mao. The younger generation tend to think for themselves. They have been reasoning thus: "If Mao made so many mistakes and the Party backed him in those mistakes, then the whole Communist system is probably at fault." Deng (Teng) vowed at the time of the Gang of Four trial to purge incompetent officials. This is proving much more difficult than even he imagined. After all, to be a Party member is a guarantee of the "good life." They are the prime beneficiaries under the Communist system. Neither the Party members nor the cadres are about to surrender their positions easily, particularly the new breed of liberals who openly oppose the policies of Chairman Mao. These men owe their positions to Mao.

In 1976 Deng Xiaoping (Teng Hsiao-ping) had grasped the scepter of power and proceeded to herd his massive nation away from the self-reliance policies of Chairman Mao. He set the nation to achieve the impossible by 1986. He, like Mao, attempted to lead his nation in a "Great Leap," but this time not on the basis of self-reliance entirely. Western expertise and finance were welcomed. Within China landlords, religious believers, and intellectuals were being "rehabilitated" so they could participate in the Four Modernizations. Former capitalists still in China were sought after to contribute their managerial skills. Chinese capitalists who had fled from Communism to become millionaires again in Hong Kong, Singapore, or the United States were urged to enter into joint ventures with the State. These Chinese of the Diaspora received red-carpet treatment when they set foot in China, and were granted special tax concessions for their enterprises. Tremendous, observable progress in many areas was achieved over the next five years.

By 1981 the economic policies of Deng (Teng) were in serious trouble. The great retreat began in the first months of 1981. Actually a decision to "readjust" had been made at a Party Work Conference held in the closing months of 1980. Once again China began one more of its frequent and infamous startling reversals of policy. Just such a reversal had been dreaded by the Chinese people. We must never forget, as has been pointed out, "the Chinese people are the most avid and experienced China watchers." They had been anticipating this switchback.

Before touching on the new policies, let's try to discover why Deng's (Teng's) economic leap fell so far short of the target. Perhaps the major reason was that that achievement required expertise, education, competence and hard work. All of these are in short supply among the government functionaries, particularly at the local level, without whom the system cannot function. The Chinese press blamed several other contributing factors including a wage spiral, galloping consumerism, the Sino-Vietnamese war, overcommitment of capital expenditure, and corruption. The corruption included grand theft and tax evasion on a grand scale. However, the foot-dragging of a significant number of unhappy hard-line Maoists still in the Party was probably the last straw. Deng (Teng) had complained publicly that "some of our Party members are not qualified to cope with the difficulties that pile up like mountains." These Party members were the biggest obstacle to modernization. Most of these functionaries were old and incompetent. The world was passing them by and power was slipping from their grasp. Apparently there were enough of them to force a retrenchment of Deng's (Teng's) policies. Deng (Teng) had tried to sweep them out of the Party as he had promised but had not yet succeeded. They were still a force to be reckoned with.

China was choking on its own red tape. Bureaucracy, it is claimed, was invented by the ancient Mandarins and expanded by the Communists, who installed a Soviet-style centralized planning system. This hybrid system produced nineteen million paper pushers. The new Chairman said: "Bureaucratism and special privilege have created a very serious situation." The *People's Daily* denounced "universal, evil practices of delay, avoidance, shifting of responsibility and negligence. . . ." Businessmen, both Western and Asian, found this barrier almost insurmountable. Many Americans, lacking Oriental patience, or any patience for that matter, had given up and gone home declaring it a hopeless business climate. The problem was easily identifiable, but solving it was another matter.

Nearly a third of China's thirty-eight million Party members had been recruited during the Cultural Revolution when radicalism was in fashion and intellectuals were in prison "digging mud" on the farms. Deng (Teng) was discovering that this was his most difficult problem. Because the Party is the supreme power in China Deng (Teng) had to be careful lest he be purged once again. He decided to back off and try again later. But Deng (Teng), in his late seventies and sometimes accompanied in public by a nurse, did not have much time left to wait.

Before this retrenchment Deng (Teng) had succeeded in making several significant changes in the system. The most far-reaching was his dismantling of Mao's most cherished institution, the Commune. Mao had reasoned that by grouping all of China's farmers into 26,000 self-sufficient communities it would greatly enhance agricultural progress. This proved to be a fallacy. The communes became a mindless programming of people with slavish adherence to theory at the expense of all human aspirations and personal motives. Men are not machines to be manipulated. For this reason alone Communism will never succeed anywhere. The peasants, deprived of all incentives, with no chance of personal gain, simply saw no point in toiling for the common good. Slavish adherence to Mao's dream led to a total of 74,000 communes by the mid-sixties. All were counterproductive. False, bloated production figures hid the truth for years. Now the commune system is being judged a total, unmitigated failure that impeded rather than promoted production. But more important, China's 800 million peasants' average annual income is less than 60 yuan (about US $75). That's below the subsistence line even in China. Double that amount would be just adequate.

The new system, called "The Responsibility System," promotes the spirit of enterprise. The Vice Minister of Agriculture pointed out that "the majority of today's peasants want to get rid of the rather heavy burden of totalitarianism, undemocratic order, and the arbitrariness of a few." These, he said, are problems left untackled for many years.

Forced to retreat, the C.C.P. embarked on a road not dissimilar to the Great Proletarian Cultural Revolution. In fact, one of the first steps was to play down the negative aspects of that revolution and stress the "accomplishments." Criticism of Mao was toned down considerably. The People's Daily said that any attack on the Cultural Revolution was, in reality, an attack on Mao and, as such, should not be tolerated. This seeming rehabilitation of the calamitous Cultural Revolution has to be significant. Several dreaded features of that period have reappeared. These include forced attendance at Marxism classes in the schools as academics are again losing ground to Marxism; the reinstitution of self-criticism as a means of mind beauty; the open attack of intellectuals again; the arrest of religious leaders; the push for self-sacrifice for the cause of socialism, not monetary incentives. Freedoms so recently granted are being withdrawn as ideology takes precedence over accomplishment. This is Maoism without Mao. It appears to be a return to the old Stalinism so dreaded and hated by the people.

The old guard of the C.C.P. and the army have apparently been the moving force behind the panic moves. Not everyone would agree. Some argue that Deng Xiaoping (Teng Hsiao-ping) is buying time to thoroughly clean out his opposition before proceeding with liberal reforms. Others argue that Deng (Teng) himself has never been a true liberal and that he merely exploited the popular resentment of the people against the Cultural Revolution to eliminate his political opponents. Speculation abounds. While all the contributing factors may not be known one overriding reality is a political system that breeds instability and stifles freedom. Faith in that system, however, has been seriously eroded. Consequently it is doubtful that China will return to the excesses of the Cultural Revolution. What we are seeing may be only a stutter in China's march out of the mists of antiquity.

Part Two

The Religious Challenge

The Impact of Christianity
on China

8

Yesterday's Cross

A Chinese Bible scholar, Mr. K. S. Lee, has spent a lifetime attempting to discover the earliest influences of Christianity upon China. He believes that Isaiah 49:11-12 refers to China. The Chinese, who are believed to be descendants of Noah's son Shem, called themselves the Sine people. The Chinese word was *Chin*. The three criteria of Isaiah 49:11-12 are that the country must be east or south of Jerusalem; must be far from Jerusalem; and must be an important country to deserve mention. China meets all these criteria. "Behold these shall come from afar: and lo, these from the north and from the west; and those from the land of Sinim" (12).

Mr. Lee is also convinced that the wise men, who came to worship Jesus, were Chinese astrologers. Astrologers in those days could be grouped into two segments, those studying the stars for scientific purposes and those who used the stars coupled with demonic power to foretell. Some of the former were the wise men who came seeking the new King. To substantiate his belief, Mr. Lee gives the following facts: the Chinese had been using the compass for one thousand years before Christ. At the time of Christ's birth they had in their possession a clear map showing the route from China to the Meditarranean sea. In 110 B.C. Zhang Qian (Cheung Ching) made a trip from China to the Mediterranean, carefully charted the entire area by compass, and produced clear maps which are in existence until today. Also, astronomy was extremely well developed in China and saw its greatest advancement between the years 500 B.C. and 200 B.C.

The Chinese had discovered a star before the Han dynasty, that is, before the time of Christ, which they named the "king" star. In a lengthy book called by the name of the star, the Chinese expressed their belief that whenever this particular "king" star appeared, a king was born. Chinese history says that this star was at its most brilliant peak during the Han dynasty. Perhaps this explains why, when Christianity first came to China, the Chinese called it "king's" religion. One of the astrologer wise men could have been a man by the name of Liu Shang (Liu Sheung). When he was seventy years of age he disappeared from China for over two years. If Christ was born in six or seven A.D., as some scholars believe, it is possible that Liu Shang might have followed the star to Bethlehem and returned to China to die. His story was never told, Mr. Lee asserts, because he feared that China's reigning king would attempt to kill Jesus just as Herod had.

Tradition says that Thomas, one of the twelve disciples obeying Christ's command to "preach the gospel to every creature," had carried the message of Christ to India and on into China. There does not seem to be any evidence of his visit to China.

The first recorded Christian influence in China dates back to some five centuries after Christ's death. How different China's history might be if there had been an earlier witness, for example one of those who had been endued with power from on high in the upper room on the day of Pentecost. Up to this time Christianity had only penetrated as far as Persia. The road to China was frequently blocked by Turks barring the high passes until the Chinese defeated the Turks in 630 A.D. Previous to this date, there had been at least some penetration of China by Persian businessmen. It was a Nestorian Christian trader from Persia who brought the first silkworm eggs out of China to Constantinople in A.D. 551.

As far as we know, the first to bring Christianity to China were the Nestorians. Nestorian Christianity had broken with the Roman Catholic church on matters of doctrine and government. The Nestorians could not accept, among other things, the doctrine of purgatory or the honorific title "Mother of God" awarded to Mary. They were probably strongest in Persia. At least it was a Persian Bishop, Alopen, who first came to China during the Tang dynasty in A.D. 635. He received an extremely cordial welcome from the Tang emperor, who issued this decree: "The Way has more than one name. . . . Doctrines vary in different lands, but their benefits reach all mankind. A man of great virtue has brought books and images from afar to present them in our capital. . . . His religion does good to all men. Let it be preached fully in the empire." Alopen was off to a good start.

Permission was granted for the Nestorian Scriptures to be translated. Three years later the first Christian book in the Chinese language was completed. It was a handwritten copy of "The Sutra of Jesus the Messiah." This is believed to be the standard version—the "Vulgate" of the Syrian Church. It was not strictly a translation but an adaptation introducing the Christian faith. The life of Christ from His birth to His death was presented for the first time to Chinese scholars who could read. Ten years later Alopen was appointed "Great Spiritual Lord, Protector of the Empire, Metropolitan of Changan (Chang-on)" by Emperor Gaozong (Kao-tsung). A Christian leader had found great favor with the emperor, who himself was of non-Chinese central Asian stock.

By this time there were numbers of Persian traders who had learned the Chinese language and taken up residence in China. Not all were Nestorians; some were Zoroastrians. We know that Jews and Muslim Arabs had also penetrated China. Subsequently a number of Nestorian churches and monasteries sprang up, one with as many as twenty-one monks. Though rejecting the symbol of the crucifix, they called themselves "The Religion of the Cross"; their churches were called "Monasteries of the Cross." Thus was yesterday's cross planted in China.

Nestorianism was the only Christian church in China for over seven hundred years. Most of their missionaries were well-educated men who were accepted for their medical skills as well as their intellectual accomplishments. During the Mongol rule the Nestorians experienced their greatest period of expansion. The mother of the great Kublai Kahn was a Nestorian. Nestorians became a privileged and powerful group. The Mongols gave them positions of preference. A Nestorian was put in charge of the Bureau of Astronomy in Khenbalig (Beijing [Peking]).

Emphasis is purposely being placed on the seeming success of the Nestorians for a reason. Within a few short years they were to completely disappear from the scene. Why? The answer to this question is of great importance. A partial answer appears in the following observations:

1. Nestorian writing became increasingly syncretic. Buddhist and Taoist terms and ideas were incorporated into their writing in order to win favor with the court. Nestorianism became less Christian the longer it stayed in China.
2. Nestorianism never became a Chinese faith. Few Chinese were won—perhaps little effort was made in this direction. It was primarily a Persian faith which did not put its roots down into Chinese soil. Wholly Syrian terms for God and Christ were used.
3. The Nestorian church was not self-supporting. It relied on the mother church in Persia or Central Asia.

4. When political turmoil blocked the routes, missionaries could not come to China. A Chinese priesthood had not been prepared for the exclusion of missionaries.
5. The Nestorian church depended on imperial patronage. Because it was attached to one government the fall of that government meant the fall of the church.
6. Though the Nestorians were trinitarian Christians, there is no evidence that they preached a redeeming gospel.

Again we come to a potential watershed in the history of the Church in China—the story of a lost opportunity. Two Roman Catholics, Niccolo and Maffeo Polo, elder brothers of young Marco who would come later, were received by the great Kublai Khan in A.D. 1262. They shared their faith with him. Impressed, the Monarch offered a challenge that was to be faintly mirrored seven hundred years later by General Douglas MacArthur after the fall of Japan. Kublai Khan challenged the Pope to send one hundred men, learned in religion and the arts, to his court. If they could prove the superiority of Christianity over other religions, then the Khan and all his subjects would be baptized. He promised there would be more Christians in his realm than in all the rest of the world. O for an Elijah to challenge the prophets of Baal! But no one came to answer the challenge—not one! The first Roman Catholic priest did not arrive in China till 1294, thirty-two years later. Kublai Khan was dead and so was the opportunity.

John of Monte Corvino, the first priest to arrive, was favorably received by Kublai's successor but strongly opposed by the Nestorians. It was virtually an Eastern-church (Nestorian) versus Western-church (Roman Catholic) confrontation. The generous Mongol court, however, granted freedom to both. By 1306 six thousand had been baptized into the Roman church. The life of the Roman church in

China at this time was to be short-lived. With the defeat of the Mongols, themselves foreigners, and the establishment of the Chinese Ming dynasty, both the Roman Catholic and the Nestorian communities completely disappeared.

Only a silk-wrapped Latin Bible remains as evidence of the Franciscan penetrations of China in the thirteenth century. The fall of the Roman church was due to the fact that there were mainly foreign membership, support, and leadership. Governmental ties with the Mongols further sealed their doom. Two centuries would elapse before the Jesuits would gain another foothold in China. The conquering Moslem Tamerlane in the late fifteenth century wiped out the last vestiges of Romanism.

The arrival in Macau, a Portuguese Colony off the coast of South China, of a Jesuit missionary in A.D. 1579 marked the resumption of Roman Catholic missions to China. Ruggieri and his later associate, Matteo Ricci, showed considerable wisdom in their approach to the Chinese. Dressing as Buddhist monks and studying the Confucian classics, they worked hard on the Chinese language. The first Chinese book ever written by a foreign missionary was "The True Account of God" by Ruggieri. Many new terms had to be adopted to express Christian concepts for which there was no equivalent in the Chinese language. Many of these terms are still in use today. These early priests were careful that the structure of the Roman Catholic Church with its papacy and hierarchy was not mentioned at first, lest it arouse the opposition of the Chinese leaders.

During the next few years the Jesuits accommodated Chinese ancestral worship in their instructions to converts. This became a real bone of contention. Arguments and disagreements as to how to fit into China's culture continued for many years. Even the proper term for God was cause for high-level disagreement. Eventually the overbearing organi-

zation of the Roman Catholic church with its insistence on
Western terminology and forms came to the attention of
Emperor Kang Xi (K'ang-hsi), second emperor of the Ch'ing
dynasty. In December 1720 he commanded, "Henceforth,
no Westerner shall preach in the Middle Kingdom. We shall
prohibit them in order to avoid further trouble." There
followed a mass exodus of Roman priests, and the faint
flame of Christian faith was almost extinguished in China.

Modern-day Protestant witness in China commenced
with the arrival of Robert Morrison on the 4th of September
1807. His journey to China was made doubly difficult by the
British East India Company. These traders from Christian
Britain feared the effect of missionary work in China and so
refused to grant Morrison passage on their ships. Undaunted, Morrison set sail for China, via New York, on a
journey that took seven arduous months.

Morrison arrived not in China but in adjacent Portuguese
Macau. He was still on the outside attempting to look in. He
must have felt very much like the Jesuit Valignani 250 years
before him. When the prospects for entering China seemed
particularly dark and dismal, Valignani stood looking out of
a window of the College of Macau towards the nearby hills
of the closed continent of China, then as now earth's largest
nation. With a voice filled with a mingling of affection and
frustration he cried out, "O Rock, Rock, when wilt thou
open, Rock?"

In the heart of this young Scot burned a zeal for the souls
of China. Morrison applied himself to the difficult language
in a day when the Chinese government forbade, on pain of
death, the teaching of the language to foreigners. It is said
that his teacher carried poison on his person so he could
commit suicide if he was discovered. Morrison learned the
language well and started the arduous task of providing the
word of God in the Chinese language. Another young mis-

sionary who came a few years later wrote, "To acquire the
Chinese language is a work for men with bodies of brass,
lungs of steel, heads of oak, hands of spring steel, eyes of
eagles, the hearts of the apostles, memories of angels, and
lives of Methuselah." That's how it impressed William
Milne in 1814.

There is no question that the absence of the printed Scriptures in the language of China was an important reason for
the failure of earlier efforts to plant the cross. Amazingly
God placed this burden on the hearts of two men simultaneously. One was in China and the other in India. Dr. Marshman, an associate of William Carey in India, worked for
eighteen years to produce a Chinese Bible. He was helped by
an Armenian, John Lassar, who was born in Macau and considered Chinese his native language. Together they produced the first modern-day version of the Bible in Chinese.
This was printed in 1822.

Both the Nestorians and the Roman Catholics before them
had done some translation work, but no evidence of this remained. There was apparently not even any knowledge of
previous translations. Indeed, in the early nineteenth century some considered the Chinese language so difficult and
different that a translation was thought a literary impossibility. Now two translations separately appeared
within a year of each other. Morrison was assisted in the
later stages by William Milne. This, too, was an eighteen-
year project. Before his own death Milne wrote Morrison,
"By God's help you have set on foot what all the people of
China can never destroy or effectively stop, what will raze
their temple, destroy their idols, change their lives and save
the souls of many." These early translations were indeed
among the greatest achievements of Christian missions.

In the meantime, Morrison was faithfully witnessing for
Christ. On July 16th, 1814 he baptized his first Chinese con-

vert. As the door to China was virtually closed, Morrison became burdened for the Chinese of the dispersion—those in Malaya and Southeast Asia. In 1818 he established a training college in Malacca, which was to be "The Jerusalem of the East." His vision was to use this as a base for the future evangelization of China when the door opened. Here in Malacca, under Morrison's ministry, Leung Faat found Christ. He was destined to become the first Chinese ordained to the Christian ministry. Over forty Chinese workers graduated from this school in the next few years.

Both the Morrison and Marshman Bibles reached only a small number of people, not because of limited circulation but because of the Confucian influence. The scholars of that day, all Confucian oriented, held the vernacular in disdain. Theirs was a literary language virtually unknown to the average literate Chinese. It was purely a classical language. Scholars considered it wise to keep it this way in order to protect their privileged status in the nation. Both of these early translations were done in the classical Wen-li style. Not until some thirty years later did a standard Mandarin translation appear. This brought God's Word to the common people of China. The present Chinese Bible was completed in 1919 and revised in 1951.

These early Bibles were feared by the Chinese. Buddhists, Taoists, and even Confucianists opposed these newly printed books. Some opposition was motivated purely by superstition. One city warned its citizens against Morrison's Bible by posting this notice, "The books that the foreigner is selling are printed with ink made of stupefying medicine. When anyone reads them for a time, he becomes stupefied and loses his natural reason, and believes and follows the doctrine. This is to warn the Chinese not to read them." The edict carried further warnings. "Again, the foreigners use much money to bribe the poorer Chinese who have no means to depend on. They also use the stupefying medicine in all sorts of food, in order to win over the little children. At times they use it for kidnapping the children, to sell to other foreigners, who then take away their marrow. The children die at once. Whenever foreigners come, families ought to warn their children not to go out." In spite of this opposition, Morrison's greatest contribution to China was probably the providing of the Scriptures in the Chinese language. His grave can still be visited in a quaint colonial cemetery in Macau.

Protestant missions had an unfortunate beginning in China. The arrival of Robert Morrison found the doors of China closed to foreigners and the gospel.

Only employees of the British East India Company were permitted residence in the Chinese city of Guangzhou (Canton). After much hesitation, Morrison accepted an appointment as translator to this company. This gave him not only living expenses but, more important, the right to reside in his beloved China. The tragedy is that the company which employed him was the principal agent of the completely immoral opium trade. This was the price Robert Morrison paid to fulfill his vision of getting the Gospel into China. Thus it happened that the first Protestant missionary and opium arrived in China virtually simultaneously under the benevolent guns of the British Navy. The Chinese would never forget. Opium was "foreign mud"—Christianity a "foreign religion." They have never been able to separate the two. Both were part of hated colonialism.

About the same time there lived in Macau a Rev. Karl Gutzlaff, a short, stocky Protestant missionary. Dr. Gutzlaff spoke and wrote Chinese fluently. He was known as a colorful exponent of pills and Scriptures. The British East India Company was about to take a ship up the coast of China trading piece goods and opium. Needing a translator, Mr. Jardine, founder of the trading agency, wrote Dr. Gutzlaff, requesting him to be their translator. The letter stressed the £ 4,000 of piece goods that the ship would carry but went on to say, "But as the expenses of the voyage cannot be defrayed from this source, we have no hesitation in stating to you openly that our principal reliance is on opium. Though it is our earnest wish that you should not in any way injure the grand object you may have in view by appearing interested in what, by many, is considered an immoral traffic, yet such traffic is absolutely necessary to give any vessel a reasonable chance of defraying expenses, that we trust you will have no objections to interpret on every occasion when your services are requested. . . ."

The letter continued, "The more profitable the expedition, the better we shall be able to place at your disposal a sum that may hereafter be employed in furthering your mission, and for your success in which we feel deeply interested." Gutzlaff wrote later, "After much consultation with others and a conflict in my own mind, I embarked. . . ."

In his published account of the voyage, after detailing the furious gales that lashed their ship, he expressed his hopes: "We hope this may tend ultimately to the introduction of the Gospel, for which many doors are opened." He continued, "Millions of Bibles and tracts will be needed to supply the number of the people. God, who in His mercy has thrown down the wall of national separation, will carry on the work. We look up to the ever-blessed Redeemer, to whom China with all its millions is given; in the faithfulness of His promise we anticipate the glorious day of a general conversion, and are willing to do our utmost in order to promote the great work.

Nor was this the only link between Christianity and colonialism. The foreign community in Canton gathered regularly for divine services. Most of them were engaged in the opium trade. The Chinese watched them come out of church and go straight into the business of smuggling opium, forcing China's doors open against her wish. No missionary favored the opium trade, yet millions of largely uneducated Chinese were absolutely unable to distinguish between the foreign missionary and the foreign trader—both were "foreign devils."

Few can argue with the assessment of Outerbridge: "The opium traffic was the single greatest impediment to Christianity in China in the nineteenth century, and a potent weapon in the hands of every anti-Christian agitator ever since." He concludes, "[The opium trade] stands forever as one of the darkest stains on the history of Western relations with the Orient."

Thus was yesterday's cross planted in China. Christianity had gained a foothold that in time would prove to be very tenuous. Our zeal outweighed our wisdom. We were neither "wise as serpents" nor "harmless as doves."

9

The Church Takes Root

The West had at last succeeded in forcing her way into China. Missionaries, riding on the stained coattails of colonial expansion, were now legally free to reside in designated areas of the country and practice their faith. Thus it was that the struggle to nurture an enduring Christian church in China greatly accelerated following the signing of the infamous treaties of Tianjin (Tientsin) in 1858 and Beijing (Peking) in 1860.

Increasingly large numbers of missionaries from Great Britain, the Continent, and the United States arrived. Then as now China was earth's most populous nation and certainly the least evangelized. The caliber of these early missionaries was often of the highest order. Scholars, linguists, doctors, and teachers came using their skills, thus preparing the way for the spread of the Gospel.

The story of their contributions to the betterment of China is certainly inspiring. Dictionaries, Bibles, and text books; hospitals, doctors and nurses; primary schools, middle schools and colleges; and orphanages, social welfare, and ministry to the blind and deaf became the visible monuments to these early pioneers. That scholarship should have been emphasized by many of the earliest Protestant missionaries to China was a stroke of genius. The Chinese, as perhaps no other people, valued scholarship and culture.

One great shadow, however, cast a pall on all these

brilliant men and their sincere efforts. Unfortunately, every missionary owed his presence in China to the victories of colonialism. Just as he shared the fruits he also had to live under the curse. Missionaries and colonialism in China were inseparable, at least in the minds of the Chinese.

Nor had the missionaries, generally speaking, taken positive steps to minimize this association. In fact, often their actions and associations unquestionably if unintentionally emphasized their links with colonialism. As we have already pointed out, two earliest Protestant missionaries, Robert Morrison and Karl Gutzlaff, were actually at times under the employ of the very Western merchants who epitomized colonialism. Three American missionaries, Peter Packer, Samuel Wills Williams, and Elijah C. Bridgman, were the advisors to the American government during discussion of the first Chinese-American treaty. Roman Catholic missionaries were at the heart of controversies that eventually led to early armed conflict.

This kind of unfortunate association would plague Christianity in China for more than just the immediate century. In 1869 a highly placed Chinese official is said to have remarked to the British Ambassador, "Take away your opium and your missionaries and you will be welcome." Both missionaries and opium were under the protection of foreign governments and above the Chinese law. The passage of time did not noticeably alter the situation. The last American Ambassador to the Chiang Kai-shek régime was a former missionary, Dr. Leighton Stuart.

The Chinese converts too inevitably bore the cursed mark of colonialism. As long as 150 years later they would still be branded as "tools of the imperialists." In addition, there were those Chinese who were willing to "convert" to Christianity in order to benefit from the concessions the treaties guaranteed for Christian converts. The historian Latourette

flatly observed, "Not infrequently Chinese professed conversion to obtain the assistance of the missionary and the
(foreign) counsel in lawsuits." The web of colonialism over-
shadowed the sacrificial, sincere efforts of missionaries
laboring at great personal sacrifice.

The Christian missionary and his converts actually
became a state within a state, not subject to the laws or
government of China. It would have been difficult to devise
a more certain means to guarantee that Christianity would
have a most difficult time becoming an indigenous Chinese
faith.

Stephen Neill in his book *Colonialism and Christian Missions* quoted a German writer, W. Franke, who makes an
even more damaging assertion: "The missionaries of the
nineteenth century," wrote Franke, "saw no reason to adapt
Christianity, even in its outward forms, to the facts of
Chinese life. The Chinese Christians worshipped a foreign
God and had entered a foreign religious community in
which there was no place for Chinese customs. He had
become a stranger to his own people and his own culture.
Any concession on the part of the foreign missionaries to
Chinese ways of doing things was unthinkable. So," concludes Franke, "Chinese Christians were regarded by their
neighbors as half-foreigners."

Only part of this statement can be accepted. It is true that
Chinese Christians were frequently looked on with disdain
and even distrust by the non-Christian community. It may
also be true that some missionaries, perhaps far too many,
"saw no reason to adapt Christianity in its outward forms,
to the facts of Chinese life," but not every missionary could
be placed in that category.

In just under one hundred years after the treaties of
Tianjin (Tientsin) and Beijing (Peking), virtually all foreign
missionaries would be forced out of China by an atheistic

régime. The labors of a century would be put through a blazing crucible. The retreat of the West from China would quickly reveal whether the churches planted by foreigners in China were sustained artificially or whether they were genuinely rooted in the soil of China.

Three times previously the church in China had been put through a test of fire and proved faulty and far from eternal. God had certainly not failed—what then had occurred? The failure lay in building the church according to our own pattern instead of the divine pattern.

Three separate rebellions within China held significance for both missionaries and Chinese Christians. The first appeared to be a popular Christian social revolution. The second and third were obvious attempts to eliminate the Christian influence. In this chapter we shall look at the Taiping (T'ai P'ing) Rebellion and what is known as the Boxer Rebellion. The Communist revolution will be considered in other chapters. These revolutions had a direct bearing upon the establishment of the Christian church in China.

Just eight years after the Opium War there broke out a rebellion in Guangxi (Kwangsi) province that raised the hopes of some missionaries. In fact, one recent Christian historian has called the Taiping (T'ai P'ing) Rebellion "a lost opportunity" because of the failure of Christian nations to back this rebellion. A nineteenth-century British Protestant wrote that there would be "four advantages which will accrue to China from success on the side of the insurgents: China would be opened to the dissemination of the Scriptures, idolatry would be firmly put down, opium traffic would be stopped, and China will be fully opened to our commerce, our science, our curiosity, and all the influences of our civilization."

This rebellion, which initially raised such high hopes, raged in China for nearly fifteen years (1850-1864), ravaged two-thirds of the empire, and probably resulted in the death of almost ten million. Optimism resulted from the very evident need for social changes and the need for the overthrow of the Manchu empire. Christian optimism stemmed from the connections which its leader Hong Xiu Quan (Hung Hsiu-ch'üan) had with Christianity and the trappings of Christianity which accompanied the rebellion.

Hung had received a Christian book in 1836 written by an early Chinese convert to Christianity, Liang A-fa. This book contained mainly translations and summaries of Bible chapters. The book did not mean much to Hong (Hung) until 1843 when he connected it to a dream he had when ill. Hong (Hung) had received instruction in the Christian faith from an American missionary, I. J. Roberts, but had never been baptized. A very confused—some claim mentally ill—man, he believed that according to his vision he was the younger brother of Jesus Christ. His mission, as he saw it, was to win the Chinese people from idolatry to the Christian faith and establish "The Heavenly Kingdom of Great Peace" (Taiping Tianguo [T'ai-p'ing t'ien-kuo]) with himself as King. His new "holy trinity" was composed of God the heavenly Father, Jesus Christ the elder son of God, and Hong Xiu Quan (Hung Hsiu-ch'üan) the second son of the heavenly father.

The Taiping (T'ai P'ing) derived their precepts primarily from Gutzlaff's translations of the Bible. They printed their own Bible and distributed it widely. The fullest versions of the Taiping (T'ai P'ing) Bible contained the first six books of the Bible and the entire New Testament. Hong (Hung), as the "younger brother of Jesus," made many annotations on the upper margins of the published editions. These revealed his own confused conception of Christianity and the be-

wildering array of mythology with which it was inter-
spersed. The startling fact remains that a mere thirty-six
years after the baptism of the first Chinese Christian convert, and eight short years after the horrendous Opium War,
a popular Chinese revolution bore the trappings of Christianity and distributed copies of the newly translated Scriptures. This was also the first popular revolution of common
folk seeking to overthrow the alien Manchu and initiate
reform throughout the empire.

The rebellion was eventually put down with considerable
help from the West. Like the Chinese capitalists, they saw
the Taiping (T'ai P'ing) as a serious threat to trade. It will be
recalled that two foreigners, Ward, an American, and Gordon, a Britisher, successively led the forces that eventually
crushed the Taiping (T'ai P'ing). It is generally considered
that the overthrow of the Manchu dynasty would have been
an accomplished fact at this time without foreign interference. Instead, this impedance to Chinese progress was
delayed almost fifty years.

It is interesting to note that after the fall of the Manchu
dynasty some Chinese were hailing Hong Xiu Quan (Hung
Hsiu-ch'üan) as the forerunner of the modern revolution.
Indeed, many of the social programs instituted by this
untrained revolutionary were remarkable in their scope. He
forbade private ownership of land and insisted on equality
for all. He attempted to develop a self-supporting economy.
This system was first devised in the third century B.C. and
later became the basis for Mao Zedong's (Mao Tse-tung's)
socialist state. Mao perverted Hong's (Hung's) religious emphasis and turned it upon himself. Hong (Hung) wrote,
"Apart from worship of the Heavenly Father, Supreme Lord
and August God, all former bad customs (in worshipping)
shall be dispensed with. . . . Every sabbath the section-chief

shall lead his men and women to the chapel . . . preaching and listening to sermons, singing hymns and praying to the Heavenly Father, Supreme Lord and August God." Against this background visualize the Chinese Communist emphasis upon learning Mao thought, prayer to "The Great Helmsman," and massive distribution of "The Little Red Book."

"The most violent outbreak of antimissionary feeling ever recorded" is probably a fair description of the Boxer Rebellion of 1900. Lasting only about a year, the effects were so disastrous that some observers in the West concluded at that time that the Protestant enterprise in China was indeed ended. The Roman Catholics, because they had larger numbers in the areas affected, lost most heavily. The best estimate is that a total of 186 Protestant missionaries or missionary children lost their lives. The China Inland Mission and The Christian and Missionary Alliance suffered the greatest losses.

Yet, with all the violent losses suffered by the missionary community, the rebellion was directed not specifically at missionaries but at all foreigners. This rebellion was designed to eliminate the foreigner and his political, economic, and social intrusions. No other group of foreigners was so widely dispersed over the interior of China as were the missionaries. Consequently they were exposed to the full violence of the Boxers because they were by calling pioneers and led far less sheltered lives than other foreigners.

It is important to note that Chinese believers were made to suffer merely because of their acceptance of a "foreign religion" and their association with foreigners. Chinese Christians were labeled "secondary devils." Christianity had not become a Chinese faith. The stories of heroism, loyalty, bravery, and suffering of the Chinese Christians is a proud chapter. There were some desertions under pressure, but the majority of Chinese Christians nevertheless remained loyal not merely to some foreign missionary but, more important, to their Lord and Savior.

The Boxer Rebellion was in actuality the spearpoint of antiforeignism originally fostered by provincial officials and subsequently by the Empress Dowager herself. The Boxers were originally a secret society formed for other purposes. Their activities became directed to antiforeignism in Shandong (Shantung) province in 1895. The murder of two German missionaries by the Boxers brought about the occupation of Jiaozhou (Kiaochow) Bay and the beautiful city of Qingdao (Tsingtao) by German military forces. Germany pressed for and got a ninety-nine-year lease on the entire Jiaozhou (Kiaochow) Bay area. By the time the activities of the Boxers had become a national antiforeign tool in 1900, Shandong (Shantung) province had been brought under control by provincial authorities. This province suffered little at the hands of the Boxers. Twenty years later my father and mother with two infants in arms, my older brother Donald and I, arrived in the seaport city of Qingdao (Tsingtao). By then the Manchu dynasty had fallen and the Republic had been established.

The Boxer Rebellion was quelled by an international military force marching on the city of Beijing (Peking). The very forces toward which the rebellion was directed mounted a superior military force and crushed the antiforeign rebellion. Rather than slow down the progress of missions in China, the Boxer Rebellion merely served to focus the attention and concern of Christians around the world on China. New missionary recruits rapidly more than filled the gaps left by the martyred.

Establishing an indigenous Chinese church was still the great need. Most missionaries failed to sense the importance of this emphasis. James Hudson Taylor, founder of the

China Inland Mission, was one of the exceptions. Taylor wisely instructed his missionaries to "wear Chinese dress and as far as possible identify themselves with the customs and even the prejudices of the Chinese people." He instructed them to steer clear of "recourse to European consular officials and win their way by love alone." Hudson Taylor also wished to see Chinese churches led by Chinese pastors, "worshiping in edifices of a thoroughly Chinese style and architecture." If only his suggestions had been followed! To this day the memory of Hudson Taylor is revered by Chinese Christians.

"In theory," Latourette observes, "recognition was given to the need of freeing Christianity from its foreign trappings." In actual practice little progress was made. Missionaries usually were very slow to place Chinese Christians in places of leadership. Unfortunately this was still true right up to the time of the Communist revolution. The opposition to missionaries and their Christianity can, to a large degree, be traced to their linkage with colonialism and their failure to Sinicize the Christian church in China.

My father was among those who early caught the vision of what the church could become under Chinese leadership. From the beginning of his years of service dating back to the turn of the century in Gansu (Kansu) province on the border of Tibet till our arrival in Shandong (Shantung) in 1920, my father, Ivan Saunders Kauffman, felt his prime responsibility was to train nationals. I well remember hearing one of father's early converts on the Tibetan border preach. In later years he came to Shandong (Shantung) and was greatly used of God. His entire theological and pastoral training had been at my father's feet.

During the remaining fourteen years my father served in Shandong (Shantung) till his early death in 1934, he put his whole life into on-the-job training programs for potential

In the eye of the poverty-plagued Chinese, the missionary always seemed to be wealthy.

Chinese leaders. Church after church was born, financed, governed, and grew through the ministry of these whom he trained. When my father was called to his heavenly reward, and when the Communists took over our part of the country-side, these churches not only survived but thrived under well-trained leadership that had long been receiving support only from the local congregations. Some of the more effective pastors and evangelists which God used in Shandong (Shantung) province were thus trained by my father on indigenous principles from the day of their conversion.

Nor were Hudson Taylor and Ivan Kauffman the only ones. The tragedy is that their numbers were far too few. About the time we arrived in Shandong (Shantung) province there was evidence that God was taking a hand in the situation. A number of outstanding Chinese evangelists were being used of God. An interdenominational Chinese-financed missionary endeavor, appropriately called "The Chinese

Missionary Society," was sending missionaries into Yunnan (Yunan), Sichuan (Szechuan), and Mongolia. The number of foreign missionaries that willingly began to transfer responsibility to the Chinese was increasing. This development occurred at an auspicious moment. There was a mounting resistance on the part of the Chinese to foreign control. Unfortunately, due to the lack of training, there was not a commensurate willingness on the part of Chinese Christians to assume financial responsibility. Those churches, established initially on the indigenous principle, however, found the Chinese people able and willing to give.

As far back as 1856 there arrived in China a missionary with a vision and a plan for the indigenous church. He was John L. Nevius. His plan called for Christians to seek to win their neighbors while supporting themselves with a trade. Nevius, a Presbyterian, urged that ecclesiastical organization should only be developed as the Christians themselves were able to handle it. He stressed the self-support principle. Churches should utilize local architecture, he urged, and should be constructed only when the Christians were able to afford it. He encouraged the sending and supporting of witnesses by the Chinese church. All of this was undergirded with emphasis upon prayer and Bible training programs.

In 1890, Nevius shared this plan with the infant Korean church. It was adopted and became the guiding force for the Korean church. Eighty-three years later Billy Graham, after addressing over one million Koreans in the capital city of Seoul on the closing night of his June 1973 Crusade, called the Korean church "the fastest growing church in the world." He said, "I urge church and theological leaders . . . to come and study the Korean church." Perhaps it is the Nevius plan that needs to be studied afresh and implemented. One wonders what would have happened if the Chinese church had been built on such a truly biblical and logical New Testament foundation from its inception. T. Stanley Saltau, veteran missionary to Korea, has this to say in his book, *Missions at the Crossroads:* "Korea has been one of the most fruitful mission fields and while there have been several factors in the amazingly rapid growth of the church here, the most important has been the methods and policies which have been used, whereby from the very beginning the responsibility for maintenance and leadership has been with the church."

I well remember the early thirties in Shandong (Shantung) province. The impressions I received as a young lad are indelible. Shandong (Shantung) province had previously seen a visitation of God under the ministry of Jonathan Goforth shortly after the Boxer Rebellion. Now God began again to sovereignly move. Shandong (Shantung) experienced a widespread divine visitation. There was deep conviction of sin and public confession as there had been during the days of Goforth. Preaching was uncompromising and clear-cut. The supernatural power of God was frequently manifest in the conversion of sinners, repentance of believers, healing of the sick, speaking in tongues, and the casting out of demons. These supernatural works of God were not restricted to a few but swept across denominational and national barriers. This was as it should be.

The Shandong (Shantung) revival, with its visitation of the supernatural, was to forcefully affect the church in China for many years to come. This was the time of the Japanese invasion of Manchuria. China was caught in the grip of uncertainty. Latourette commenting on this period had this to say: "To many [in China] the churches and their faith seemed the only stable element in a distraught and shifting world." Latourette wrote, "At Christian gatherings there were emotional scenes, with the casting out of demons, speaking with tongues, and the public confession of sins. New churches were erected, summer conferences were held, and Bible study flourished. Church membership rapidly increased." God was preparing His church for what lay ahead.

Directly or indirectly, there developed out of and around the Shandong (Shantung) revivals, the most encouraging indigenous Chinese church movements. In fact these were the first truly indigenous (growing naturally out of the soil of China) churches to gain national status. At long last there were churches that did not owe their existence directly to any missionary or maintain any links with the Western denominations. These churches were gloriously free to follow the guidance of the Holy Spirit in the structuring of the body of Christ. The Holy Spirit is, after all, the only authorized architect. It was He that declared, "I will build My church—and the gates of hell will not prevail." Only the church which He builds is eternal!

We shall take time to look briefly at only three of the truly indigenous churches that sprang up out of the heart of China in the early part of the twentieth century. The first to gain nationwide prominence was the True Jesus Church, established by Paul Wei in Tianjin (Tientsin) and Beijing (Peking) in 1917. Rapid growth was experienced in Shandong (Shantung) province under the ministry of Barnabas Chang. Under the Spirit's guidance emphasis was placed upon witnessing, tithing, and local church government. This strongly fundamental church expected, and experienced, the supernatural manifestations of God's power as the sick were healed, demons were cast out and believers spoke in "other tongues as the Spirit gave them utterance." Communal living was a vital part of the early days of the True Jesus Church especially in Shandong (Shantung) province. Soon True Jesus Churches were springing up throughout China and among the overseas Chinese in Korea, Japan,

Taiwan, and even Honolulu. By 1949 there was reported to be a membership of 125,000. Compare this with the 196,000 in the Church of Christ in China which was a union of several major denominations and one gets a picture of the solid, rapid growth of the True Jesus Church. In just over thirty years under Chinese leadership it had become almost as large as the Church of Christ in China, which had well over one hundred years of missionary effort behind it.

The year 1926 saw the birth of another truly indigenous church under the teaching of the remarkable Nee To-sheng, better known to the West as Watchman Nee. They called themselves "Christian Assemblies," but were popularly known as "The Little Flock."

With no links with the Plymouth Brethren or any other Western denomination for that matter, the local church under Watchman Nee developed a number of features similar to the "Brethren." Decrying formal church organization or even "churchy" edifices, great stress was placed upon the local church, local leadership, and local financial support. Strong emphasis upon Bible study and Bible teaching predictably generated evangelists and teachers of unusual ability. It is also important to note that a number of business ventures were initiated in order to assist with the finances of the ministry. Having no central government, statistics were never considered important; therefore, we can only estimate the size of the Little Flock.

Shandong (Shantung) province and the Shandong (Shantung) revival, which my father was very privileged to experience, gave birth to the most interesting and invigorating of the new Christian groups in China—the Yesu Jiating (Ye-su Chia-ting) or the Jesus Family. This indigenous movement grew out of the personal experience of Jing Tianying (Ching Tien-ying). Jing (Ching) was no second-generation Christian. His family were Buddhists with a strong Confucian tradition. Desiring a good education for their son, they sent him to the finest school in the district, a Methodist school. There, following a prolonged spiritual battle, he accepted Christ as his Savior. He concluded that Christ was greater than Confucius because Christ had died for his sins. In the year 1920, following a humbling act of restitution that involved his wife, from whom he was at the time separated, both of them received the infilling of the Holy Spirit. The following year the Jesus Family came into being.

Selling all of their possessions and giving the proceeds to the poor, Jing Tianying (Ching Tien-ying) and his wife commenced their ministry with the establishment of a uniquely Chinese commune on a piece of land left him providentially by his great-grandfather. With no textbook outside the Scriptures to guide him, Jing (Ching) developed a fellowship of believers that eventually spread throughout North China and deep into the interior. To an amazing degree the Holy Spirit structured this church so that it was uniquely prepared for the coming of the Communists. In later years Mr. Jing (Ching) said to his friend Dr. Vaughan Rees, "Little did I think . . . how the Lord would lead, or what He had in store for me. How foolish and ignorant I was. Now I see what He has done," explained Mr. Jing (Ching). "He has raised us up for this purpose, that the Communists might see what Christianity is."

Wisely using agriculture as a base, Yesu Jiating (Ye-su Chia-Ting) developed extraordinarily effective land policies. These policies paid off in abundant harvests. In 1930 they began to tithe (that is, give to the poor) one-tenth of the harvest of their land. In 1942 there was a great famine in North China, so they decided to give away 20 per cent of their harvest. One of the founders, Mr. Heng-shin, tells what happened: "The Lord blessed us . . . that we felt we should add a tenth each year. This year we are giving away nine-tenths." On forty-three acres of land they supported five hundred people and gave away 90 percent of their harvest to the poor. The Communists, who boast that their land policies "were better than that of either Marx or Lenin" could never compete with the Jesus Family. The best the Communists have been able to do is one acre per person for life support. Contrast this with forty-three acres for five hundred people who gave away 90 per cent of their harvest!

Here are a few further instances of how the Holy Spirit prepared His "Jesus family" for the coming of the Communists.

1. There was no central control. This made it very difficult for the Communists to control. Those denominations with a central control like ones in the West were easily controlled first by the Japanese and later by the Communists.

2. They would accept no foreign funds. During the great famine of 1942 money poured into North China from abroad, mainly from the U.S.A. The Yesu Jiating (Ye-su Chia-ting) would not touch this money. By 1949 all churches that had received foreign funds (for any purpose) were completely liquidated. This was not their motive for refusing the money, though. At the time Mr. Jing (Ching) explained, "Those foreign churches would rob us of one of our sheet anchors. It is our financial needs which drive us to our knees and force us to cry to Him."

3. They did not have church buildings as such. In their commune a central building was used for worship six or seven times a day—but it was also used (often simultaneously) in producing the products the Jesus Family needed. Thus, when the Communists took over all church buildings, the Yesu Jiating (Ye-su Chia-Ting) was not affected. Outside their commune the people were taught to set aside an area in their home for worship. This, too, proved very wise.

Remember, these policies were not instituted as an answer to Communism. They were guided to these policies by the Holy Spirit a full twenty years before the Communist takeover. The Jesus Family, born in the Shandong (Shantung) revival, considered the supernatural as normal. Casting out of demons, the ministry of angels, speaking in tongues, divine healing, miraculous supply of every need—these were part of the accepted normal worship of God. I knew this to be true from my own, and my father's, contacts with the Jesus Family in the days before my father's death in 1934.

Soon the Bamboo Curtain would fall. The church in China was about to be subjected to fiery trials. We have seen God and men at work. Not every human effort would endure. God never promised that man's creation was indestructible. Only those bodies of believers drawn together and molded together by the Holy Spirit are guaranteed eternal life. The gates of hell will never prevail.

10

The Bold Ones

The years of Christianity's greatest impact upon ancient China roughly parallel the rape of China by the West. This parallelism could conceivably lead to the conclusion that the twentieth-century Christian influence in China was entirely Western—false! The strongest Christian voices in China, especially in the years immediately preceding the Communist takeover, were Chinese. No Western voice spoke as boldly or as effectively as the voices of such godly Chinese men as John Sung, Wang Mingdao (Wang Ming-tao), and Watchman Nee. To their number could be added a host of other dynamic Chinese Christian voices that have received little or no publicity in the West.

Two of the better-known Chinese witnesses were indeed John Sung and Watchman Nee. Brief reference will be made to their lives and ministry in order to tell more fully of those lesser known, but just as effective, heralds of the Cross.

John Sung

It is true that no Chinese "Apostle" appeared to catch the imagination of both East and West in the early years of Christian endeavor in China. The man that God chose to signally use as the trailblazer was Sung Ju-un, the son of a Methodist minister in Fujian (Fukien) Province. Considered by his parents as unsuitable for the Christian ministry, young Sung was permitted, by his reluctant father, to study in America. The next seven-and-a-half years saw him excel in academics, plunge into a spiritual wilderness, and become confined to a mental institution because his Christian zeal and fervor did not fit the pattern of liberal theology.

Fast-moving events finally put him aboard a ship bound for his father's home. Aboard ship he struggled with the temptation to use his doctorate in chemistry to provide for his family. Following a great prolonged personal struggle, he emerged from his cabin to throw his diplomas, medals, and Phi Beta Kappa key overboard. Renouncing the world and its promise of fame, he echoed the declaration of the Apostle Paul, "What things were gain to me, those I counted loss for Christ."

God was to grant John Sung just fifteen years of public ministry. Perhaps no evangelist in history accomplished so much for God in so short a time. He was a powerful fearless preacher in the manner of Billy Sunday; a tireless zealot who never spared his own strength or his audience.

His exploits are still talked about today. He often ministered three times a day—not just talks, but powerful, anointed sermons. For example, during one Bible Conference conducted in Xiamen (Amoy) over a thirty-day period, John Sung took his audience through the entire Bible. Beginning in Genesis, ministering four and five hours a day, chapter by chapter he expounded the Word clear through to the last chapter of Revelation. When published, these messages occupied 554 pages. Has anyone else ever even attempted such marathon expositions of the Scriptures?

The greatest proof of a man's ministry is the fruit that remains. Today, more than thirty years after his early death from cancer and tuberculosis, there is abundant evidence of the effectiveness of his ministry throughout Southeast Asia. Many of today's Chinese Christian leaders in Asia were converted or set on fire by John Sung's ministry. The churches in Indonesia, Singapore, Malaysia, Thailand, and many other areas owe much to this man and his anointed ministry. Undoubtedly such evidence abounds in mainland China also. Leslie Lyall has done the church a great honor by writing a biography of John Sung, "Flame for God in the Far East."

Watchman Nee

A comtemporary of John Sung was Watchman Nee, who on June 1, 1972 went on to receive his victor's crown. Watchman Nee is probably the best-known Chinese Christian leader, owing to his translated messages which are still widely circulated in the West. It was in 1926 that Watchman Nee organized an indigenous Chinese Church popularly known as "The Little Flock." Largely Brethren in concept, this vigorous evangelical church grew to something over seven hundred churches with more than 70,000 members in just over twenty years.

Shortly after the Communist takeover, Watchman Nee was arrested and imprisoned. He spent the remainder of his life in prisons, in work camps, and under house arrest. In July of 1972, Communist officials were still telling inquirers that Watchman Nee was being "educated." One can only imagine at this point what this godly man endured during seventeen years of political thought reform.

Watchman Nee was often controversial. Early in 1938 his most famous book in the Chinese language was published. *Rethinking Missions* was first given as a series of messages to his coworkers, then edited by Watchman Nee himself. This book hit the Chinese churches and the missionary-oriented denominations like a bombshell. A storm of criticism broke over Watchman's head as churches closed their doors. Christians left their denominations and united with the Little Flock.

Rethinking Missions had as its foundation three basic postulates: Denominations are not scriptural and have become corrupt; the local church is sovereign and cannot be governed by any outside body; and the churches in China are not following the Bible example and must return to the Apostolic pattern.

This bold interpretation stunned the churches of China. Watchman Nee insisted that every local church must be self-supporting, self-governing, and self-propagating. His emphasis of dependence on God drove the Christians to their knees. Soon a general spiritual awakening became evident. Eventually, *Rethinking Missions* became the most influential book of the Chinese church.

Yes, Watchman Nee was one of God's bold ones, daring to teach what he believed, even though it ran counter to the grain of the established church. Now we know that Watchman Nee was used by God to prepare China's church for the very dark days that lay immediately ahead.

Wang Mingdao (Wang Ming-tao)

The "St. Paul of Red China" is not a title easily earned. It certainly would depict a man totally dedicated to the proclamation of Christ's Gospel, fearless in the face of persecution, and endowed with the spiritual stature to command the respect of fellow Christians. Wang Mingdao (Wang Ming-tao) was such a man—one of God's bold ones.

No Chinese Christian leader was more fearless in his opposition to atheistic Communism and the pseudo-Christian organization which it brought into being. Wang Mingdao (Wang Ming-tao) was the pastor of the largest church in Beijing (Peking) and highly respected throughout the nation. Sin was his major opponent. He was an incessant thorn in the side of the Communists and a courageous example of all of China's Christian community. He was careful never to attack the government, but he continually warned against their atheism.

Wang Mingdao (Wang Ming-tao) was born into a Christian home that early bore the scars of suffering for Christ. At the height of the Boxer Rebellion, just months before his birth, Wang lost his father. Hounded by the Boxers, cornered apparently with no hope of escape, Wang's father took his own life rather than fall into the hands of the ruthless Boxers. Wang's expectant mother and older sister somehow escaped with their lives. Wang was born a short time later. His early years were marked by a cruel struggle for mere existence. One of his earliest memories was of walking the railroad ties in Beijing (Peking) collecting pieces of coal that fell from the passing freight trains in order to survive Beijing's (Peking's) bitterly cold winters.

Up until his conversion at fourteen, young Wang was clearly headed down the wrong road. Already he was involved with opium and women. His teachers considered him hopeless. His widowed mother was at the point of despair. Through the witness of a classmate, young Wang surrendered his rebellious life to the Lord and experienced a complete transformation. The Christian life to him became a serious business. He became obsessed with the desire to be Christlike. When his classmates would point out his faults or failures, young Wang would go into the school washroom and beat his chest until it was black and blue in an agony of mingled despair and repentance.

Just a year after his conversion, his life became an inner conflict when God called him into the ministry. Wang Mingdao (Wang Ming-tao) had already set his heart on becoming a political leader. The tragic condition of his country called for strong Christian leadership. He was determined to provide it. Abraham Lincoln, apostle of emancipation, became his idol. But, "No man can serve two masters." Was it to be politics or Christ? Wang had come to feel that those who studied for the ministry were inferior; perhaps they couldn't keep up with the grueling university studies. He never accepted the second best; he always gave himself wholeheartedly to every project. Politics, not preaching was his choice.

The hardships of his early life often took their toll. In times of sickness he seemed to be able to reach out in faith and accept healing from Christ. He wrote many times of God's healing power in his own life. At eighteen, he became ill and the heavens seemed brass. Gradually, he realized that no healing would come until he settled the question of God's call on his life. Once he fully surrendered his life to Christ's service, he was healed.

Wang Mingdao (Wang Ming-tao) largely educated himself for the ministry; rather, he was taught by the Holy Spirit. He refused to go to seminary because he saw too many faults in those missionary-dominated institutions. This was to be a strong asset later in life when the issue of the foreign connections of the church became the Communist's favorite weapon. Wang Mingdao (Wang Ming-tao) was in no way a product of direct Western missionary effort. He was not trained in their theological schools. He was not ordained to the ministry by Western missionaries. He had never been employed by Western missionaries. He never received any form of financial help from them. Indeed, he was often openly critical of the Western approach to missions in his own country. His church in Beijing (Peking) owed its success solely to the blessing of God upon his own God-given ministry.

This eminent pastor was an outspoken evangelical. His ministry was underscored by an impeccable Christian life. The Communists could find no fault in him as a man of God. The major emphasis in his ministry was teaching on man's personal relationship to Christ. He permitted no compromise with sin. For a number of years after the Communist takeover his church in the capital city was a source of embarrassment to the atheistic government. The church was always packed. Loudspeakers on the outside of the church often reached an additional thousand people. His flawless character, his clear Christian message, and his undaunted courage held the Communists at bay. It is believed that over the years Pastor Wang Mingdao (Wang Ming-tao) preached to more Chinese than any other man.

Wang Mingdao (Wang Ming-tao) broached no liberal theology. He was known to accost leading liberal churchmen on the street and call them to repentance. Before long, these liberal clergymen became the unwitting tools of the Communists when they cooperated in the establishment of the "Three Self Church." Wang battled against what he called "this apostate church" from his pulpit and in his publications. At only twenty-seven years of age Wang Mingdao had begun to publish the "Spiritual Food Quarterly" to stem the tide of liberal theology in the Chinese church. He warned the people and liberal Christian leaders of the dangers of cooperating with an atheistic régime. He was later proved right. Eventually, all church doors were closed and the puppet leaders of the Three Self Movement were thrown in jail or sent off to forced labor.

Pastor Wang was subsequently put on public trial in Beijing (Peking). All his congregation were forced to attend. Three charges were brought against him: He was anti-government; he was anti-"Three Self Church"; and he preached unfamiliar and independent messages. No chance was given for defense. In spite of the government's desire to either jail him or kill him, public opinion in his favor forced his immediate release. No printer, however, would print his courageous messages. Pastor Wang responded by buying his own lead type and printing press. Two books rolled off that press, typeset and printed by himself. *Truth or Poison* attacked theological liberalism and *Obey God—Not Man* was a clarion call for resistance to all but Christ.

His last public sermon was preached to a crowded Beijing (Peking) church on August 7, 1955. His text was Matthew 26:45: "The hour is at hand, and the Son of Man is betrayed into the hands of sinners." It was a bold, clear reference to the future as he saw it. That night he and eighteen student members of his congregation were arrested and sent to prison. This time, when Pastor Wang was brought to trial, he was given opportunity to speak. At no time in his writings or during his trial did he say anything against the government. During the trial he fearlessly lashed out at the liberals and the Three Self Movement as betrayers of the crucified Christ. He was sentenced to fifteen years in prison despite the public support which he had.

For the next months he was subjected to endless mental torture. Two shifts of party political experts worked on him day and night. Every form of brainwashing technique was employed on the aging pastor. At last, after thirteen months of this torture, his mind shattered. He broke and signed a confession. The day of his release he was forced to read it before a large crowd assembled for the purpose. His self-criticism read in part, "I am an antirevolution criminal. I am grateful to the government for pardoning me and saving me from the depths of my sin. . . ." His confession was carried on the front page of every newspaper. Wang Mingdao (Wang Ming-tao), God's bold one, had finally been humbled. A few days after his release, he was seen walking up and down the streets of Beijing (Peking) from morning till night shouting, "I am Peter. I am Judas. I have betrayed my Lord."

His deranged mind could find no place for self-forgiveness. He had betrayed his Lord, though a careful reading of his "confession" shows that he did not, in fact, betray Christ.

A few weeks later, his mind restored, he took his dear wife and went to the government authorities. "The statement I was forced to sign is false. I have not sinned. Imprison me if you will, but I will not betray my Lord!" he announced. Wang was immediately imprisoned, and there the "St. Paul of Red China" spent the remaining years of his life. China has never had a clearer, more courageous Christian voice than Beijing's (Peking's) Pastor Wang Mingdao (Wang Ming-tao). China's own "Mr. Valiant-for-truth" endured twenty years of imprisonment before his release.

Li Hanwen (Lee Han-wen)

Trudging the primitive roads and paths of his beloved China, Li Hanwen (Lee Han-wen) did not attract much attention. Nothing about his height or dress made him different from the casual travelers, except perhaps the knapsack on his back.

Lee had graduated from the North China Theological Seminary in Beijing (Peking), a school that inspired a goodly number of China's evangelical Christian leaders. A native of Beijing (Peking), born into a non-Christian home, he had his first confrontation with Christianity at middle school. His personal surrender to Christ came at the time of his graduation. During his seminary days God kindled in his heart a great love for all the souls of China. His was no tiny vision.

Our first glimpse finds young Li (Lee) starting out on his own to preach the Gospel. He believed God had called him to preach in every one of China's twenty-one provinces, a fantastic undertaking in any day and especially in the early 1900's. Most of the time he slept on the side of the road unable to afford a night's lodging. Once Li (Lee) lived for two weeks on two loaves of bread. Recalling these experiences later, he said, "When you are penniless you are rich in Jesus Christ." Everyday he preached the Gospel in some town or village through which he passed. We do not know how long or for how many uncounted miles his burden propelled him. All we know is that when he arrived in China's largest city in 1948 he was a powerful and compelling Bible preacher.

Undaunted by the massive multitudes of Shanghai, China's largest and most sophisticated city, Pastor Li (Lee) started big. He borrowed the German Lutheran church seating over a thousand people and on a Sunday afternoon commenced his pastoral ministry. Within months it was packed to capacity. A year later, the congregation purchased their own property in the French concession. This tireless dynamo ceaselessly preached evangelistic campaigns and taught the Word. He never preached topical sermons. All his mesages were verse-by-verse expositions of the Living Word. He was another in the long line of great Chinese Bible preachers.

In 1949, Pastor Li (Lee) startled his congregation one morning when he boldly announced, "John the Baptist has arrived. Jesus will not be far behind." The Communists had moved into Shanghai in force. The wise pastor was warning his beloved flock and assuring them of the nearness of Christ. He felt that the coming of Christ would not be far behind the coming of the Communists. For many Christians it was not.

This was a fruitful year of ministry. The crowd gathering to hear him preach the Word often blocked the streets outside the church. The police eventually placed a restraining order on ministry at that spot. With inspired wisdom Pastor Lee divided his congregation into smaller units and dispersed them into various areas of the city. This increased his pastoral load but also prepared the church for the days of the scattered church. Could Pastor Li (Lee) have foreseen this or had the Lord revealed it to him?

Tragedy struck the Li (Lee) household in 1950. Their only daughter, a bright seventeen-year-old who loved Jesus with all her heart, contracted typhoid fever. The Communists had ordered her to report to a work gang in a distant village but illness prevented her ever leaving home. As death seemed imminent, some members of the congregation, Pastor Li (Lee), and his wife gathered around her bedside. Looking up at her father, his face now wrinkled with care, hair streaked with grey, heart burdened for some of the Christians who had already capitulated to the Reds, the daughter said, "Father, nothing is more important than prayer. Do your best to preach the Gospel. Have pity on those who have deserted you. Have courage to preach the true Gospel. Speak for God." Her eyes moved from friend to friend around her bed, then lighted on her mother. "Mother," she said, "trust the Lord. Love the Lord no matter what happens. The world is nothing but vanity." Her face turned upward as she exclaimed, "I see daybreak now. Jesus is coming for me. Good-bye."

Those present reported her face was radiant with the glory of the Lord as she passed into eternity. Members and friends wept, but not a tear moistened the pastor's face or that of his wife. "God does all things well," they seemed to be telling their congregation by their courage.

God gave Pastor Li (Lee) ten more years of relative liberty in preaching the Gospel, probably because his congregation was now meeting in homes. That freedom came to a sudden end in 1960 when he was arrested and sent to a forced labor camp in nearby Anhui (Anwei) Province. There he found warm Christian fellowship with some one hundred pastors, deacons, and Catholic priests. All denominational barriers quickly melted in the heat of the brick furnaces where they worked.

Writing to a friend in Hong Kong, he said, "Our hands are burned and swollen (making bricks), but our faces shine with joy. We sing and praise the Lord constantly as we work. We experienced what God's children did when they were slaves in Egypt making bricks for the Egyptians." Their spontaneous joy made a great impression on fellow prisoners. "Many businessmen and landlords in camp ask us why we sing as we work," he wrote. "What a wonderful opportunity to tell them of Christ."

Pastor Li (Lee) stressed, in his letters to his now widely scattered members, the wonderful unity all the Christians found in Christ. He wrote, "At this moment we are making bricks, but they are not to build walls separating one denomination from another. Oh, how we love one another!"

After two years of hard manual labor at the work camp, old Pastor Li suffered a heart attack. For the next months he was all alone in a Shanghai jail cell attempting to regain his strength. There he entered into a spiritual communion with Christ few men have ever known. He lived with Jesus; he talked with Jesus. The two of them occupied that Communist cell. Christ never left him. Often his letters to his wife would be stained with tears as he told of the loveliness of Christ.

His love and concern for his congregation was constant. Whenever he could, he sent out a letter to his congregation (through intermediary sources). One of his members in Hong Kong received a letter in which he apologized to the Lord. He was suffering from an infection and could not eat, think, or talk. He felt like he was failing in his duties as a shepherd. God had given him a flock, and he was not looking after them. His pastor's heart cried, "God I cannot work for you. Please work in me." "That night," he wrote his people, "God instantly healed me of the painful infection."

Released from prison, Pastor Li (Lee) was reunited with his beloved wife. They had just a few more years together before the Lord called him home in the Spring of 1965. Very late every night, when he was sure all the guards had retired for the night, he would reach for his precious Bible hidden in the back of an old clock case. Together he and his wife would read the Word, have a season of praise, and then pray for everyone in their congregation by name. One night he said to his wife, "My dear, don't cry when the Lord takes me away—praise God, because that will be the day of my release."

How do I know so much about Pastor Li Hanwen (Lee Han-wen)? In 1948, he was giving a series of Bible studies in Isaiah. He went through the entire book verse by verse. Among those who found Christ through those studies was a wealthy restaurant owner's wife. Soundly converted, she took her four children to hear Pastor Li (Lee) at every service. Her husband refused to give up his life of sin. Within days of her conversion, Pastor Li (Lee) put Mrs. Wang to work teaching a Sunday School class. She taught her own children, as well as many others, to love and serve Christ.

Later most of the family fled to Hong Kong. Mrs. Wang, speaking many different dialects, was my secretary for a number of years. Her eldest son, David, is now General Director of Asian Outreach. The father held out for over twenty years and finally recently completely surrendered his life to Christ. He, too, is actively serving the Lord. This amazing Wang family is only one of the absolutely countless families touched by a great pastor, Li Hanwen (Lee Han-wen)—faithful to the end. His works do follow him.

Timothy Dzao

One of God's bold ones finished service for his master during 1973. Just before his passing I spent a fruitful afternoon with the man I consider to have been one of China's great pastor-evangelists, Timothy Dzao.

Since 1949 he baptized over seven thousand new converts in Hong Kong alone, even though half of his time was spent as an evangelist in other areas of Asia. Few Chinese pastors in my estimation have the world vision and burden that Pastor Dzao demonstrated.

In 1941 Timothy Dzao, after returning from a preaching mission to Borneo, founded the Ling Liang evangelistic mission. Established in Shanghai as a Chinese missionary enterprise, it today reaches around the world. Chinese missionaries are supported in Europe, Indonesia, India, Sabah, Congo, Malaysia, the Philippines, and even the United States. His Hong Kong congregation sent US $10,000 to help build a Chinese Church in Los Angeles.

Timothy Dzao's ministry within China before coming to Hong Kong was also very fruitful. He established three churches in Shanghai which grew to well over two thousand believers. In Nanjing (Nanking), Hangzhou (Hangchow), and Suzhou (Soochow), over five hundred believers were in each church. No shallow evangelist, Timothy Dzao was a Bible preacher. One of his contributions to the Chinese church is a weighty thirty-volume "Bible Treasury" of Bible expositions and devotional reading.

John Sung, Wang Mingdao (Wang Ming-tao), and Watchman Nee all ministered in China at the same time as Timothy. Asked to recall his personal impressions of these men, Pastor Dzao looked away and said, "John Sung was a powerful uncompromising evangelist; Wang Mingdao (Wang Ming-tao), a pastor whose ministry centered on a

Christ-honoring personal life; Watchman Nee, a persuasive Bible teacher who could make you believe that white was actually red." Such were the bold ones that were used by God to build an indestructible church in China.

Timothy Dzao had a message which he wanted me to convey to the churches of the West. "I believe," said the veteran evangelist-pastor, "that the time has come for the Chinese to preach the Gospel in the West." He gave two reasons for this conviction. "First, I believe the time has come that the Chinese church must acknowledge its debt to the missionaries who came to China with the Gospel. Second," continued Dzao, "God has given us Chinese brilliant minds and a unique ability to understand the Scriptures which were written in an Oriental context. I believe that God wants to use us Chinese to bless the West and lead many to Christ."

The massive missionary enterprise in China may yet pay unexpected and unsought dividends. Is it inconceivable, as Timothy Dzao suggests, that God will use Chinese evangelists to turn many in the West to Christ? Don't the Scriptures teach that if you cast your bread upon the waters it will return again after many days? This is, in fact, already happening as men like Calvin Chao, Moses Chow, Leland Wang, and many others penetrate the West with the living Gospel. Yes, God is beginning to use the Chinese Christians to bless those who in the past have blessed China.

Of one thing we can be sure. God still has His bold ones in China. Some day, their story, too, will be told.

11

Through the Fire

At least twice a day during the tempestuous so-called "Cultural Revolution" the workers in the communes were paraded before the portrait of Chairman Mao. There they would be instructed to bow before his picture and pray for his guidance, his wisdom, or just for strength to do what he wanted them to do.

Imagine the shocked reaction of the commune leaders when a new member sent from the city refused to bow before the great Chairman's picture. The young "reactionary," as he was termed, was taken to the young local Red Guard chief. Asked to explain his actions, the young man replied fearlessly, "I am a Christian. I will not bow before anyone but the true God." Angrily he was told, "We will give you one more chance." Again he refused to bow. Following a severe beating he was again ordered to bow before Mao's picture. He refused.

In a rage the leader ordered his young Red Guards to break the stubborn prisoner's legs just below the knees. The leader was not satisfied until the Red Guards had propped the now only partially conscious young Christian up on his broken bloody stubs before Mao's picture. The young Christian's faith remained unbroken but those who knew him and related this story to me say that he will be a cripple for the rest of his life.

Zechariah the prophet could just as well have been describing God's plan for the Chinese church when he wrote, "And I will bring the third part through the fire, and will refine them as silver is refined, and try them as gold is tried; they will call on my name, and I will hear them: I will say, it is my people: and they shall say, The Lord is my God" (Zechariah 13:9).

The date October 1, 1949, was a watershed in the history of the Christian church in China. That date not only marked the inauguration of The People's Republic but, infinitely more important, it marked the commencement of a baptism of fire for China's church. This church was going to be refined and brought through the fires of severe testing.

Only God knew what lay ahead. The years immediately preceding 1949, and the year following, China erupted with tremendous spiritual activity. Churches became bold and blessed in their evangelistic endeavors. Ships were chartered to bring hundreds of missionaries, who had sought refuge elsewhere from the Japanese war, back to China. Revival fires were burning in widely scattered areas of the country. God raised up a brilliant Chinese evangelist, Calvin Chao, to spearhead Inter-Varsity Christian Fellowship on the campuses of China's universities. So great was the impact of God's moving upon the university students that conversions became almost commonplace and significant numbers began to offer themselves for full-time Christian service. Ultimately Calvin Chao became number five on the Communists' "most wanted man" list. Today, he continues his vital work with Chinese university students in the U.S.A.

"If you want to see the power of God, the atmosphere must be one of great difficulty; if you want to see the miracle power of God, the atmosphere must be one of impossibility." So wrote the respected Donald Grey Barnhouse in a China report dated 1950. "The enemy of souls has put the murk of Communist ideology down into the minds of heathendom, and has now changed difficulty into impossibility in China." He continued, "It would seem that our Lord loves to work under such circumstances, and there is every evidence that He is doing so."

Reports of crowded churches, massive Bible Conferences, and successful evangelistic endeavors encouraged everyone despite the continued successes of the Communist armies in their bid to take over all of China. At this time, there emerged a significant number of Chinese missionary societies, sending Chinese missionaries to the more remote areas of China. Finances came from the Chinese Christians themselves as God's blessing continued. Three million copies of the Scriptures were distributed by the Bible Society in a single year. The Bible became the bestseller throughout China. No other book was in such demand. The city of Beijing (Peking) was the scene of a massive evangelistic campaign arranged by The Beijing (Peking) Youth for Christ committee. God was moving by his Spirit in what was to be the last days of freedom that the Chinese church would know for many faith-testing years.

Missionaries for the most part were amazed to see that when the victorious Communist troops overran an area there was no looting or raping and, most surprising of all, no pressure was put on churches, Christians, or even missionaries. Though this was difficult for them to understand, they accepted it with gladness and plunged more deeply into their appointed ministries. Grateful for what appeared to be an honest administration, they were often fooled by this initial Communist graciousness.

In 1950 Zhou Enlai (Chou En-lai) addressed himself to the Christians of China with this message: "So we are going to go on letting you teach, trying to convert the people. . . . After all, we both believe the truth will prevail; we think your belief is untrue and false; therefore, if we are right, the people will reject them, and your church will decay. If you are right, then the people will believe you, but as we are sure you are wrong, we are prepared for that risk. . . ."

Subsequent events were to demonstrate that they were not so "sure you are wrong" and were unprepared to take the risk. On balance, it should be noted here that some influential Communists, notably Ya Han-chang, never deviated from the view enunciated in 1950 by Zhou Enlai. Obviously, their moderate position was overruled as the persecution of religious groups became a main attraction during the Cultural Revolution.

The leading Chinese evangelicals for the most part saw through it all and tried to warn the church of what was to come. Watchman Nee, Wang Mingdao (Wang Ming-tao), and others knew the true nature of Communism. But far too many missionaries and Chinese church leaders failed to understand the significance of the Communist strategy.

Looking back now, two basic reasons can be seen for the initial hands-off policy of the conquering Communists. First, they felt it was unwise to antagonize the Christians until their position as the new rulers of China was more secure. Once China was completely in their grasp they could get down to the business of eradicating the undesirable elements such as missionaries, pastors, and lay Christians.

A second reason was that many of the most capable people in China were either true Christians or were sympathetic to Christianity, having been educated and trained in Christian schools. The Communists needed their expertise and help until their own people could be trained to take over. It was a decision they were forced to make. No taint of mercy or compassion should be seen in their initial failure to strike hard at Christianity.

Article 88 of the Constitution of the People's Republic of China declares, "Citizens . . . of China enjoy freedom of religious belief." This probably was borrowed from Dr. Sun Yi-xian's (Sun Yat-sen's) stated convictions. The Communists, however, did not interpret this as one of the basic human freedoms. Indeed, it was treated as separate from such freedoms as speech, press, and assembly. Nor, was any mention made of freedom to practice one's religious belief. Future rationalizations or explanations of Article 88 were ludicrous and showed no concept of what religious freedom is.

The outbreak of the Korean war in June of 1950 coincided with the carefully timed and planned commencement of efforts to eliminate Christianity from China. A significant number of Chinese church leaders became tools of Mao's régime. They fully cooperated in producing a series of Manifestos and Declarations which served well the purposes of the Communists. These signed documents spoke of "Christianity consciously or unconsciously, directly or indirectly, becoming related to imperialism," or "The Disposal of American Subsidized Missionary Institutions and Groups." One of the favorite Communist tools was to call for the unification of all churches. This eventually led to a pseudoChristian government-sponsored church.

It is obvious that some Chinese Church leaders were caught between conflicting convictions. They were aided in their thinking by the undebatable fact that Christian missions, though not an "imperialist plot" as claimed, did benefit immeasurably from Western imperialist policies in China.

A document published by the Beijing (Peking) régime in 1951 outlined "Foreign Preachers' Intrusion into the Interior and Intervention of Domestic Affairs." It stated among other things that Robert Morrison, the same man who translated the Bible into Chinese, drew up the draft of the Nanjing (Nanking) treaty, and Rev. Gutzlaff prepared the draft of the Chinese text. This, incidentally, is the treaty which all Chinese resent the most.

With such a barrage of antiimperialist charges, whether true or false, being leveled at former missionaries, a strong reaction was not unexpected. The force of all these charges was that sufficient truth was mixed with error to make them completely believable to some church leaders.

Unquestionably some of these church leaders were further nobly motivated by a desire to do what they could to assist in the rebuilding of their shattered country. In other words, there was a mixture of patriotism and antiimperialism in their thinking. The result was early cooperation with the régime.

Some church leaders, while conceding that "Protestant Christianity . . . has made a not unworthy contribution to Chinese society," underscored the need for the government to control all religious activity for the purpose of "putting into execution the political, social, and economic principles of the New Democracy."

Pastors were party to the adoption of a new slogan, "Love Country—Love Church" (note the order). Christian leaders backed a new church called the "Oppose-America, Aid-Korea, Three Self Reform Movement of the Church of Christ in China," more popularly known as the "Three Self Reform Church," or "Three Self Movement."

This Communist-inspired "church" created ambivalence in the Christian community. Good were the aims of self-government, self-support and self-propagation. Bad were the obviously ominous signs of government control of the church. Good was the hope that perhaps this would permit at least a partial freedom to worship. Bad was the agreed-upon "Manifesto" which stressed not faith in God but the evils of imperialism. It was purely a political tool. Good to some and bad to others was the government's insistence that all denominations and groups should unite to become one church called "The Three Self Movement." With the signing of the Manifesto, the die was cast. This was the beginning of the end for the organized church in Mao's China.

The exodus of missionaries was now in full force. They had not been ordered out but the message that they were not wanted or needed in the new régime came through loud and clear. The largest missionary force in China, the China Inland Mission, ordered the evacuation of all their missionaries in January of 1951. Some felt that this move would strengthen the Chinese church as it would now be forced to assume full responsibility. All Roman Catholic missionaries except the aged, inform, or ill were ordered to remain at

Not only were Christians forbidden to enter their churches but many places of worship were also desecrated.

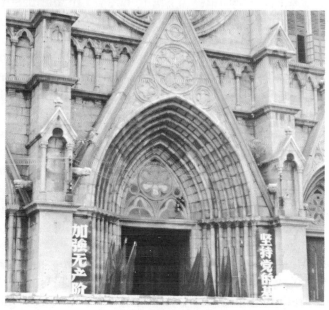

their posts. The Protestant evacuation was practically complete by early 1952.

Pressures on the church became severe. Attendance and membership were on a descending scale, especially in the major denominations. Only the independent, indigenous churches showed a gain from 1949 to 1957. This gain was in fact quite a dramatic one as their numbers almost tripled in a period when others suffered tragic decline.

Evangelical Protestant church leaders one by one were arrested and sentenced to imprisonment or labor camps. In 1951, Isaac Wei, son of the founder of the True Jesus Church, and several of their leaders were imprisoned on charges that their faith healing, speaking in tongues, and other practices were "unscientific" and "harmful." In 1952 the founder of the Jesus Family, Jing Tianying (Ching Tienying), and Watchman Nee were arrested and sentenced. In 1955 Wang Mingdao (Wang Ming-tao) was at last silenced.

Faith-testing times indeed! Some could not stand—others stood firm. That's why God takes His church through the fire. A Catholic priest who refused to be a tool declared, "If I betray my God and my soul, who could then guarantee that I would not betray my motherhood and my people." A Methodist bishop boldly said to his accusers, "I have thrown in my lot with Christ and His church. I'm not going to be on the fence. If I have to, I'm willing to die for Him." A humble woman, graduate of John Sung's Bible School, was thrown in prison. Told she would be released if she would only declare there was no God, she replied firmly, "No, that I will never do. I am very peaceful in jail here with my Lord." Years later she died in that jail cell, still strong in her faith, still peaceful with her Lord.

It was during this period that brainwashing techniques were viciously employed to break the will of Christians. One who endured the worst the Communists could throw at him

declared on arriving in Hong Kong, "I came to a final conclusion about Communism. . . . It tends to hypnotize the
human race into believing that wrong is right." Communist
brainwashing experts have been known to claim, "If God
himself was sitting in that chair, we could make him say
what we wanted him to say."

Brainwashing techniques were fully justified in Communist thinking. They referred to it as "thought reform or to
transform thinking." Any means seemed to justify the end of
eradicating that which was evil and corrupt in Chinese
minds. More than one writer has pointed out that the process was a humanistic means to achieve spiritual goals. By
stressing guilt, creating shame, demanding atonement and
recantation, a "new birth" was achieved. This "group
therapy" did not always take the form of brutality, but the
fervor with which it was pursued led frequently to extreme
physical and mental pressure.

To share with you just a faint inkling of what was involved, this is the true story of a young lady I know. Her
father was a Christian physician in China. She was accused
of being a spy and a reactionary simply because she had
attended missionary primary and secondary schools.
Arrested, she was made to live in a room with five Communist cadres who twenty-four hours a day attempted to
break her. Five women at night—five men in the day. The
light was kept on all night. She was forced to write her background over and over. The purpose of this was self-
searching, self-confessing, and self-criticism.

After several months of this pressure, she thought of
suicide, but each time was driven to prayer. She prayed, "O
God, if there is anything evil in my life please take it out and
allow me to go free." As they were unable to break her, she
was eventually sent to a remote area of China to serve the
party with her professional skills. I had the privilege of

baptizing her soon after her escape to Hong Kong. Only God knows what China's Christians had to endure during this period.

A beautiful woman is a virtual prisoner in her own home, constantly watched by cadres who live with her. Her face continues to glow with the presence of God. She is not living in the past, but her past was an inspiration to me and many, many others.

Jane was an orphan girl from a poor village who came to the big city during a famine in her area. A pretty teenager, she soon found work in a dance hall and rapidly became the queen. Men begged for her favors. A lonely orphan, she soon became the third wife of a millionaire twenty years older than herself.

Even though she now could have anything money could buy, she was disturbed by a great emptiness within. A friend persuaded her to attend an evangelistic meeting conducted by evangelist Timothy Dzao. There she found Christ and as a result ran into fierce opposition from her husband and his family. Eventually she led her husband to the Lord. He, too, demonstrated a completely changed life.

Following their conversion, they felt their relationship was wrong in the sight of God. After their separation he continued to support her. They remained close friends. Jane built a small house in her private garden which she called "The Ark." In the next few years, Jane led many influential people to Christ in that "ark," including forty members of her ex-husband's family. He became a lay preacher.

Jane has since been through many brainwashing sessions. She is reduced to poverty and physical loneliness. Those who have seen her recently say her inner beauty still remains. Her witness to all she meets remains strong and clear. This in itself is a modern miracle.

An elderly Christian lady was put under reeducation by the cell leaders in her city. Several times a day she would be visited by experts at mind-breaking. They attempted to get her voluntarily to tear up her Bible and remove the picture of Christ from the wall of her room. She steadfastly refused. The visits and pressure would come any time of the day or night. There was no privacy as over a period of many months the pressure was increased.

Finally one day the dear old lady's mind snapped. She sent for the ones who had tried so hard to break her will. In their presence she tore up her precious old Bible and threw the picture of Jesus at their feet. When they left the room she died at her own hand, her mind unable to function properly.

A well-known Bible woman was one of the first Christians arrested in her area. They determined to make an example of her. Not just brainwashing but cruel inhuman treatment over a long period finally destroyed her mind. She was released to wander, penniless and alone, through the villages of her area with a blank look on her face. She is considered "mad," as she begs her daily bread from house to house.

She is still living as I write. Something beautiful happens when she meets a Christian she had known "before." Her eyes light up in a momentary recognition. A fleeting smile crosses her otherwise vacant face giving silent and moving testimony of an inner faith that has somehow survived.

The Communists were not, and are not, satisfied with individual attempts to change minds. Their satanic pseudo-psychiatry is aimed at changing the thinking of every person in China, earth's largest nation. Sometimes more drastic action is necessary, hence, the "Cultural Revolution." This was, from the Christian viewpoint, a massive outbreak of militant atheism. Christianity was marked for annihilation along with all other religious faiths. The young Red Guards were convinced that these totally unnecessary remnants of the past must be eradicated in order to build a new society in China.

The crusading young Red Guards set out to destroy the old. Christian churches, Buddhist temples, holy places, sacred books, Bibles, pictures of Christ, crucifixes, images, all were crushed beneath the heels of the overzealous youth. All churches were closed, even the "government-sponsored" Three Self churches. All pastors were prohibited from carrying on public ministry. Most went to prison, work camps, or thought-reform camps. Many were brutally treated by the highly motivated young Red Guards. News of the outbreak of violence against Christians drove the church into hiding.

Individual Christian families felt the impact of the revolutionaries. The entire Luke family was at home when the Red Guards barged in. The two sons had graduated from a university under Communist instructors. They could not accept the Christian faith of their godly parents. Because the father had received his college education in America the entire family, including the sons, was blacklisted as undesirables by the Communists.

Entering the house, the Red Guards wantonly destroyed most everything in sight. They discovered the life savings which the Lukes had carefully kept for their sons' inheritance and pocketed it. Then they demanded all Bibles and Christian books. The parents surrendered two Bibles and two copies of the book Chinese Christians value most next to the Bible, *Streams in the Desert*. The Red Guard leader threw the books at the elder Luke saying, "Destroy these books," and with that they left.

Repulsed and disgusted by what they had seen, the two sons apologized profusely to their parents. Mr. Luke responded by saying, "Boys, the money I had saved for your inheritance is gone, but I have something far greater to give you." To each son he gave a Bible and a copy of *Streams in the Desert*. Since then both boys have accepted the Lord. I have talked with friends who have worshiped the Lord with them in recent months.

Shortly after the Cultural Revolution, my associate visited the library of Beijing's (Peking's) Qinghua (Tsinghua) University. Lining the walls were 1,300,000 volumes. He asked the librarian if the library had a copy of the Bible. She replied, rather uncertainly, that there might not be a Bible in their library. He moved on to another room in the vast building reading newspapers from years gone by.

The librarian came bustling into the room saying, "Sir, I referred your question to my superiors and they have located a Bible. Would you care to see it?" He followed her to a shelf where a lone Bible stood. One Bible among 1,300,000 volumes! A quick glimpse revealed the Bible which had been printed in 1950 in Shanghai by the Bible Society had never been checked out. It was not available for loan.

Surrounding that lone Bible he noted eighteen titles critical of the Bible, titles such as *The Poisonous Essence of the Bible* and *The Bible Is the Sugar-wrapped Poison of Imperialism*. Opening one book, he noted that Jesus Christ was defined as "a nonexistent man rumored to have claimed that he was the son of God." These had been well read.

Not just the Luke boys but thousands of other Chinese were repelled and disgusted by the wild excesses of the Cultural Revolution. The clay feet of the great Chairman were soon clearly visible. Their hopes and dreams crashed around them as they saw what happens when restraints are removed. Communism and massive doses of Mao's thought had not transformed human nature.

The Cultural Revolution succeeded in virtually anni-

hilating the visible church in China. Those visiting China
reported that they could find little, if any, evidence of the
survival of China's church. The Red Guards had done their
work well—or had they?

12

The Church Becomes Visible

Despite, or possibly because of, thirty years of widespread repression, persecution, and martyrdom, the Christian community in China is now many times larger than during the peak years of missionary endeavor. In fact, at no period of China's ancient history have the Chinese people been so responsive to the Gospel.

The former Anglican Bishop of Fuzhou (Foochow), Moses Hsieh, told reporters during the Spring of 1980, "Generally we have more Christians in China now than before the Cultural Revolution." Just how many Christians there are in China is very difficult to ascertain. China's government certainly does not want to admit to the explosion of Christianity in China following the end of the Cultural Revolution, so we can't expect an accurate figure from them. The Christians themselves are widely scattered and are not tied together organizationally. No one is keeping a membership roll covering all of China. There is no source to which we can go. What we can do is talk with as many Christians in China as possible and get an estimate as increasing contacts are made throughout the country. In 1980 Dennis Bloodworth, Singapore-based journalist of the *London Times*, estimated that there may be as many as eight million Protestant Christians in China. His figure seemed to be an exaggeration to some but, in fact, may have been fairly accurate then. Now Christianity seems to be spreading across China almost like a prairie fire.

173

In the Spring of 1981 a pastor in the Hangzhou (Hang-chow) church of the Three Self Patriotic Movement esti-mated that there were five million Christians among the thirty-eight million people in that one province (Zhejiang [Chekiang]) alone. Our best estimate at this writing is that there are probably over twenty-five million Christians in China. Some researchers are estimating as high as fifty million. Whatever the actual figure it certainly represents completely unprecedented church growth. From less than one million in 1969 to over twenty-five million in thirteen years is dramatic growth for any country on earth. For this to have taken place in China is especially significant.

After 150 years of dedicated Christian missionary effort there were less than one million believers when the Com-munists took over in 1949. Now perhaps three million Chinese every year are joining the ranks of those who acknowledge Jesus Christ as Lord and Savior. And this is taking place without any organized effort to evangelize the nation. Evangelism is spontaneous rather than taught. In fact, traditional evangelism may not be the most significant aspect of this dramatic church growth.

To discover cause and effect requires first a brief journey into the past. The full story of Chairman Mao's Cultural Revolution may never be told. But it was during those pitch-dark days of agony that preparations were under way that would be one of the most significant factors in the future growth of China's church. The ideological madness of the revolution focused upon the destruction of the "Four Olds." One of these was religion. Consequently all religion came under intense attack. Christianity, because of its past links with the West, may have been a particular target of hatred. Christianity is Christians so pastors, laymen, and laywomen from all walks of life were forced to endure brutal mental and physical torture. Even the government-authorized church group was compelled to cease functioning. Most pastors and lay leaders were thrown into prison or sent off to hard labor. It was in the prisons and labor camps that God purified and prepared a people that would one day become irresistible magnets attracting a disillusioned generation to Christ.

Many pastors and lay leaders spent fifteen to twenty years in prison. Some spent up to eight years in solitary confinement. Others suffered in silence as their loved ones, husband, wife, or children were snatched from them. This was the purifying fire that produced saints. Perhaps this is the only way. The most attractive Christian characters are seamed with the scars of suffering.

The Cultural Revolution wound down in 1969. The entire country slumped in almost total exhaustion. The now notorious Gang of Four, led by Chairman Mao's wife, took control of domestic affairs and the media. A strong leftist sledgehammer of propaganda effectively screened reality. Visiting Western churchmen returned from China to laud the new Maoist society, claiming that it was a demonstration of "true Christianity." They said traditional Christianity was dead in China.

However, news began to leak out of the existence of house churches. The church in China was still alive. House churches represented the only way believers could function in those agonizing days. In fact, in the darkest period, worship was conducted behind blanketed windows, in whispered tones, with only the immediate family in attendance. As pressure began to ease in the early seventies the Christian remnant became bolder. Reports of large gatherings of believers in the rural areas gave the first indication that God was sovereignly moving. At the heart of all such gatherings was a living saint or saints who had been purified and tempered by suffering. These lay persons shared God's Word from a miraculously preserved Bible or Bible portion. Then, as prison doors began to swing open one by one, a powerful new factor was injected into Chinese society. These purified saints had walked and talked with God, their only companion during their years of incarceration. They came forth as pure gold, shining so brightly that they became the chief magnet attracting increasing numbers to Christ. Watchman Nee, well-known Christian leader, and countless others less well known but equally God-saturated walked out of their agonizing confinement. Many were old and infirm. Watchman Nee died a few months after his release. But others are still vigorously carrying the torch.

An entire generation of young people, most of whom had been caught up in the maelstrom of the Cultural Revolution, became disillusioned with the entire political system. Education had passed them by while they struggled for the revolution, and now there were no jobs. The death of Premier Zhou Enlai (Chou En-lai) and Chairman Mao Zedong (Mao Tse-tung) and the arrest of the Gang of Four completely shattered their foundations. An unprecedented spiritual vacuum was thus created. Into this vacuum came the impact of these godly men and women who held no bitterness against their persecutors. They demonstrated a peace and joy that became the envy of thousands of these lost young people. Soon reports of high percentages of young people in house meetings all over China were confirmed. Today they make up the majority of Christians as indeed they make up the majority of the population.

The hearts of one thousand million Chinese are searching for something to satisfy. Not all, by any means, are being influenced by Christians. There has been a widespread return to religion of all kinds. Fortunetellers are practicing openly and are often considered to be the most important people in the community. They certainly have the highest income in rural areas. Incense is once again openly sold in the market places. Taoist priests are being called on to assist in family functions. Temples are reopening. Priests are busy training young priests. In fact, young people are turning to religion in such numbers that it can almost be considered the "in thing."

This return to religion followed the violence of the disastrous Cultural Revolution. John Gardner observed, "Violence is counterproductive and produces changes of a sort you don't want. It is a very dangerous instrument and can destroy those who wield it." Jesus said: "All they that take the sword shall perish with the sword." Communist violence backfired.

China's youth are seeking peace of soul after experiencing a lifetime of violence. They are turning to religion in highly significant numbers. I am delighted to report that the Christians of China are rising to this challenge of a new generation of young people who are searching for that something which materialism cannot supply.

The Communist Party knows a crisis of confidence when it sees it. Strenuous efforts are currently being made, at all levels, to offset the impact of religion on today's youth.

The People's Daily defined religion as "the vain and erroneous responses of man to his feelings of impotence and fear in the face of natural and socialistic forces."

The Ren Min Daily News clearly stated the C.C.P.'s twisted view of religion: "Religion by itself is conservative and backward. Religion tries to exploit people by trying to sell them tickets to a life of heavenly blessing. Religion's message to the hard workers and peasants is to tell them only to endure and patiently wait for grace from heaven and forget about men's rights on earth. That is why we say religion is the opiate of the people. It is like bad wine to one's nerves."

The *People's Liberation Army Daily* in March 1980 expressed concern over the number of soldiers who have accepted Christ. The paper leveled strong criticisms at soldiers who "have as their ideals false democracy and the so-called rights of man, taking in anarchy and ultra-individualism, even going so far as to believe in Christ for spiritual solace."

It is the youth that the Party is primarily concerned about. A Chinese youth newspaper published an article on how a Communist deals with people who are Christian believers. It says nothing of imprisonment, torture, brainwashing, or persecution. These are better left unsaid. What was said was revealing enough. The article commences thus: "If a person is over eighteen years of age, in our Constitution he is free to choose whether to believe or not to believe in religion." Thus it is obvious that no one under eighteen years of age is free to believe in religion. There is absolutely no guaranteed religious liberty for anyone under eighteen years of age, although occasionally it is permitted.

In paragraph two, the article states that "while we cannot force a person to not believe in religion, we should stick to our belief that there is no such thing as a savior or god. We should try to encourage them to concentrate on The Four Modernizations and not try to escape reality through religion."

Paragraph four states, "If, after all our efforts to convince them they still want to stick to their belief, then if he is a member of the Communist Party, he must be asked to leave the Party."

The final paragraph contains a warning that although the Constitution guarantees the right to believe in religion there are other laws that can be applied against believers on various pretenses: "Let us be aware of those who are using religion as a means to interfere in our political affairs, in our social affairs, and in the educational system of our nation. Some might use the mask of religion to hamper our production and peace and order, or even deceive our possessions and cause poor health. . . . These things are all against the law of our nation. Therefore, if any person is discovered with this motivation, we should report it to the authorities and give him the right kind of reprimanding."

In the Fall of 1981 the Fujian (Fukien) *Daily* reminded its readers, in a province of substantial Christian influence, that although China's Constitution guarantees religious freedom to ordinary people, "a Communist Party member in particular should not be confused with an ordinary person." The paper acknowledged that Christian believers have begun to appear inside the Party and its Youth League. Then it made it very clear that Marxism is based on total atheism, and no true Communist may believe in religion or join a church. Apparently this problem was widespread enough to merit an article in the Fujian (Fukien) *Daily*.

Several conclusions can be drawn from just these sample articles:

1. Beijing's (Peking's) Communists are puzzled by the current interest in religion and are trying to cope with it.
2. The official position of the government is an unchanged commitment to atheism.
3. No one under eighteen years of age is "free" to believe in religion. In spite of this, so many young people are becoming Christians that it has alarmed the Party leadership.
4. No one can be a Christian and a member of the Chinese Communist Party or of the Youth League. Obviously some Party members, and many Youth League members, have become Christians.
5. Believers may be, and are still being, arrested on the pretense

of interference in the Socialist Revolution. The charge then
would be conveniently civil and not religious, thus avoiding
the charge of religious persecution.

Fresh new opportunities for Christians to outwardly
express their faith emerged with the almost lightning-like
changes that occurred with the ascension of Den Xiaoping
(Teng Hsiao-ping) to the top power position in the Party.
This brought about a significant easing of political pressure
upon Chinese society. A greater degree of personal freedom
was soon evident throughout the country.

In 1978 the Four Modernization Drive was launched. This
was a concerted effort to modernize the tragically anti-
quated fields of Agriculture, Industry, Defense, and Science-
technology. To have any hope of making progress along
these lines the Party was forced to grant more freedom to
the people. As a result of this taste of freedom the Democracy Wall became a *cause célèbre* as the youth of China
freely expressed their hopes and dreams, as well as their
disenchantment with the system. Another spin-off was the
official recognition of the existence of Christianity in Communist China and the subsequent opening of churches as
well as Moslem mosques and Buddhist temples.

China's Communist Party seems to have been forced to
the recognition of religious believers against its will. Government leaders are calling it an "indefinite interim existence of religious practice and belief."

It is difficult, however, not to suspect the Communists of
duplicity. Do they have hidden motives for officially recognizing the existence of religious believers?

The recognition of Islam was certainly appreciated by the
oil-rich Arab States. They undoubtedly are in a position to
help finance China's modernization. The Chinese minor-
ities, living on the borders of the Soviet Union, are largely
Moslem. It is not difficult to see that the present recognition

of Islamic believers will be to the advantage of Beijing (Peking). Similarly, the recognition of Buddhism will please the largely Buddhist nation of Japan and many of the wealthy Chinese of Southeast Asia. These are people whom China is counting on heavily in their modernization drive. It is significant that the indigenous religions of China, such as Confucianism, have not been given the freedom to openly practice their faith.

The Western world, on the other hand, is nominally Christian. While seeking the technical expertise of the West, it is obvious that increased liberty for Christians in China has highly pleased many in the Western world. From a pragmatic point of view, then, China's Communist Party has decided, at least temporarily, to tolerate religion while at the same time planning for the day when religion will no longer be necessary. At the same time, all of China's religious believers will logically be more likely to voluntarily cooperate in the Modernization Drive. The basic goals of Beijing (Peking) have not changed.

In 1979 the Three Self Movement was revived by the Religious Affairs Bureau. This concept had its roots in a conference of Presbyterian missionaries held in Swatow in 1881. They addressed themselves to the question of how the then infant Chinese Church should proceed in its development. A resolution was passed urging that "the native church must become self-governing, self-supporting and self-propagating." In the ensuing years there was great variance in the application by missionaries of what was a biblical principle. Unfortunately most were not too insistent upon this principle, nor was it easy to implement, given the low level of income and education of most Chinese in those years.

Shortly after the Communists came to power a group of Chinese clergymen, mainly linked to the YMCA, drew up a

Manifesto in conjunction with the late Premier Zhou Enlai (Chou En-lai). This manifesto placed the State above God in order of allegiance. Leslie Lyall has branded this a "Manifesto of Betrayal." The Three Self Patriotic Movement was then formed to unite the believers under this banner. Through the means of self-government, self-support, and self-propagation, the Communist Party sought to permanently sever all ties of the Chinese Church with the West. The motives were political rather than biblical. Eventually, during the mid-fifties, the Three Self Movement became a government tool to brutally suppress those who refused to demote God to second in authority in their allegiance. If appeasement with the State to permit the Christian Church to continue functioning was a motivation of the leaders of the movement, it was a failure. In fact, most churches were closed in 1956 because of their refusal to cooperate with the Three Self Movement. By 1966 all churches were closed and eventually even the Three Self Movement itself was unable to function.

If the major goal of the Three Self Movement was to encourage the development of a truly indigenous church along New Testament guidelines then it would have had much broader support, both from inside and outside of China. Their past records do not support this contention. The name is something of a misnomer because such men as Wang Mingdao (Wang Ming-tao), Watchman Nee, Jing Tianying (Ching Tien-ying) and Isaac Wei would not have been imprisoned through pressure from the Three Self Movement if the name had any relevance. These men were all outstanding leaders of indigenous self-supporting, self-propagating, and self-governing Chinese churches. They had virtually no links with the church in the West. Foreign influence was not an issue at all; only their politics were unsatisfactory. All spent years in prison because they could not acquiesce to the policies and practices of the movement.

Coinciding with the resuscitation of the Three Self Movement, China's official organ, the *People's Daily*, published what it billed as "A Comprehensive Policy for Religious Freedom." Reading between the lines of Marxist verbiage, it reiterates the Marxist view that religion being a "product of history . . . will follow its own course of birth, development, and disappearance." The reason for granting more religious liberty at that time was clearly stated. "This will help," the paper claimed, "to unite the vast believing population and the patriotic people in religious circles and mobilize all positive and active factors toward the Four Modernizations."

A brief reference to the power structure might be helpful here. The Communist Party is the major power base. It created a Religious Affairs Bureau to oversee and control all religious activity in the country. The Religious Affairs Bureau, in return, carries out its mandates through several created vehicles covering all religious believers, whether Moslem, Buddhist, Roman Catholic or Protestant. The Three Self Movement is the agent to govern all Protestant activity. Bishop Ding (Ting), who heads this agency, said in an October 13, 1980, speech that "because of the Three Self Movement the patriotic consciousness and national pride of the Christian has increased greatly." There was no mention of spiritual goals. In November 1980 the Third National Christian Conference was held in Nanjing (Nanking). At that conference a new agency was created and dubbed the China Christian Council. The same man was elected to lead both groups, causing widespread confusion and some skepticism as to the role of the new agency.

But we must give them an opportunity to speak for themselves. They have given three reasons for the reactivation of the Three Self Movement:

1. To be able to negotiate with the government about resuming control over church property.
2. To inculcate the Three Self principles among those who were converted during and after the Cultural Revolution.
3. To develop relations with overseas Christians according to the lines of the Three Self principle.

Their officials have explained that the purpose of the China Christian Council is to "provide nurture for Christians, train Christian leaders and publish Christian literature." Why these could not be accomplished by the Three Self Movement that is headed by the same man no one has satisfactorily explained. Perhaps it has something to do with the badly tarnished reputation of the Three Self Movement because of its pre-Cultural Revolution activity.

Be that as it may, the opening of selected churches for public worship has been a gleam of light for many. It contrasts so strikingly with the violently imposed atheism of the immediate past. One by one church buildings have been restored for the use of believers. Perhaps significantly these are mainly in tourist centers where they would be most visible. All are under the control of the Three Self Movement or the China Christian Council.

It has certainly been an exciting time for the Christian tourists to be able to sit in church and worship the Lord with Chinese believers who have come through the fires of persecution. When the first church opened in Shanghai in the Fall of 1979 tourist friends of mine happened to be in the city and hastened to attend. When the Holy Spirit had broken down the atmosphere of fear and suspicion, Chinese and Westerners tearfully embraced and prayed for each other. It was an unforgettable experience for those present.

In fact, it was a scene to make heaven rejoice and the Communists quake. Those who attended the Morse Memorial Church the following Sunday heard one of the "Three Self" pastors warn the people that they were to be courteous to foreign guests but they were not to embrace them and weep in their presence. Also they were told not to ask foreign guests for Bibles or Streams in the Desert.

These public services have subsequently been occasions for numerous encounters between the Christians of the West, who have long prayed for China, and the hard-pressed Christians of China who had been told by the Communist propaganda machine that there were no more Christians in the world. Science, they said, has eliminated the need for religion. Consequently, just the presence of foreigners in the Church strengthened their faith.

In 1981 I was in Shanghai on a warm summer night. I made my way at 5:15 to Grace Church not far from my hotel. I was told the gate to the church opened at 6 o'clock. By the time I arrived there were about one thousand people standing outside virtually blocking traffic. As the doors opened people poured into the church and quickly filled every available seat. Extra chairs were quickly set up and just as quickly filled. Then small camp stools were placed in the little remaining space. I sat in the balcony thrilled by the electric atmosphere of expectancy. I took out my pocket calculator and counted 2,700 people inside the church. Hundreds of others were seated outside where they could enjoy the service through the open windows. At 6:30 a song leader stood up and said, "In the evening service we have many new believers" (I learned later that there were also many seekers). "We want to teach you some songs to memorize so you can sing them as you walk and as you work." The first song he taught was "Just now your doubtings give o'er, just now throw open the door. Let Jesus come into your heart." I

was thrilled beyond measure as I heard that beautiful invitation sung. Three thousand voices sent its message out on the
breezes of that summer night.

At 7 p.m. the service proper began. Looking around at the
congregation I saw a generous sprinkling of grey hairs
among the primarily youthful audience. Many had newly
printed small hymnbooks. A few had Bibles: some old and
yellow with age, that had been miraculously preserved;
some new Bibles, printed by Asian Outreach or the Bible
Society in Hong Kong. The lady next to me showed me her
old Bible. She said, "It was my mother's. She has now gone
on to meet the Lord." I asked how she hid it from the Red
Guards. She smiled and said, "Mother hid it under the eaves
of the house—see," as he pointed to the tattered leather
cover. "The rats were nibbling on it."

There was no commotion in the service, no sign of inat-
tention. Eager faces focused on the tall, distinguished
seventy-four-year-old pastor as, with Bible in hand, he stood
to bring God's message. His was a vigorous, anointed
message from I Corinthians 1:27-31: "But of Him you are in
Christ Jesus, who was made to us wisdom from God . . . and
righteousness and sanctification and redemption." It was a
thoroughly biblical message from an obviously Spirit-filled
man of God. He, too, had spent years in prison for his faith.

Visiting tourists, however, are blissfully unaware of one
striking feature of the reopening of selected churches. During the decade-long era of violence which Chairman Mao
called a Cultural Revolution, the cross became a special hate
target of the rampaging Red Guards. On my first trip back to
China I saw clear evidence of their hate. Many church buildings, identified by their architecture or from memory, were
still standing. Now used as schools, warehouses, or factories, one feature of their architecture was glaringly absent.
Whether simple Gospel halls or foreign pinnacled cathe-

drals, the Red Guards had stripped them all of their crosses. Their hatred for the cross had driven them to chipping away crosses carved in marble over the entrance to the cathedrals. All crosses, without exception, were destroyed. They had even invaded the cemeteries throughout China and destroyed the gravestones marked by a cross. I discovered this when I went to visit my sister's grave. The cross had obviously become a focal point of their hate.

Now, as churches reopened one by one, the cross was being restored to its former place. I must confess I had not paid much attention as a missionary's son to the crosses that marked the Christian meeting places. Now, suddenly, they had become the most notable feature, noticeable either by their presence or their absence on church buildings not yet restored. As I traveled I noted that the Communist hatred of the cross had fanned the flame of love for the cross in the hearts of the Christians. How proud they were to wear a cross as a symbol of their faith.

Some, still partly paralyzed by fear, would form a cross with their crossed fingers close to their chest to indicate to me that they were Christians. How significant it is that the government is now aiding and abetting the open restoration of the cross as a highly visible symbol of the Christian faith. In city after city the cross on church steeples now towers above the Red Star and all other symbols of a waning Marxist faith. Mao's picture, once omnipresent, is fast becoming a rarity. The cross is now more visible, more significant than ever. Again the cross has triumphed.

As the doors of church buildings began to open one by one, China's Christians were faced with a serious question. Do we or do we not attend the services in the official churches? The question stems from a basic distrust of the government's motives. Christians have worshiped somewhat furtively in their homes for more than a decade. During this period, the Church has experienced the most dramatic growth. Now the government is encouraging them to return to the long-closed church buildings. Many Christians suspect that this may be a government attempt to lessen the impact of the house churches. In fact, one Three Self pastor that we interviewed frankly stated he believed this was indeed one of the government's reasons for opening church buildings. Bishop Ding (Ting) admitted under a Beijing (Peking) dateline of 31 July 1979 that "he and some others of the religious community have drafted a proposal to reinforce the management on churches and temples. . . ." Therefore, to say that government control is an objective is not idle talk. Others fear that with the next violent swing of Beijing's (Peking's) policies all who worship will be easily marked for retribution. After all, this has happened before to China's now cautious Christians. Consequently the question of whether to attend the open churches was one that had to be faced.

What is undeniable was that as quickly as church buildings were reopened they were filled to capacity with Christians eager to once again worship God openly. In some cities multiple services were soon necessary. The Three Self Movement acknowledged that they could not open churches rapidly enough. Former tenants had to be moved out and funds had to be found to restore the buildings to usable condition. One Three Self pastor in Shanghai told me that his congregation paid for all the costs of restoration. Not one penny was received from the government. Other congregations were paid back rent by the government for the use of their building for up to fifteen years. The news of churches reopening spread rapidly across China and believers in other cities began to agitate for a church to open in their community. However, the pace of opening churches was agonizingly slow. Government bureaucracy is not easily overcome.

It was a source of amazement to me that so many Christians chose to worship God openly. I expected a greater degree of caution. There may have been several reasons for the openness. For some it was a return to what they had once known as the only way to worship God—a long-awaited return to normalcy as they saw it. To others it may have been a way of giving open public testimony to an atheistic regime of their Christian faith. For others, it may have been a form of defiance, a way of saying to the Party, "We have absorbed the worst persecution you could throw at us and we are still firm in our faith." Many of the young people attending the open services had never known persecution for their faith, as they were post-Cultural Revolution converts. Whatever the motivations, it is an undeniable fact that unprecedented crowds are attending the services.

What is also undeniable is that many of the Three Self pastors being appointed are men of strong Christian convictions. Some are unquestionably evangelicals. This, too, offers a gleam of hope. It is entirely possible that persecution has had a refining influence upon these men, most of whom are now in their twilight years. The experiences of the immediate past may have helped them to sort out life's priorities and conclude that one's relationship to Christ must take first priority. Although some of the sermons being heard are innocuous, fence-sitting orations, others are ringing declarations of faith in Christ and a challenge to Christ-honoring lives. The hymns heard most often are the hymns beloved by the church around the world. On Easter Sunday churches rang with "Christ the Lord is risen today, Hallelujah." Sermons were preached on the Resurrection of Christ in spite of the fact that this was one of the four reportedly forbidden subjects, the others being the Crucifixion, the Kingdom of God, and the Return of Christ.

A congregation has several officially appointed pastors, each coming from a different denominational background.

The Three Self Movement has wisely insisted that the denominational structures are unnecessary. Baptismal candidates can choose their own method of baptism. How the new convert would know which method to select is a moot point. The denominational background of the present pastors, all men in their 60s and 70s, inevitably surfaces in how they conduct a service or how they train new converts. The congregation is made up of people from all faiths, from Anglicans to Seventh-day Adventists to Pentecostals. In some places services are also conducted on Saturdays, ostensibly for those who cannot attend on Sundays, but they are also a convenient way to accommodate Adventists. The Church buildings, too, have varied denominational backgrounds. Virtually no new church buildings have been constructed since the 1950s.

The Three Self Movement seeks to be the only Christian organization in China. They claim that they, and they alone, have the right to lead the Christians of China. Efforts are being made to bring all Protestant activity under their control, as this is what the government has decreed. It is only their voice that is being heard in the West as only their leaders are given government permission to travel in the West. What printing of Christian literature is permitted by Beijing (Peking) is under their control as well. In fact, the Three Self Movement has gone one step further and decreed that no one else has a right to supply Bibles to China's Christians. This, they say, includes anyone outside of China.

They have been able to print some Christian literature, including hymn books, a correspondence course, and a quantity of Bibles, but only in quantities that completely fail to reflect the demand. Yet they attempt to portray the efforts of overseas Chinese and concerned Christians from the West who are supplying Scriptures as being "unpatriotic." They claim it violates the principles of Three Self. What is important is that this position of the Three Self leaders not only has denied the Scriptures to the majority of China's Christians but, even more seriously, it violates a biblical principle. There are not two churches, one in China and one in the rest of the world. We are all part of the body of Christ according to Scripture. When one member of the body suffers, or is in need, all must respond. Christ is the Head of one church universal. Sensitive response to the need by the Church around the world does not need to violate the biblical principle of an indigenous church.

What must be made very clear is that the Christians who are thoroughly enjoying the open churches are beautiful people. Their faith, too, has been tested. Those I have met and talked with are people at whose feet I want to sit and learn. They have so much to teach me. Just being in their presence has blessed and humbled me.

I think of a brilliant heart surgeon I met in church in Shanghai. His face was wreathed with a luminous smile as he told me how thrilled he was that the church was open once again. We stood talking in the courtyard of the church after the morning service. He said, "Every Sunday for almost fifteen years I rose at dawn and stood in the street outside this closed church and prayed that the doors would open again." I looked at him through misty eyes, realizing that I was looking at a saint whose love for the open church exceeded mine. I just know myself well enough to know that I would not have risen at dawn for fifteen years, especially on Shanghai's bitterly cold winter mornings, to stand in the street and pray for the doors to open.

Saints such as this illumine the open churches. Indeed, many of the pastors have emerged triumphant from damp prisons and merciless labor camps to once again openly proclaim the Gospel of Christ. I think of the old pastor who preached the first sermon when the church opened in his city. As he stood he held a borrowed Gospel of John. His own Bible had long since been taken from him. As he read from John 3:16 and began to preach he broke into tears. Composing himself, he apologized, saying, "I'm sorry. I just never thought I would ever again have the opportunity of preaching the Gospel openly in my country." Saints such as these are God's jewels. Matthew Henry once called them "a royal diadem in God's hand."

The visible reopening of church buildings by the Three Self Movement is dramatic but it does not begin to measure the size of the Christian community. By far the majority of China's Christians are not to be found in the open churches for several reasons. There are just not enough churches open to accommodate China's believers. In fact, so rapid has been church growth since 1979 that even if all the former church buildings and gospel halls were instantly reopened the majority of Christians would still have to worship elsewhere. There would just be no room for them because the church of prerevolution days numbered less than one million believers.

Some groups and individuals prefer the house churches. They have spurned church buildings since their earliest days. These are largely indigenous groups such as the Brethren-style "Little Flock" of Watchman Nee, and the Pentecostal "True Jesus Church" and the "Jesus Family." These groups were the fastest growing of all Christian groups before the Communist takeover. They are still strong in some areas. For the most part these groups are not really interested in the open churches. They much prefer the home churches, believing they follow a more biblical pattern. In addition to these groups a considerable number of pastors and house-church leaders who once pastored traditional churches have told us they now prefer the house church. They like the intimacy. It seems to lend itself more readily to a more Chinese style of life and worship. Even Bishop Ding (Ting) has said that in Nanjing (Nanking) some of the Christians prefer the house meetings. He indicated that they may decide to keep both forms of worship. This remains to be seen.

Some who at first eagerly attended the open churches have since returned to the house churches. They found the minutely prescribed worship service in most of the open service too great a contrast to the more informal gathering of believers in the house churches. It is understandable that the lay leaders of the house churches know little or nothing of the missionary-dominated training of the older pastors in the open churches. Consequently their form of worship is considerably more spontaneous.

Obviously, then, many of China's Christians will not associate themselves with the official churches of the Three Self Movement, even when attempts are made to force them to do so.

And then there is the vast majority of new believers who have never worshiped in a church building. Most of them live in the villages and have known only the house church. The house church represents the norm.

It is the house churches, representing possibly 80 per cent of China's Christians, that contain some of the most dynamic aspects of China's church. The cities are honey-combed with small groups meeting wherever and whenever they can—university campuses, in the parks, in homes and warehouses. But it is in the countryside that the majority of believers are found. Of course, this reflects the vastly larger rural population. Villages where the majority of the people are Christians are not unusual. They can be found in several areas of China where the church growth is the most rapid. There are even reports of whole communes containing forty or more villagers that are primarily Christian. These country folk, once the slaves of superstition, are now placing their faith in a living God.

Accounts of divine encounters among them are neither rare nor unreliable. We should not be surprised by these angelic visitations. The Psalmist declared, "He shall give His angels charge over thee, to keep thee in all thy ways" (Psalm 91:11). The Apostle Paul testified, "For there stood by me this night the angel of God, whose I am, and whom I serve" (Acts 27:23). Hebrews 1:14 asks, "Are they (angels) not all ministering spirits, sent forth to minister for them who shall be heirs of salvation?"

A very poor Christian couple made their living with wooden carts on which they hauled stones and logs. Their fifteen-year-old son often assisted them by pushing from the rear. About a year ago they were straining to get a very heavy load of stones up a hill and, as they reached the top, the wife rushed around to the front to help her husband keep the cart from going down the hill too quickly. As she did she tripped and fell in front of the cart. Her husband was unable to stop it. The wheels of the heavily loaded cart passed right over her body, crushing her bones. Local doctors said she would have to be taken to a major hospital in the city where they would do a bone transplant, which might be of some help. But the couple were unable to afford such an expensive operation.

Lying in the hospital, she found no relief in all the medications from her incessant pain. As she waited on the Lord, she decided to stop taking all pain-killing drugs and just trust the Lord for her healing. That night, her fourth in the hospital, two angels visited her. They lifted her by the shoulders and pressed down on her pelvic bone. A feeling which she later described as "resembling boiling water" passed through her body from head to toe.

When she awakened the next morning she kept saying, "Thank you Lord! Praise the Lord!" A lady in the next bed inquired, "What's the matter?" She ecstatically replied, "My body is well again. The angels have operated on my bones." When the doctors came that morning to examine her, she told them what happened during the night. The doctors were amazed to find, on examination, that her bones were perfect, so perfect that she was permitted to check out of the hospital by noon of that very same day.

A few days later she went to the market and bought some fruit and candies. Then she stood by the side of the road and stopped people as they passed, telling them her testimony of God's healing power. To each who would listen she gave some fruit and candy—her Thanksgiving offering!

An old couple living in China's austere countryside made their living by mending shoes. Business was not good. There was little money in the pockets of the farmers. Drudgery turned to joy following the visit of a Christian to their humble dwelling. The first time they heard the Gospel story they accepted Christ, and with Him came inner peace and purpose in life.

Not many years after their conversion, the old gentleman became very ill. The next-door neighbor was a government official of a rather high rank. One morning as he was brushing his teeth outside his door, he saw two persons dressed in white, going into the old couple's house. Then he saw them walk the old man out of the house, one on each side holding his hands. As he watched, he saw all three of them disappear into the sky! Dumbfounded, he stood staring upwards. Nothing he had ever heard of could explain what he, a Communist official, had just seen.

The stillness of the morning was broken when he heard the lady next door begin to cry loudly. He rushed over to the house and found the husband had died. He did what he could and then said to the bereaved wife, "I don't understand. Why did I see two persons in white holding your husband's hands, taking him up into the sky? I'm sure I recognized your husband." Immediately the dear old lady understood that those were God's messengers come to take her husband home. Her tears of grief turned to tears of joy. Her dear husband was now safe with Jesus!

Unable to understand the angelic visitation, and now seeing the old lady so peaceful in the presence of her dead husband, he asked, "What religion do you believe?" She replied, "We believe in Jesus. There was a man in the Bible named Lazarus. He died. God sent His messengers to take him up to heaven to enjoy God's presence forever. That is what has happened to my dear husband."

The official stood transfixed by all he had seen and heard. Before long he said to his neighbor, "I want to believe too." That very same day the widow went off to find the person who had first told her about Jesus. The official went home and prepared his family for the arrival of guests. That day the entire family knelt and accepted Christ as Savior. He still holds his government position but must be very careful in his contact with fellow Christians.

The Book of Acts is being continued in China as, in answer to simple faith, God meets His people.

As the many thousands of house churches became more visible following the arrest of the Gang of Four certain characteristics appeared to be common to most of them. This is particularly remarkable, given the fact that there had been virtually no contact with one another. Obviously, then, this uniformity was not brought about by the common consent of some ecclesiastical leadership. Nor was it coincidence. The majority of China's Christians, guided solely by the Holy Spirit, had been led back to the patterns of Christianity in its first century of existence.

As I attempt to spotlight these common characteristics you will be able to judge for yourself the similarity to life in the early church. As in the Three Self Movement, most of the house churches are virtually bereft of denominationalism. Once this had assumed tragic proportions, as Chinese converts confessed to being "German Lutherans" or "Southern Baptists" (in the far north). Very little, if any, of this has survived. Christians have discovered the unity there is in the body of Christ. No denominationalism existed in a prison cell or work camps. The emphasis was upon "the tie that binds." Fortunately, the stress on denominational differences has been largely washed away in the river of suffering. China's Christians could teach us much if only we were ready to learn.

The church in China is, to a great extent, family oriented. Persecution and the absence of foreign influence have made it so. As a general rule it would be accurate to say that during the darkest days of persecution there were as many "churches" in China as there were Christian families. Government efforts to destroy the traditionally close knit family unit have been largely unsuccessful. Families worship together. This is their church. There is certainly a message here for the West where the breakup of families is now so commonplace. As more freedom was permitted gatherings represented many family groups and those from non-Christian families who were newly converted.

I am thinking of a particular family in North China. The parents left China over twenty years ago. The two daughters were forced to stay behind. Years of education in Mao's China dulled their Christian faith. Following the excesses of the Cultural Revolution they rededicated their lives to the Lord. Both girls witnessed to their husbands and eventually won them to the Lord. The husbands won their parents. The parents have been witnessing to other members of the family. Today when that family worships the Lord there are at least nine adults present. Open worship for them is still not advisable. This is typical of China's family-oriented church.

China's church as yet is not weakened by nominal Christians to the extent that it is in most other areas of the world. Those who were nominal Christians before "liberation" have not survived the years of Communist pressure. Nominal Christians have long since fallen by the wayside. Those who meet to worship have decided that Jesus Christ means more to them than life itself. Most of them have pastors, family members, or friends who have paid with their lives for their faith in Christ. They have accurately counted the cost of their Christian faith. None are Christians for social or economic reasons. There are no "rice Christians" left in China. The church is not a social club or a symbol of acceptability. The church in China can offer no financial or educational benefits to its Christians except that which God may be pleased to provide. Consequently the motives for becoming Christians are unclouded. This makes for a purer church.

This does not mean that all of them have achieved spiritual perfection, or that they are not subject to temptation. They have their spiritual battles. A letter, received from China, was written by a young Chinese Christian. He had been sent from his home town to work in a commune hundreds of miles away on the island of Hainan. There he was isolated from Christian fellowship. He confessed in his letter that he had become a lukewarm Christian until a personal experience revealed to him how much God loved him.

Hainan Island lies right in the heart of the typhoon belt. In the summer and late fall it is pounded by repeated gales. Winds of 150 miles per hour are not unusual. During a typhoon he was asleep in a dormitory with many of his fellow commune workers. He was awakened by someone calling his name. He sat up in bed and again heard his name being called by someone outside. He didn't want to go out in the storm. Flying debris can be lethal. The voice was so insistent he dressed and went out. As he did the building collapsed behind him. Several were killed and all were injured.

In his letter he was praising God for his miraculous deliverance and for the discovery that God knows his name. He asked God's forgiveness for his period of lukewarmness. He testified to a boldness in witnessing such as he had never before known.

I have noted that the Chinese church that meets in the home is primarily a Bible-centered church. The focus of all gatherings is the Word. This is partly if not primarily because copies of the Word of God are so scarce among the house-church Christians. Very few Bibles exist among them. One Bible among twenty or thirty is common. We know of cases where there has been only one Bible among more than one thousand Christians in an area. The few that do remain are highly valued and passed from hand to hand. Long passages of Scripture have been committed to memory. Often this is the only Scripture available when most needed. Others have hand-copied Scripture portions as a substitute for their own Bibles taken from them during the Cultural Revolution. Bibles are not selfish personal possessions but something precious to be shared. As the church continues to grow the call for Scriptures accelerates dramatically. The house churches are not supplied by the Three Self Movement. The temptation is to attempt to get vast quantities in at one time, ignoring the long-range effect this will have on house church-government relations. China's Christians have suffered enough. Our response must be sensitive to and considerate of all the factors involved.

An interesting feature of many of the house churches is that sermons as we know them are seldom preached. The

leader will give a brief Biblical exposition, and then everyone in the group will share what that Scripture means to
them. The Bible is their daily bread, their only means of
spiritual survival. They have learned to share their faith and
participate in worship. One reason for this participation is
that the house churches are not clergy-dominated, as we
shall see later.

The Chinese church is a witnessing church. How do I
know? I have met and talked and worshiped with many who
have been led to Christ inside China since the dark days of
the Cultural Revolution. This is not an inverted self-satisfied
group of spiritual superiors. Sharing their faith can be extremely dangerous, but share it they do.

Witnessing frequently occurs within the family circle.
Family members who have demonstrated the lasting values
of faith in Christ by their daily lives find it easy to answer
the queries of their families. This has greatly contributed to
the family-church concept that blends so well into China's
culture.

My surveys reveal that the joyful, peaceful life of the
Christian is what most frequently prompts the non-
Christian to inquire. This becomes the perfect opening for
the Christian to share his faith even with those outside the
family.

The church in China is surprisingly youthful. This is evident both in the open churches and in the house churches.
In fact, the percentage of young people is on the increase as
young people find in Christ the satisfaction and reality they
had found nowhere else. This is not a decrepit old church
that has barely managed to survive and can be expected to
disappear as the old folks die off. On the contrary, few of the
older Christians have survived. The church in China is alive
with the enthusiasm and faith that characterizes the young.
These young people are far older than their years. Life for

them has been difficult. They have found meaning and purpose in Christ. As has been pointed out, it is this response on the part of China's highly indoctrinated youth that troubles the Communist Party to such a great degree. On the other hand, it is a portent of further growth in China's church as youth tend to attract youth.

During the years when most pastors were under some form of detention, the house churches by necessity became lay churches, thus greatly multiplying the leadership. Frequently the gatherings are led by laywomen. These godly women have long been giants in the Chinese church. I know of one whom God called at the height of the Cultural Revolution to leave her home in North China and go as a missionary to an area of South China. There she established a thriving Christian fellowship attended for the most part by young people.

I met one of the young people she ministered to. Ho told me how she had torn a page out of her own daily devotional book and given it to him. He told me that this was the only page of Christian literature that he possessed in two years as a Christian before fleeing China.

A group of young people from Hong Kong visited China for a week. There they contacted a Christian who took them to a gathering of Christians led by a Bible woman. The young people were able to take a Chinese Bible in with them. This they gave to the Bible woman. The sequel to that story occurred later.

Four young people subsequently made good their escape to Hong Kong by paddling a flimsy homemade raft on the coldest night of the year across the choppy waters of Mirs Bay. One of those four was a Christian. Here is part of his story.

Just over a year before he had failed in an attempt to reach Hong Kong. Captured, he was beaten by the Communists and released in mental distress. Having no one to turn to, he wrote to a friend whom he knew had escaped to Hong Kong, asking for help and advice. The friend gave him the address of a trusted Christian to go and see.

The Christian lady took him to the Bible woman. The Bible woman talked and prayed with him and gave him a Bible to read. Through that Bible he found Christ and became a strong Christian. Just before paddling to safety in Hong Kong, he returned the Bible to the lady because he knew how scarce Bibles were in China and that he could obtain another one in Hong Kong. On reaching Hong Kong he came to see us and told us this story because the Bible that led him to faith in Christ was the one those four young people had given to the Bible woman months before.

This, then, is a partial picture of China's living church. It is a picture that bristles with life and light. Unquestionably the Holy Spirit has been the most important factor. God has been, and is, sovereignly at work in China. As the government of China maintains a degree of pressure upon the church, and contact with Christians outside of China is limited, the Chinese church will continue to be obedient to the promptings of the Holy Spirit.

Deep in China's vast Far West lived an old sheepherder on the slopes of the forbidding mountain ranges. He was the first Christian in his native village, but both fellowship and teaching were lacking. Unfortunately, his life was not a good testimony. One of our coworkers recently accompanied a Christian pastor in that remote area on his preaching rounds. As they approached the village, the old shepherd met them and, in desperation, declared, "I have just lost one of my sheep."

Meat is virtually unknown in the diet of those mountain people. A sheep is an extremely valuable possession. The pastor invited the shepherd to come to the house meeting at which he would be speaking that night. The shepherd was torn between going to search for his lost sheep or attending the meeting. He decided to attend. During the gathering the Christians prayed that the old shepherd would find his sheep.

The next day the pastor was leaving that village to preach in another village. As he was leaving the old shepherd came running: "I have found my sheep! I have found my sheep!" he cried. When asked how it happened, he told this story:

"I rose very early, before daybreak this morning, to search for my sheep. After I had walked a long way I came upon a house. Seeing me, the people of the house came out and asked what I wanted. I told them I was searching for my lost sheep. They asked me, 'Can you identify your sheep?' 'Yes,' I said. 'It had long curly horns and a certain spot on the feet.' 'Oh,' they replied, 'We have that sheep in our house. We found it wandering by itself so we brought it home.' " His parting message to the visitors was, "Seek ye first the kingdom of God, and his righteousness, and all these things shall be added unto you."

This true story is also a parable. The flock of the Lord is rapidly increasing in China, but there are far too few shepherds to care for them. At the end of 1979 our co-workers visited a village that was part of a large commune in Xinjiang (Sinkiang) Province. Upon inquiry they were told there were few Christians in that village. On a return visit six months later they were told, "Now there are few unbelievers in the village." Since then there has been a spiritual awakening in that entire area. On the most recent visit, our coworkers were told, "This is now a Christian commune" (a commune is made up of many villages). When inquiring further they were told, "There are now many Christian communes" in this province. Never before has the Christian community grown so rapidly in China. But there must be shepherds, whether laymen or trained clergymen.

Because of the shortage of spiritual leaders, new Christians sometimes are led astray, or mix their animistic roots with Christian practice. For instance, in one area spiritualist mediums are very active. People approach them to know the future. For a fee the medium goes into a trance, and three men appear. They are Mao Zedong (Mao Tse-tung), Zhou Enlai (Chou En-lai), and an army general eulogized by Mao, Zhu De (Chu Te). The medium then purports to relay their message of the future. Some Christians have participated in those séances out of ignorance. The village people are very simple folk and are easily led astray. Some uninformed Christians keep their images or worship paraphernalia until taught otherwise.

In another province where the church is growing very rapidly there have been sad occurrences. One sincere but simple man desired to imitate the faith and dedication of Abraham, so he slew his nine-year-old son. He was arrested by police. Also in that area a long-haired man claims to be Jesus. Simple village people go to him and ask him to lay hands on them. As he does those people become demon-possessed. So great is the shortage of Christian workers that in the same area there are only three Christian workers to minister to tens of thousands of mostly new believers. As they talked to us they wept from exhaustion and concern for the flock of God. They are never able to stop to refresh their bodies or their spirits. The call for their ministry is so great that they just keep traveling. The laborers are so very few.

When we asked the Christian leaders of another area what they needed most, they replied using two Chinese sayings: "Now is the time of hunger, give us food," and "Give us charcoal in the snowstorm, not a flower for our dress coat."

The message was clear. Give us Scriptures and Bible study materials now. The flock, and particularly the newborn, must be fed. Later may be too late.

13

House Churches, Prisons, and Saints

The indomitable Christians of China are finding ways to propagate their faith, whether inside or outside the now well-publicized official churches. The few thousand Christians attending the official churches are only a token force. As has been stated before, by far the greatest majority of believers are part of the myriad small house groups, or home churches that sprang up all across China during the days of persecution and the absence of church buildings.

The fact that the house churches have been, and still are, frowned on by the Beijing (Peking) Government, primarily because they are more difficult to control, makes it somewhat more difficult to write about them. Those within the home churches often feel that it is not wise to attract undue attention to themselves. They recognize that the government knows of their existence, but they hope that by keeping a low profile the government will keep its heavy hand off. They have survived persecution but they do not wish to ask for more.

While there is an obvious determination among these believers, there still exists an aura of caution and sometimes fear. This is understandable based on what they have experienced in the past. In fact, in several known instances, once an official church is opened, Three Self leaders have literally forced the closing of house churches in that city. Consequently, I feel strongly that we who are observers must respect their desire for anonymity. It is not our responsibility to shine the spotlight on them if they desire, for whatever reason, to remain in the shadows. It is my hope that the shadows will soon disappear.

Living under somewhat similar circumstances, the Christians of the New Testament worshipped God in identical fashion. The Christian Church began as a "house church." Soon house churches had sprung up all across the Roman Empire. It was not until many years later that the first buildings dedicated exclusively for Christian worship were erected. A study of the New Testament church reveals that the church in the home was a virile and powerful force that shook the world of its day.

This form of Christian gathering fitted Chinese culture much better than the imported variety. If the Chinese are anything consistently, they are family-oriented. This is possibly their single most consistent characteristic. Consequently, to make the home the focal point of Christian worship almost guarantees not only family participation but the faith of succeeding generations. The house church seems to truly belong in the Chinese culture. A return to open worship in designated church buildings, segregated from the powerful family unit, may be a retrogressive step.

Of course, one form of church does not have to exclude the other. Those who attend the open churches do not have to abandon the house-church concept entirely. In fact, the largest and fastest-growing Protestant congregation in the world combines both methods with undeniable success. I refer to the Full Gospel Central Church in Seoul, Korea, pastored by Dr. Cho Yonggi. True, it does have a massive sanctuary, but it is the ten thousand or more house meetings held every week that are a strong contributing factor to the church's dramatic growth. It now has over five hundred thousand members, thus demonstrating that a marriage of the house church and the open church can produce the world's largest congregation. There is some indication that such a marriage may be about to occur in China. I pray it does.

Space and caution permit me to share only a few further glimpses of the house churches.

I interviewed a young man twenty-eight years of age who had come across the border into Hong Kong. Like so many of China's young people, during his impressionable school days he had rejected the faith of his parents and had accepted the philosophy and ideology of Communism. Four years before leaving, he surrendered his life completely to the Lord through the counsel and help of a Christian friend in China. Subsequently, he became part of a house-church fellowship in China and was baptized. He, like most of China's young people, was sent by the government to the countryside to work. Like many, he returned home illegally to live in his parent's home and supported himself by a nongovernment-sponsored trade.

He came from a city of about four hundred thousand people. It was estimated that fifty thousand Christians meet regularly in house-church fellowships in that one city. Among all of those Christians, it is believed there was only one ordained pastor from before the revolution. That pastor was over eighty years of age but still had an active ministry of Bible teaching and counseling to Christians who came to visit him in his home. In that community there was a house-church fellowship meeting almost every night of the week with varying numbers present.

He told me they had four kinds of meetings:

1. Prayer meetings—This was the most unrestrained kind of meeting as few accusations could be laid against the Christians for praying. The largest numbers gathered for prayer meetings.

2. Bibles Studies—Bibles were too scarce and precious to be taken to these meetings, so the one leading the meeting copied out in longhand the chapter to be studied ahead of time, using carbon paper so that a number of copies could be made at once. Then each person was given a copy which he later took home. Therefore, after completing a study of Matthew, for example, each Christian would have his own hand-written copy of the entire Book of Matthew plus his own notes. At the Bible study everyone was expected to take an active part in discussing the meaning of each verse.

3. Witnessing Meetings—The Christians encouraged each other with testimonies of what the Lord was doing among them. Miracles, such as relatives being released from prison, were a special joy.

4. Practice in Preaching—Every Christian man or woman was expected to speak on some occasions, so training was given on how to preach and teach God's Word to others. Meetings were moved around frequently from one home to another for the sake of safety.

Tucked away in a mountainous region of Zheijang (Chekiang) Province is a village of about ten thousand souls. It is estimated that one out of three people in the village are Christians. They told us that in 1976 they began to worship openly. There are more than fifteen meeting places with an average attendance of two hundred at each service. Services are generally held in the evening and last from 7 p.m. until 11 p.m. There is time for singing, for testimony, and supplication. Sermons are usually more than an hour in length as the people are so hungry to be fed. There are about ten people who travel from meeting to meeting to expound the Word. Many are young people.

This group has learned much in the school of prayer. Some of the Christians rise at 4 o'clock every morning to pray for their country. Those who have prayed with them were impressed by the spirit of urgency in their praying.

In a major city of China lives an old pastor well past ninety years of age. He suffered much at the hands of radical Red Guards. His church was taken from him; his personal library destroyed, including his Bibles; his son was imprisoned. The old pastor was publicly stoned and humiliated. Then as a final humiliation his feet were shot off at point-blank range.

At his invitation, I visited him. He had written asking for a Bible not knowing the condition of things on the outside world. He only knew the Communists had said, "There are very few who believe in God left in the world." The old pastor wrote, "I do not have a Bible to teach my people. If Chinese Bibles are scarce I will be happy to copy the Bible and send it back to you." When I entered his bedroom he greeted me with a broad toothless smile and a warm welcome in the name of the Lord. Sitting on the edge of his bed, he expressed his delight in meeting a Western Christian again. When I asked him to tell me about his treatment, he only said, "Many times, Brother Kauffman, I prayed to die. Now I'm so glad God did not answer my prayer because I am now enjoying the most fruitful years of my ministry" (I learned of his suffering from others). It was difficult to see how an old and feeble man sitting on the edge of his bed with no feet could be having the "most fruitful years of his ministry." In answer to my query, he told of a congregation of over fifteen hundred believers. Startled, I asked how that could be. He then told of how God directed him to train house-church leaders in God's Word. They then go out and hold hundreds of house meetings weekly in the city and surrounding areas. Breaking into his infectious smile, he said, "I never had a congregation this large before the Communists came." I happen to know that he was a highly respected evangelist and pastor before the "liberation."

As a general rule, it is not wise for Westerners to make contact with the house-church Christians. Already there have been some unpleasant aftereffects of such encounters. This old pastor felt he had nothing to lose. His home is known in the area as a gathering place for believers. "Aren't you afraid?" I asked.

"No," he said, "I wrote the authorities asking for permission to hold services. They have never answered my letter so it is their problem, not mine."

Similarly, a few house-church leaders have initiated contacts with Westerners, but they are the exception, certainly not the rule. This visit did give me a personal glimpse into a house church. All ages attend, as there is an increasing boldness to worship together. In fact, so rapid had been the multiplication of the believers in China that a crisis of leadership has arisen. An older man immigrating from China to the West said that before liberation Chinese shepherds (pastors) were often looking for sheep (a congregation); now it is the other way around—many sheep are looking for shepherds.

As mentioned before, out of the prisons and labor camps of China are emerging saints of tremendous spiritual power. The most notable among them—China's "Valiant for Truth" —was released early in January 1980. Pastor Wang Mingdao (Wang Ming-tao) was China's bold evangelical pastor in Beijing (Peking) who refused to bow his knee to any form of compromise. He was first arrested in July of 1955, released inexplicably thirteen months later, and was rearrested in 1958. Twenty-three years of imprisonment in Shansi (Shanxi) Province have not dimmed his famed faith or courage. He was finally released to live with his blind wife in Shanghai. Pastor Wang is almost deaf. He told a visitor, "When we were married we became one—so we only need one pair of eyes and one pair of ears between us." Pastor Wang is only one of many great saints to emerge from China's prisons.

Many of China's most outstanding Christians have spent from twelve to twenty-two years in prison. Now, miraculously, the prison doors are being opened. Not because the government is less atheistic, but because the Sovereign God wills them to open. Through those heavily guarded gates the saints are now marching out to rejoin the living Church in China.

As yet, we have not discovered any "prison epistles" written within the walls of China's prisons, but our associates have met and talked with some of these living saints. It is still too early to share their stories in full. The following are guarded excerpts from the experiences of just one of those "prisoners of faith."

At the time of her arrest twenty-two years ago, she was in prayer when the authorities arrived to arrest her. She was not surprised, as the Lord had already prepared her heart. In fact, just as they arrested her the Holy Spirit came and filled her with uncontainable joy. As the car in which she was being away jostled down the road, she was overflowing with joy and sang all the way. The authorities naturally suspected that she was demented.

As she was being registered at the prison she had time to witness at length to one of the officials. So powerful was her anointed witness that right then and there he accepted Christ. As he registered her she said to him, "Today is not the day I came to register myself, and I will never really be a prisoner here—Christ will constantly be with me. I am free. This is the day when you have registered your residency in the Kingdom of God."

Sometime later, all the inmates were given an envelope containing the length of their sentence. The other inmates asked her how long her sentence was. She answered, "I don't know. I just put the verdict away without looking at it."

"Why?" they asked. "Don't you want to know how many years you are getting?"

"It doesn't matter," she replied, "whether it is ten years or one hundred years, each day will be a day with my Lord."

In one prison they were inhumanly crowded—ten prisoners to a tiny cubicle. They were not allowed to speak to each other or doze off during the day. A guard periodically looked into the room through a glass opening in the door. Many fell ill—others lost their minds. One prisoner whispered to her, "We can see that your religious faith really gives you strength." Another day the guard burst into the room and shouted to her, "Stop your smiling."

"I'm not smiling," she replied.

"Yes, you are," shouted the guard.

When he left the other prisoners said, "Your eyes are always smiling and your face glows with joy even when you are not smiling." Most of her fellow prisoners were not Christians, that is, until she led numbers of them to the Lord.

During one period of time she was sent off to work seventeen hours a day in the rice paddies. Daily she stood in water almost waist high until her body was a mass of sores. For a woman in her late sixties who was not used to such work it was nearly unbearable. But even worse for her was having to listen almost continually to the foul language used by the other workers. When she complained to the Lord about it, she felt she heard him say, "Are you holier than I? I left the absolute purity of heaven to live in your sordid world."

Many times the Lord spoke to her, sometimes in most unusual ways. She recalled that when she was young she had a dream. She found herself going up a mountain leaning on the arm of a man. She heard the words from the Song of Solomon, "Who is this that cometh out of the wilderness?" She found herself leaning on the arms of her beloved Lord. Years later she was taken to a prison located in the mountains. As she was walking up the mountain, she suddenly realized the scenery was the same as what she had seen in her dream as a young girl. God had prepared her for this walk up to the prison on the arm of her beloved Lord.

Recently released from twenty-four years of imprisonment, now over eighty years of age, this old saint was not yet ready for retirement. Before her imprisonment she would take her accordion and go from house to house singing and witnessing. On her release she was delighted to get her old accordion back. The years of disuse had taken their toll. She spent weeks repairing the cracks and limbering up the keys.

The only alternative open to Christians in China was to meet in private homes.

Now she is back in ministry again. She goes to the park every day and plays hymns. She had forgotten many of the hymns so she was thrilled with the hymnbook we brought her. As the crowds gather she explains the meaning of the hymn she is singing. Thus she continues to witness. Her wrinkled face wreathed with the joy of the Lord—eighty years old and still going strong! What an impact these prison saints are having on both the Christians and the non-Christians!

Not all the saints have gone to prison, by any means. This does not mean they have not suffered for their faith! Someday their stories will be told. When they are, all of us will learn again and again of our Lord's total sufficiency.

A Christian in North China had been harangued, interrogated, and berated repeatedly by the Red Guards. Her early association with foreign missionaries was the focal point of the pressure. Eventually, after hours of interrogation under bright lights, she was brought to public trial. She had not slept for days. The interrogation was carried on twenty-four hours a day. Shifts of Red Guards tried to break her spirit and force her to confess to being a spy for America. Weak from lack of food and exhausted from lack of sleep, she was led out to face a crowd of thousands in one of the Cultural Revolution's now infamous public trials. Standing on a raised platform she heard the crowd haranguing her as a "lackey of the imperialists." Too weak to stand, her knees began to give way. A guard saw it and kicked her, forcing her to stand erect. Her head dropped. A guard pulled her by the hair and forced her to look at the crowd. Unable to stand it any longer she breathed this prayer: "Father, please help me. I'm so tired. I must have some sleep." Soon she lost consciousness but did not fall. Miraculously she remained erect, her open eyes staring at the crowd, but she saw nothing and heard nothing. The trial lasted for over five hours, she was later told. As the trial was ending she regained consciousness just as she heard the trial leader say, "Do you confess to all the charges that have been laid against you today?"

She replied, "What charges? I have been asleep. I heard nothing." God had answered prayer and given His beloved sleep.

Miracles are as commonplace among the Christians of China as they were in the Book of Acts. Those of us who are now in direct contact with these long-isolated Christians are hearing many testimonies of miraculous healings. It seems that most of the testimonies concern healings from incurable cancer and, as I previously pointed out, often involve the appearance of angels or some other form of divine visitation. Many of those healed are Christians; others have become Christians as a result of a healing, either their own or a family member. There seems to be little evidence of "healing evangelists." Most healings take place when the person is completely alone—often in the middle of the night while the patient is asleep.

A typical testimony follows: The gentleman whom we shall call Mr. Huang came from a family of Buddhists. He, too, was a worshipper of the Buddha. His health began to deteriorate until he could not keep any food in his stomach at all. After a thorough examination, the doctor diagnosed his case. "You have a cancer of the liver in the terminal stage. There is nothing we can do for you."

Mr. Huang then returned to a small town near his native village to await the inevitable. While there he heard about a doctor in the town and decided to get a second opinion or perhaps obtain some medicine that could prolong his life. This doctor was a Christian. In fact, it was this doctor who accompanied the man as he gave his testimony. The Christian doctor confirmed the first diagnosis as cancer of the liver in an incurable, terminal stage.

The Christian doctor told the man that there was no medicine that could prolong his life but that if the man would believe in Jesus Christ he could have eternal life. He carefully explained the Gospel to the man and urged him to believe on the Lord Jesus Christ. The doctor also explained that Jesus was the Lord and had the power to heal any sickness if it was His will. "But whether Jesus heals you or not is not important," the doctor said. "What is important is that you have eternal life."

Mr. Huang said, "I want to believe in Jesus." The doctor called in another Christian man and the three of them knelt in his office as Mr. Huang became a new person in Jesus Christ.

Returning to his home, he told his wife of his faith in Jesus Christ and asked her to remove all the idols from the house and burn them. She did as she was told, knowing the hopelessness of her husband's condition. From then on, Mr. Huang's condition deteriorated rapidly. Every night he and his wife knelt and prayed together. He thanked the Lord that whatever happened to him physically he now had eternal life. He was gripped by terrible pain. His wife fixed some herbal and chicken soup but it only made matters worse. In fact, over the next weeks he became so weak that the family began preparations for his funeral. The coffin was purchased and the grave dug on the hillside.

One night a man in a white robe appeared to him in his sleep. The man was holding a knife. Not knowing what he intended to do, Mr. Huang struggled with the man in white, but the man prevailed and touched Mr. Huang with the knife. He awoke the next morning at 8 o'clock and was hungry for the first time in many days. After eating a nourishing bowl of egg-drop soup, he fell asleep. When he awakened he clearly saw two men in white robes standing by his bed. They said, "You have been saved." He reached down and found all of the swelling gone. Being extremely hungry, he ate a hearty meal. When his brother came to pay him a last visit, he was amazed to see him sitting up and strong. He told his brother that Jesus had touched him during the night and he was completely healed.

Each area of a city or village has an appointed Security Chief. His job is to see that the policies of the Communist Party are enforced. In essence, he is the Party watchdog and enforcer. His power has been awesome.

In a certain city of southern China, dramatic growth had been experienced in the Christian community since the end of the Cultural Revolution. From a dedicated core of Christians, the body of Christ has grown to some fifteen hundred known believers in that one city. This fact became known to the government authorities. Apparently the Security Chief in the area was not very zealous in enforcing Party policy, that is, until he received a directive from his superiors to stamp out the Christian gatherings in the area. He proceeded then to arrest several of the known lay leaders of the house churches. Shortly afterwards, he was found to have advanced nasal cancer. His superiors were putting strong pressure on him because of the continued growth of the Christian community. So he continued to function as the Security Chief.

One night he and a group of agents secretly surrounded a house where the believers were meeting. Their mission was to gain evidence of anti-Party teaching and then arrest the participants. That night, listening outside in the darkness, he heard a clear presentation of the Gospel. He heard of God's mighty power to forgive and cleanse from sin. The message spoke conviction and hope to a man who had just been told that his cancer was terminal. At midnight that same evening, he called at the home of one of the lay leaders of the house church, not to arrest him but to pour out his hopelessness to someone.

That same night the Communist Security Chief found
Christ as his personal Savior. Subsequently, as the believers
laid hands on him and prayed for him, he was miraculously
healed of cancer. Today, he is an active witness for Christ in
that city.

Some sixteen or twenty million people at a time were
believed to be in China's labor camps. It was claimed that
the primary purpose of these infamous camps is not punishment, but thought reform. Whatever the stated purpose, the
camps are dreaded by the people.

A zealous Christian lady was sent to one of these labor
camps. She was not young anymore but her faith was
indomitable. Some years before, she had lost the hearing in
her right ear through disease. One day in the dining hall, as
she bowed her head to thank God for the food, she was
observed by an ill-tempered guard. He thought, "I must
make an example of this stubborn woman." He walked over
and struck her bowed head a sharp blow. The blow was so
severe the woman lost consciousness.

Taken to her dormitory bunk, blood and water drained
from her ear all night as friends in the camp tried to comfort
her. Next day she discovered that complete hearing had
been restored to her once deaf ear. Friends who visited her
said she had an incurable case of Christian joy!

Reports indicate that casting out of demons is a common
occurrence in the Chinese Church. Given the Satanic nature
of atheistic Communism, frequent cases of demonic possession are not surprising. This is the story of just one such
deliverance, told in an abbreviated form:

A young girl from a non-Christian home was ordered to
leave her hometown and travel several hundred miles on
foot to a distant farming village, where she was to become
part of the commune. This was a highly unpopular government policy; nevertheless, it had to be obeyed. After many

days' journey, she arrived at the village only to find they had no place for her to sleep. The village elder told her of an abandoned Buddhist temple nearby. She could sleep there. A lonely, frightened girl in her early 20s, she lay on a thin straw mattress in the dark, cavernous interior of the abandoned temple. Her thoughts were of mother and home. She had never been away from home before. Staring into the blackness of the night she saw what appeared to be a black ball moving about in the air. As she watched, it circled and came closer to her, finally striking her on the forehead. When they found her the next day she was just regaining consciousness. Those who tried to help her found her to be uncontrollable—a virtual wild person. Unable to help her, they sent for her parents to come and take her home.

Back in the city she was taken to the hospital where every form of treatment was tried, ranging from drugs to acupuncture to shock treatment. Eventually the hospital authorities said, "We can do nothing for her; you must take her home." At home the girl was unmanageable. The desperate parents had a special metal chair built and embedded in concrete to which they chained their wild daughter. The brokenhearted parents tried everything to find help for their only daughter. Fortunetellers and illegal Buddhist priests were consulted. Their advice was followed but no help came. The daughter was no better but rather grew worse.

"Shall we kill our daughter to put her out of her misery, or shall we commit suicide? We cannot live like this. All the neighbors superstitiously blame us for our daughter's condition." The parents were desperate.

One evening, there was a knock on the door. A neighbor lady came in. "I know someone who can help your daughter," she said.

"Oh, who is it? Please tell us where we can find him."

"His name is Jesus Christ," replied the neighbor lady. "He

can completely restore your daughter and give you a happy time."

The anxious parents asked, "Where can we find this Jesus?"

"I will come," replied the neighbor, "at 8 o'clock tonight and take you to a man who can help you."

At 8 o'clock that night, when passage through the streets was not as obvious, the neighbor took the distraught parents to the home of the lay leader of a house church. For two hours, the Christian witnessed to them of Jesus Christ and of their need to repent of their sins and receive forgiveness and eternal life. At 10 o'clock that night, the parents knelt and accepted Jesus Christ.

How do I know it was 10 o'clock? Because back in the home their son was staying with the demonic daughter while the parents went out. At exactly 10 o'clock the daughter turned to her brother and calmly asked, "What am I doing chained to this chair?" She had been instantly delivered from the demon the minute her parents had accepted Christ and allowed Him to become Lord in their home.

Perhaps what is happening could best be expressed in the words of a house-church Christian. This is part of a letter which we received from one of our Christian contacts in China after Mao's death. Many of the Christians use a form of hidden meaning in their words so that only fellow Christians can understand what is really being written. One will have to read between the lines:

"Over here our people of the same spirit are even more revived, more progressive, and becoming more perfect in Christ. We have greater freedom and are meeting quite openly now. Everything is so convenient compared to the past. Every week we have great meetings—very crowded, and very warm in the Spirit. Many people have turned away from their old superstitious ways and from their old beliefs.

Also, quite a number are coming back to us who were previously with us but, because of the difficult situation, had
left us. Therefore, we are adding new members very rapidly.

"Great miracles and supernatural events with powerful
manifestations are happening frequently. These manifestations of God's power not only are more in quantity but also
greater in quality. In the past few decades we have not seen
such wonderful things. Comparing now with the past, we
can expect even greater things from Him. He is really working among us. The time is ripe for Him to reveal His own
glory. . . ."

14

Lessons from China's Church

During the years of Communist pressure the Church in China has discovered that many of the elements that we have traditionally come to believe are imperative to the survival of the Christian faith have been swept away. Yet, the Chinese Church not only survives but is a living, growing Church. Perhaps no church in history has grown so rapidly.

By once again looking at the significant features of the Chinese Church we may be helped to discover what the true essentials are. A look at the Chinese Church may force us to reexamine the program, emphasis, and direction of our churches in other parts of the world. Learning from one's own experiences is not uncommon. Learning from the experience of others is true wisdom, exercised by too few. There is much we can learn from the experience of China's Church, IF we will. The subsequent easing of governmental pressure on the Church in China has not nullified the lessons to be learned.

Samuel Johnson long ago observed, "Knowledge is of two kinds: we know a subject ourselves or we know where we can get information on it." Hong Kong, with its proximity to the mainland, and, more recently, in its role as the doorway to China, has been an excellent vantage point.

The Holy Spirit has been molding His Church in China during the past quarter of a century and more. There has been virtually no influence on the Chinese Church from the

Church community outside of China. The Church in China has learned its lessons the hard way. The Holy Spirit has been virtually its only teacher. Through incessant persecution, most of the peripheral trappings of modern-day Christianity have been taken from it. Yet, the Church has not merely survived but, more important, it may well be the closest to the divine pattern that exists anywhere in today's world. The similarity of the Church in China in its present form to the Church in the Book of Acts is certainly not accidental, nor is it incidental.

There are compelling lessons we can learn from the Church in China. My fear is that those lessons may not be what we want to learn. It may be that we would rather close our eyes to what the Lord is attempting to teach us through the experience of His Church in China.

It is my conviction that the Chinese Church has a powerful message for every church in the world today. I feel like St. John must have felt on the Isle of Patmos when the Lord said to him, "Write the things which thou has seen, and the things which are, and the things which should be hereafter" (Rev. 1:19). What the Lord was about to show him contained powerful and indispensable lessons for the churches. Knowing that not everyone wanted to hear what God had to say, John was inspired to write, "He that hath an ear to hear, let him hear what the Spirit saith to the churches" (Rev. 2:7).

The lessons to be learned have not been placed in the order of their importance. I am not capable of doing that, nor will I attempt to. I believe the experience of the Church in China raises pivotal questions that we must answer. In this chapter we will only look briefly at five lessons to be learned. In the course of these pages we have mentioned the features in passing. We now look at them in more detail in an attempt to discern what the church in China may be saying to us.

(1) The Unimportance of Cathedrals

For well over a decade the Church in the PRC was virtually without "church buildings." From the Cultural Revolution on, "church buildings" were confiscated by the government. Christians were not permitted to use them for worship. The two church services conducted openly in China were primarily propaganda showpieces, disguised to present to the world a facade of religious tolerance.

Aside from the two known showplace "churches," all other places of Christian worship from stained-glass cathedrals to Gospel halls were denied to the Christian community. These church buildings were once the focal point of much of the Christian activity in China. Now they were being used for other purposes that better suit the aims of an atheistic regime.

What effect has this denial of church buildings had on the Chinese Church? Well, it has definitely not resulted in the death of the Church. The Church in China has learned that church buildings are not at all essential to the continuance of the Church. Admittedly, it was a hard lesson for many Christian groups in China to learn. Most had been nurtured to believe, as most Christians in the West, that the first thing a congregation must do is construct a church building. This building may be primitive or ornate, but it was the number-one priority of most new congregations. The missionary taught them so.

This was definitely not true in the New Testament Church. Nor was it the teaching of the most vibrant indigenous Chinese churches which had been birthed in revival before the Communist takeover.

The Little Flock, the True Jesus Church, and the Jesus Family are the most obvious examples. In their case the Holy Spirit had most definitely instructed them to do without traditional church buildings. As a result, they were better prepared than most Christian groups in China to face the forthcoming repressive actions of a godless government.

One effect of the absence of church buildings was to drive the Church into the home. What better place for the Church to function, especially in a culture that stressed strong family ties? Was this not the only place where the New Testament Church functioned? Will any other form of Christian gathering be able to survive the storms which prophecy proclaims will buffet the Church in the end time? Can the enormous amounts of money now being spent on church building be justified when experience has proved they are not essential? These are just some of the questions raised by the experience of the Church in China.

(2) The Sanctity of the Home

The home in China has become the focal point of Christian activity. When the church building was taken from them, there remained only the home. When the persecution of Christians became pervasive and severe, where else could the believers gather? The home is the most difficult place for a government to monitor. There could be limited coming and going to the home without raising suspicion. The home became the virtually unassailable gathering place of Chinese believers.

One important by-product of this was the return to the biblical concept of a lamb for a household, or "household salvation." You recall that at the time of the exodus the children of Israel were told to "take to them every man a lamb according to the house of their fathers, a lamb for a house: And if the household be too little for the lamb, let him and his neighbor next to his house take it . . ." (Exod. 12:3-4). Several principles are enunciated here: (1) a lamb for each household; (2) no household is too large for the lamb;

(3) the lamb was never too small for the household. The family covered by the lamb may reach out and invite the family next door to share the shelter of the lamb. Sometimes the household was too small for the lamb.

Apparently this was the background of Paul's promise to the Philippian jailer, "Believe on the Lord Jesus Christ and thou shalt be saved, . . . and thy house." For the same reason, an angel appeared in a man's house and told him to send for Peter, "who shall tell thee words, whereby thou and all thy house shall be saved."

Household salvation was common in the early Church. Lydia, the seller of purple, "was baptized and her household." My findings are that this is a fundamental principle of the Chinese Church. Not only does the Church meet in the home but conversion tends to be a family experience. Whole households turn to Christ—whole villages in China are known to be Christians.

To be sure, this biblical promise has been put to severe tests many times. Christian families in Communist China have frequently seen their children taken from them to be raised and educated in state-run schools. The educational system in China has stressed ideology rather than academics. Many Christian parents have seen their children become acknowledged Communists. Some children of Christian parents even became Red Guards during The Cultural Revolution, taunting and tattling on their own parents. Claiming the promise of God in these circumstances has certainly not been easy. Yet, family after family in China has found that God stands behind His promises. I could fill a small-sized book with stories of children who have come back from Marxism to become active members of the Body of Christ. I have such people working on my staff in Hong Kong. The Church in China is primarily a family Church—a Church that has rediscovered the sanctity of the home.

This raises pertinent questions. By separating the Church and the home geographically, have we violated a biblical principle and thus created many of our present family problems? Is the biblical promise of household salvation still valid? Do we need to return a significant portion of the function of the Church to the home? Have we failed to prepare our people for the days of persecution which Scriptures seem to indicate lay before us? Historically, has not every Church under persecution rediscovered the home as the place of worship? It does seem that God somehow always brings His Church back to the home as a place of worship.

(3) Centrality of the Word

The Church in China has rediscovered the Bible. It is true that many Chinese pastors and evangelists in pre-Communist days were powerful exponents of the Word. Men like John Sung, Watchman Nee, and Wang Mingdao (Wang Ming-tao) will rarely be excelled as expository preachers. People sat for hours under their ministry, drinking in the verse-by-verse biblical expositions. However, for the most part this was clergy centered. That is to say, laymen were listeners.

Shortly after the Communist takeover, all pastors and professional clergy were imprisoned. All individual congregations were left without pastors. By one means or another, the government separated the pastors from their congregations. The Chinese Church was left without its teachers.

A second factor was the Communist drive to eliminate all Bibles from China. This campaign reached its peak during the Cultural Revolution. Every home was searched for Bibles. All Bibles found were destroyed. The Chinese Church was left with just a few old Bibles that had been

miraculously preserved. One Bible to thirty or more
believers is commonplace.

I asked a young refugee, who had found Christ in the People's Republic two years before, whether he owned a Bible.
"No," he replied.

"A New Testament?" I asked.

"No."

"Did you personally have any Christian literature as a
new convert?"

"Yes," he replied. "An old Christian lady tore one page
out of her daily devotional book and gave it to me."

This combination of the loss of their teachers and the
scarcity of Bibles drove the average Chinese Christian into a
new appreciation for the Word of God. Frequently, we do
not properly value what we have until it has been taken
away from us. In many areas of China, Bibles are too scarce
and too precious even to be taken to the Christian gatherings. A government raid is always a possibility when Christians gather, so all that is brought to the meeting is
notebooks into which the Scriptures are handcopied.

A typical service finds a lay believer designated to lead
that day. He or she reads the verses to be studied at dictation
speed. Every Christian copies the verses as they are read.
Thus over a period of time, when the study of a book of the
Bible is completed, they will then have the entire book, verse
by verse, plus commentary.

Each believer is expected not only to participate in the
discussion but also to be able to teach God's Word. Many
groups devote one night a week to what they term "practice
teaching." This night is given to teaching the art of Bible
exposition. The goal is for every believer to become a
teacher of the Word. Imagine a Church in which every
believer can expound the Word of God. The Word of God is
central in the life of the Church in China. I heard of one

older Christian who, over the years, has produced several handwritten copies of the entire Bible and given them away to new converts.

The centrality of God's Word in the Church in China and the recent easing of government pressure on the Church has brought about a revival of the once very popular Bible Conferences. In "preliberation" China, Bible Conferences were extremely popular. Given the quality of Bible teachers in that period, it was no surprise. Now, however, in a hostile and difficult environment, Bible Conferences are once again being held. Firsthand reports of these conferences are reaching us in Hong Kong. Attendance is usually on a representative basis. That is, one person from a house church is selected to go to the Conference. His or her responsibility is to absorb and learn all that is possible and upon return share it with all the fellowship.

Another interesting development is the emergence of traveling Bible teachers. These capable Bible expositors travel almost constantly from town to town and village to village. They meet with the house church and share God's Word, even for a series of studies held several nights in the week. One of these teachers was a former Communist cadre, another the daughter of a preliberation pastor. The risks for them must be enormous—financial remuneration almost nil. Their status in a Communist society would be that of what is called "black persons," that is, without status: no food stamps and no provisions of government from housing to medicine are available to them. In a socialist state, the government provides most everything. Yet, reports indicate that a growing number of competent traveling Bible teachers have emerged. They specialize in teaching others to teach.

How important is the Word of God to the average Christian in the West? Is our dependence upon a professional clergy so strong that the average believer would never attempt to teach someone else the Word of God? By failing to break the Church down into smaller groups have we robbed the average believer of the privilege of sharing God's Word with others? Does the Bible really occupy a central place in the daily life of your church and its people? How important is the Bible to you personally today?

(4) The Value of Persecution

Perhaps few churches in history have endured the degree of persecution which the Church in China has. A fundamental goal of the Chinese Communist Party has been to eradicate all religions from China. Force was the means employed. It is a basic tenet of Marxism that "force is the midwife of history." The Christian Church drew more attention from the Communist persecutors than most religions. Two reasons seem apparent. First, the Christian Church posed the greatest threat to Marxist theory. Second, Chinese Christianity had strong historical links with the Western world witness its tragic record of colonialism. Consequently, the suffering of the Chinese Church has been prolonged and pervasive.

Few individual Christians escaped some form of persecution. Many paid with their lives. Some were executed, others starved to death in prison camps, others died of beatings or as a result of overwork and undernourishment in labor camps. Known pastors and leaders of the Christian Church paid the highest price, but no one escaped. Some day their sufferings may be chronicled in a book. For now, their specific stories cannot be told.

Not one of us, and particularly not one of the Christians in the PRC, would wish persecution on any fellow Christian. It has been astutely observed, "The chief pang of most trials is not so much the actual suffering itself as our own spirit of resistance to it." Suffering, both mental and physical, go hand in hand with persecution. Every form of persecution has been good for the Chinese Church.

Henry Ward Beecher once observed that "there is no good accomplished but through the medium of somebody's suffering." It has been difficult enough for the Chinese Church to endure suffering. How tragic if we learn nothing from their suffering or from all persecution has done for the Chinese Church.

"Persecution often does in this life what the last great day will do: completely separate the wheat from the tares," observed Milner. The proportion of tares to wheat in the preliberation Church in China may not have been any greater than in any other Church around the world. It did have too high a proportion of rice Christians. Many united with the Church in order to obtain employment, education, clothing, or just food for survival. The same thing can be said of the Communist Party in China today. Most of China's "Communists" are undoubtedly rice Communists. The State certainly promises to supply all material needs. Be that as it may, the years of persecution have most certainly separated the wheat from the tares in the Church.

There are no rice Christians left in the Chinese Church. Nor are there likely to be many who could be termed hypocrites, or those who go to church for social or business benefits. The PRC may indeed have one of the "purest" Churches on planet earth. To be numbered with the Christian commmunity in the PRC is to attract some form of persecution. From a materialistic point of view there would be little, if any, attraction to being known as a Christian. Therefore, the Christian in China would most likely be a true believer, with a warm personal relationship with the Lord. Only that kind of relationship would make it "worth it all." Their other-worldly outlook would offset the sufferings of today. Like the apostle Paul, they can say, "I reckon that the sufferings of this present time are not worthy to be compared with the glory which shall be revealed in us" (Romans 8:18).

Persecution has driven the Chinese Church to question, "What do I really believe?" Is faith in God a myth, a superstition? Would one be better off as a Marxist? Is Christianity a "foreign religion"? Does it meet our needs here in China now? Is it merely an opiate, as the Communists claim, or is it reality? Those without a strong personal relationship to the Lord may possibly have come up with the wrong answers. The true believer has been immeasurably strengthened in his faith.

The person who has questioned his faith, or has had his faith put to that test of persecution, can stand more erect. Jesus said, "Blessed (happy) are they which are persecuted for righteousness' sake." (Matt. 5:10) The Chinese Church has entered into a dimension of positive faith that would be little known to those of us who have not passed through the fires of persecution.

(5) The Attraction of Joy

The Communist world is a joyless world. Color it grey. Revolution is a nasty business. Mao Zedong (Mao Tse-tung) described it as "an act of violence whereby one class overthrows the authority of another.... Revolution," he declared, "is not a dinner party."

As a way, revolution is intolerable, especially if you are one of the masses. Literally millions in Europe, Asia, and the Americas have "voted with their feet" against living in the unhappy world of Communism. Hong Kong is made up primarily of refugees from the Communist revolution. All of them, even those who live in hillside hovels, could go back to China to live if they so desired. They will tell you that behind the propaganda smiles, which inevitably characterize all photographs released by China, there is deep sadness.

Boris Pasternak, in *Dr. Zhivago*, wrote, "When the Communist revolution came . . . he decided this was the fulfillment of his dream. Instead of that, he found he had only exchanged the old oppression of the Czarist State for the new, much harsher yoke of the revolutionary superstate. . . . I'm strong for any revolution that isn't going to happen in my day."

Certainly Communism always promises a bright future, but what is going to compensate for the deprivations of the long, dreary present, especially if the bright future keeps receding? Louis Fisher, an expert on Russia, concluded, "Communism is a man-made Frankenstein monster obeying no man, consuming the birthright of every man to be free." The loss of freedom never generates joy.

This background is necessary if we are to understand the attraction of joy. Just as those value freedom most to whom it is denied, so those value joy most in whom it is absent. Joy is absent in Communism. Thus joy is the single most attractive element in the Christian faith to those who live in a Communist state. This is a lesson to be learned from the Church in China. This gives new meaning to Nehemiah 8:10, "The joy of the Lord is your strength."

In the interviews that we have conducted with refugees in Hong Kong, we have been told over and over again that joy was the missing element in their lives. Because joy was missing, they consciously or unconsciously were searching for it. When they saw people living as they were, under the most difficult circumstances, who at the same time were joyful, they naturally wanted to discover the secret of that joy. The deep consistent joy of Chinese Christians was the powerful magnet which attracted them to a forbidden faith.

Our research clearly indicates that the majority of young people who find Christ in China are attracted to Christ by the joy they see in the lives of Christians—Christians who work beside them in farm or factory or with whom they attend school. This is why I say that joy is the single most attractive element in the Christian faith.

The Christians of China have had little opportunity to preach openly or use the media as tools of evangelism. When the churches are closed, and overt evangelism becomes virtually impossible, how does one witness for Christ? The Church in China has proven that a joy-filled Christian life is the most effective form of evangelism. The joy of the Lord is their strength!

These observations lead to a series of questions. Can others see the joy of the Lord in our lives? Have we failed to grasp the tremendous significance of joy in the Christian life? Have we eliminated joy from our form of worship, substituting joyless ritual for the exuberant Christian faith found in the early Church? Have we thus made Christianity less attractive in a world that is feverishly searching for real joy?

These observations are a matter of history, but they could very well become prophecy. We must not permit ourselves the unwarranted luxury of supposing that only the Chinese Church will be deprived, hounded, and persecuted. What that Church has experienced may well become common to all churches everywhere before the return of Christ. A quick survey of the present situation in several other areas of the world reveals that churches on every continent are encountering similar pressures. Indeed, even so-called Christian countries are increasing their control over the Church.

Experience is a safe light to walk by. The wise will learn from the experience of the Church in China. It is my fervent hope that their experience may transmit fresh direction for the Church universal. The Chinese Church could well provide us with some principles for today's missionary strategy.

Part Three

The Contemporary Challenge

An Indigenous Church

15

Conflict of Minds

All men may have been created equal, but not all men think alike. The Chinese have had long years to appraise the foreigners who have invaded their land whether as merchants or missionaries. Being a highly practical people, they have come to simple conclusions about foreigners. "Foreigners are too shallow" is a common judgment. Of course, each foreign nationality has identifiable traits. The British are hypocritical and calculating. The Americans are naive and frank, and so on. Whether we agree with their judgments is immaterial.

A Chinese is trained from his earliest years never to show his emotions. To do so would be to display weakness to others. They say, "If the heart is firm, the body is cool." Any display of emotion is a sign of weakness. Imagine the Chinese reaction to the jovial, backslapping American who is as quick to anger as he is to laughter. We, in turn, accuse the Chinese of being inscrutable just because they have been taught to hide their emotions. Their emotions are just as powerful as ours. But self-control keeps them where they belong—hidden inside. This is virtuous to the Chinese mind.

In any interpersonal relationship trust is a vital ingredient. Basically, the Chinese are an extremely honest people. They are taught that "rice obtained by crookedness will not boil up into good food." Another proverb declares, "Though you are starving to death, don't steal." One must, however, understand something of their culture to understand their code of honesty. The greatest virtue in Chinese culture is filial piety; that is, faithfulness and respect to parents. This takes precedence over every other virtue. "Under Heaven," declares their proverb, "no parent is ever wrong." Let's see how this works out in practice.

In ancient times a king's father committed a crime. Faithful to his office, the son brought his father to trial and dutifully sentenced him to death. He fulfilled the requirements of his office—then secretly helped his father to escape.

This king is greatly admired in Chinese thinking. The story is as well known to today's young people as to their great-grandparents. Not to have helped his father to escape was to be an unfaithful, impious son. Not to have condemned him to death was to be a weak king who was not to be trusted or respected. Very neatly both requirements were fulfilled. He was a great man—so the Chinese believe.

The sage Confucius gave to the Chinese people a rich cultural heritage. Even in pre-Confucian days, China was rich in poetry, art, and music—all evidence of true culture. There is nothing shallow about the Chinese. Contemplation and meditation flow deeply. They don't make snap decisions or relish change in any form. Caught in the vise-like grip of their long cultural heritage, they are not free to do so.

A distinguished Chinese scholar addressing Westerners once said (1937), "To understand the mentality of the Chinese people, and the philosophical background of their conduct in life, one can do no better than study their proverbs." In China everyone uses proverbs everyday. They are the "condensed philosophy" of the people and have come from philosophers as diverse as Confucius and Mao. I find them not only revealing but scintillatingly delightful. Here are a few samples to whet your appetite:

"To talk good is not to be good; to do good, that is being good."

"The first part of the night think of your own faults; the latter part, think of the faults of others."

"If you do not ask their help all men are good-natured."

"To get up early for three mornings is equal to one day of time."

"You can't clap with one hand."

"To understand your parent's love, you must raise children yourself."

"You can't cut off the sunlight with one hand."

Many of our own proverbs are phrased just a little differently by the Chinese. See if you can recognize these:

"When a thing is done, don't talk about it; it's difficult to gather up spilled water."

"Too many pilots wreck the ship."

"There is many a good man found under a shabby hat."

"Everyone has a black pig in his house."

"The bamboo stick makes a good child."

Imagine the impact of foreign missionaries on this rich cultural background. It was inevitable that missionaries, too, would come in for a fair share of criticism. "The characteristic of missionaries which we detest most," said a group of Chinese Christian young people, "is their self-importance, their tendency to talk as superiors to inferiors." Dennis Clark says these prayers have been heard: "Oh, Lord, deliver us from the missionaries." "Oh, God, break their pride." "Father, forgive them (the missionaries) for they know not what they do." Obviously, humility is one subject most foreigners have flunked. We, who are really cultural novices, often adopt a disgustingly superior attitude. We treat the Chinese like primitive children.

Missionaries arriving in China were often fresh from institutions of higher learning. Whether these were universities, seminaries, or Bible schools, there was a tendency to some feelings of superiority. These frequently were extended to the "ignorant" heathen, the Chinese. The only problem was that the Chinese were usually more philosophically sophisticated than the Western intruders. Philosophy is more significant in the life of the common man in China than in any other civilization in the history of the world. Philosophy takes the place of religion in the average Chinese mind, especially the intellectuals. Philosophical sophistication extends to an amazing degree, even to the most illiterate peasant. Two thousand years ago a swineherd was made prime minister of the Chinese empire largely because of his knowledge of the classics. The Chinese have long believed that "one who knows the Chinese classics has nothing left to learn."

Ignorant of China's vast cultural background, the foreigner usually excused his own ignorance by claiming the Chinese were inscrutable. Reference is often made, even in current missionary literature, to China as an enigma, the inference being that she is completely unsolvable, her people beyond understanding. As long as this attitude persists, I see little hope for real Christian empathy or even communication.

There must be a reasonable degree of mutual understanding. Up to now it has been mainly a one-way street. Most educated Chinese have spent a great deal of time studying our history and our culture. We, on the other hand, have done little or no study of China and her culture. The key word is "mutual."

I fully agree with the noted professor of Oriental languages, H. G. Creel, "It is not China that is ignorant of and indifferent concerning the culture of the West but the West that knows almost nothing about China and makes little attempt to learn. And the West is paying and will continue to pay the price of ignorance."

China and her peoples are not beyond understanding, but the road to understanding is not easy. Perhaps this chapter can throw at least some light and produce some faint guidelines for understanding.

It is my conviction that if we are to win the Chinese for Christ and unite them with the body of Christ we must be willing to submit ourselves to their cultural disciplines. By this I mean we must fit into their culture rather than, as in the past, attempt to force them to fit into ours. Christ was not a Westerner. Christianity is not a Western religion or a Western culture. Christ and His church will probably be even more at home in China than in the West. We must try to understand and appreciate, and I mean genuinely appreciate, their culture.

The Chinese are quick to sense hypocrisy, and just as quick to discern, and respond, to real love and understanding. No insurmountable barriers exist for the "foreigner" who is willing to learn and love. Working with the Chinese in a spirit of love and humility will be a very rewarding experience. You will be loved as you have seldom been loved before. Lasting ties will be formed that nothing can break. These are the Chinese as I know them.

This does not mean that Chinese philosophy, or the Chinese mind, is easy for a Westerner to understand, or that I fully understand many of the concepts of China's master thinkers. For instance, Hui Shi (Hui Shih), who lived some three hundred years before Christ, was a master at expressing philosophical concepts in paradoxes. "The sun begins to set at noon; a thing begins to die at birth." "The egg has feathers." "A fowl has three legs." "A brown horse and a dark ox makes three." Perhaps his most famous was "A white horse is not a horse." He explained that "white" is a color; a "horse" an animal. A horse is not a color, therefore "a white horse is not a horse." Such paradoxes delight the nimble mind of the Chinese, but throw some of the rest of us into embarrassing confusion.

It is important that we understand some broad principles. First, the Chinese mind is basically humanistic. "Man is heaven and earth in miniature," his proverbs tell him. Man occupies the center stage. Nothing else is as important. There is considerable evidence that in China's very early history, about a thousand years before Christ, spiritual beings played a significant role in the Chinese mind. This seems to have all but disappeared by Confucius' day. Confucius brought Chinese humanism to its climax. Confucius was concerned only about man and nothing else. The Chinese have inherited that attitude. "Man is of all creation the spiritual intelligence" is their conviction.

Confucius had no interest in materialism. His sole interest was man. Asked to define knowledge, he said, "Knowledge is to know man." Wisdom he defined as "attending to the welfare of the people." Government existed only for the benefit of man. When told that a stable had burned down, he asked only if any person was hurt. He had no care for the stable or the horses. Here is complete humanism. This is the underlying philosophy of the Chinese mind. All Chinese attitudes and actions are an outgrowth of this concept.

Even Confucius, however, could not evade the gnawing reality of the spiritual; though he professed no belief in God, he did speak occasionally of "heaven." By this "heaven," he was referring to the vague principal deity of the Chinese in his day. This was not a personal God such as the Christian concept of God. It was a very hazy concept that there was an other-worldly moral force that was somehow related to man. For instance, he felt entrusted by "heaven" with a mission to set things right in the Chinese world and he hoped "heaven" would not allow him to fail.

Lest you are tiring of this exploration of Confucius, may I remind you that Confucianism was the molder of the Chinese mind for over two thousand years. No Christian attempting to communicate the Biblical concept of God to the Chinese can afford ignorance of Confucianism. Even the religions of China such as Taoism and Buddhism were largely humanistic, owing to the powerful and pervading influence of Confucius. Taoism tried many ways to make the body suitable for everlasting life here on earth. Buddhism as the Chinese revamped it became basically humanistic. The term Buddha in China does not refer to a person or a being, but a spiritual force—the Confucian concept. No other civilization on earth scaled such heights of humanism. Man and only man is important. This was the basic conviction around which Chinese culture was fashioned.

Such distinctively Chinese qualities as politeness, filial piety, and ancestor worship are humanism in action. Because man is so important, be polite to him, reverence your family, and care for them after they have died. Virtue was the supreme goal of life. This reverence for man, though creating a barrier to the Christian Gospel, does engender qualities that have made the Chinese virtually indestructible. "If a man is evil men fear him but heaven does not; if a man is virtuous men oppose him but heaven does not." This is the type of guidance the Chinese have had for endless centuries.

In our recording of Chinese history reference is frequently made to the conflicts centering around governmental changes. We tend to lose sight of the fact that Confucian concepts provided China with long years of quiet existence. Because every literate person in China was drilled in the Confucian classics they inevitably exerted a powerful influence upon both governors and the governed. The great teachers' exhortations on virtue were a restraining influence on potential evildoers. If a ruler was not good to his subjects then he could and should be overthrown.

There is in Chinese thinking no such concept as man being created to bring glory to God. It was the other way around. Gods were a convenience for man, often invented to fulfill various roles in the betterment of man's life. Eventually this led to a proliferation of gods, all dedicated to helping man. God did not create man. Man created gods. Obviously Christianity's monotheism found no easy entry point into the Chinese mind. It was not too difficult to persuade a Chinese to accept Christ, as he could always use additional help. Christ was merely added to his pantheon of gods. The command "Thou shalt have no other gods before me" made little sense to the Chinese mind. Worship in the Chinese context is divided among a host of beings thought to be helpful to man. Man, not God, is supreme.

In addition, there are a host of lesser dignitaries which fall into three categories: natural objects, deified humans, and members of the Buddhist and Taoist pantheon. The first group is obviously a result of an original and persistent patheism. These, too, were mere servants of man, worshiped in order to receive personal benefit. The second category involved the ultimate result of humanism, the deification of man himself. A third-century general, Guan Yu (Kwon Yu), became the god of war, and Chang Lao-tsze, an official of high literary talent, is now worshiped as the god of literature. Naturally, Confucius himself was eventually deified. In this context the eventual virtual deification of

Mao Zedong (Mao Tse-tung) seems very natural—"nothing new under the sun." The final category represents the distinctly Chinese interpretation and adaptation of Buddhism and the evolution of Taoism. A city god, a patron of the soil, a fisherman's god, a kitchen god, and so on endlessly, all were designed to improve man's often difficult lot in life. These man-made gods were the rivals of the Christian Gospel in China.

All of China's faiths offer salvation. Confucianism offers salvation in this life alone by conformity to an extremely conservative formula of life. Taoism offers salvation through withdrawal, a return to the harmony of nature. Buddhism in China became a method of self-control leading eventually to a final absorption into nothingness. Chinese Buddhism teaches that this occurs on this earth, in this body. All, in common, offer a man-centered salvation. Fortunately these offers of salvation can be the starting point for the presentation of salvation through Christ. Christ came to take up where man's best efforts fail, and to do for us what we cannot do for ourselves. Here, then, is an open door or at least a wedge into the Chinese mind.

Westerners are forceful and direct. Chinese may be just as forceful, but they are never direct. A direct approach is crude and rude because it provides the other person no escape. Consideration for the feelings of other persons is instinctively important to the Chinese mind. This is partially attributable to the excellent training of Confucianism, where virtue involved concern and consideration for others.

This is the Confucian principle of reciprocity, defined by the master himself as "not doing to others what one does not wish them to do to oneself." Since everyone is seeking happiness, general happiness can only be found in seeking the happiness of the other person, as well as for oneself. Confucius stated it in this way: "The truly virtuous man desiring to establish himself seeks to establish others; desiring success for himself he strives to help others succeed. To find in the wishes of one's own heart the principle for his conduct toward others is the method of true virtue." Too idealistic, you say, and you may be right, but this is the lofty ideal toward which Chinese philosophy and culture has pointed for centuries. Undoubtedly, this explains some of Mao Zedong's (Mao Tse-tung's) success in promoting honesty and cleanliness.

The indirectness of the Chinese has powerful roots in their concept of "saving face." Few tragedies are as dreaded by the Chinese as "losing face." Thus, when confronting another person, think not only of yourself but of the other person. Give the other person a chance to "save face." You may be right and he wrong, but you do not have the right to cause him to "lose face." Loss of face often causes extreme results such as suicide.

The Chinese tell the story of "the poor man and the burglar." A thief entered a poor man's house one night. The poor man was awakened, but in fear pretended to be asleep. The thief saw quickly what was going on and reasoned, "He has seen me and knows that I intend to rob him, but he does not want to wake up and cause me to lose face. What delicacy of feeling. How thoughtful of him." So, the thief, in deep gratitude, crept out of the house without stealing anything. The poor man was incensed when he saw the burglar go without pilfering a single item. "Does he think me so poor that he wishes to spare my house? He'll make me lose face before the neighbors." Jumping out of bed, he called, "Thief, thief, steal something, even if I am a poor man—or what will my neighbors think of me tomorrow?" Each was thinking of the other person's "face" and also of his own "face."

Difficult as this may be for a Westerner to understand, it is deeply ingrained in Chinese life. Obviously, the crudeness and rudeness of the intruding Westerner was and is a constant source of irritation. This applies equally to Western

The test of every religious, political, or educational system is the man which it forms.

governmental representatives, traders, tourists, or missionaries. The merits of Chinese culture are not the issue. As guests, "especially ambassadors of Christ," it is our responsibility to know, understand, and appreciate the culture into which God has sent us.

Donald A. McGavran in his book *How Churches Grow* has an entire chapter which he titles "Cultural Overhang." He points out that missionaries often come to a mission field "imprisoned" by patterns and methods which worked in their own culture back home. McGavran writes, "The fashion in Christian thinking which fits the Western scene becomes the intellectual equipment which missionary candidates and visiting nationals obtain in Western seminaries."

Here is a clear portrayal of the conflict of minds; the "fashion in Christian thinking"—how expressive. We all know that fashions are both localized and highly impermanent. This is true of thinking as well as clothes. McGavran, a recognized authority on missions, calls upon us to recognize "cultural overhang." "He who is conscious of it need not succumb to it."

The apostle Paul took great care, in moving about his world in the service of Christ, to know and to identify with the people to which he ministered. He could speak meaningfully on Mars Hill because he knew the cultural traditions of Greece. In his defense before legal authorities, he always related to the local law and government. This cultural identification is a vital part of becoming "all things to all men, that I might by all means save some, and this I do for the Gospel's sake" (I Cor. 9:22-23). To be sure, the Gospel we proclaim often runs counter to the cultural involvement of both our own country and those of other countries. The point is, I and my culture must decrease. It is Christ that must be seen as relevant to the culture to which God has sent us. His love must shine through the foreignness of the emissary.

Sometimes merely what we eat or drink has immense bearing on the acceptance or rejection of the Gospel. An invitation to share a meal with a Chinese family can easily produce a crisis in one's dedication. How far are you willing to go in accepting and identifying with the culture to which God has sent you? How would you react if you were served a dish of chicken feet (skin and claws intact) or fish-head soup with livid eyes staring up at you waiting to be devoured? Refusal or even hesitation in certain circumstances could close a heart, or a home, to the Gospel you have come to proclaim. The Scriptures say, "Destroy him not with thy meat, for whom Christ died" (Rom. 14:15). This is merely the other side of the same coin—pushing your culture till both your culture and your Christ are rejected. It's easy to do. Crucifying your culture is not easy. It is all you've known up to this point in life. The Bible takes a serious view of this matter of cultural identification.

It is my conviction that unless a missionary is willing to give up, crucify his own culture, he can never sufficiently identify with a foreign culture. This is part of what D. T. Niles had in mind when he said that a missionary is "a representative of the foreignness of the Gospel in any human situation." The less "foreign" the missionary, the more acceptable his Gospel. Becoming less foreign should, therefore, be the goal toward which every missionary must constantly strive at all costs. And how can I become less foreign? By knowing, understanding, and loving the culture into which I have been commissioned to go! Merely the call of God to a mission field or adequate Bible training are not enough. Between you and the people lie two divergent cultures—theirs and yours.

If the cost of cultural crucifixion seems just too great, think of the perfect "culture" which the Son of God voluntarily surrendered in order to become the Son of Man. Christ, in His cultural identification with our world, made God and all His superhuman attributes understandable to us. "He that hath seen me hath seen the Father." Not only did we come to understand God but we can come to love Him through His Son, Jesus Christ. Our goal is to lead men and women to love, worship, and serve Jesus. No cost is too high. "The Christian missionary has to make a deliberate, conscious, and sustained effort to live and work and think and speak in the framework of that culture into which Christ has sent him."

A Chinese proverb advises, "Whenever you enter a country, inquire as to what is forbidden; when you cross a boundary, ask about the customs." Cross-cultural communication may be a twentieth-century term, but the Chinese knew all about it centuries ago when they wrote, "Wherever you go, speak the language of that place," not just the language of the lips, but the language of the heart and mind.

No, not everyone thinks alike. To move from one culture to another is to precipitate a conflict of minds. To end that conflict is vital to Christian witness.

16

Chinese Christianity

The Christian Church was planted in China by Western missionaries, but for the most part it never became a Chinese Church.

In the mind of the average Chinese of that day there was no such thing as "Chinese Christianity." To them Christianity was obviously a foreign religion. The buildings Christians worshiped in, the hymns they sang, and the leadership bore the unmistakable marks of foreignness. As a result of the overpowering influence of Westernism, the Church of the missionary era was frequently weak and deformed. It lacked the stamp of Chinese authenticity.

Therefore, some major changes had to be brought about through a cataclysmic shakeup and the refining fires of persecution. Each agonizing step through which God has taken the Chinese Church has been carefully calculated to produce the desired result. When I refer to the Chinese Church in this book I mean the Church in the mainland of China only. I see the Chinese Church during the past thirty years as a lump of clay in the Master's hand. God has been molding and shaping that Church to His own specifications.

I do not intend to go into detail on the many weaknesses of the Church during the missionary era. Our purpose is to see how God has been working in the Chinese Church. To see what God has been doing, however, we must point out some of the problem areas that obviously need to be changed.

In speaking of the Chinese Church, it should be noted at this point that there were two distinct and divergent directions in which the Chinese Church was moving during the final days of the missionary era. It must be acknowledged that a segment of the Chinese Church was truly indigenous in almost every sense of the word. Naturally, this was the most rapidly growing segment of the Church.

However, most Chinese still looked on Christianity as a Western faith, and certainly the Communists demonstrated clearly that this aspect of Christianity was what they despised most. Consequently it is this aspect that must be examined.

What frequently evolved in China was not a pure Chinese Church; rather, it was in many cases a somewhat pitiful hybrid. Looking back now, it is possible to see that we missionaries failed to "Sinicize" the practice of the Christian faith. There was virtually no Chinese Christianity. I am not speaking here of theology, I am speaking of the practice of the Christian faith.

What is not under discussion here is the message of God to man. The Bible is God's message to men—all men in whatever culture they may live. I fully agree with Professor Lloyd Kwast's view as expressed in this statement: "Biblical writers were inspired to write what they did by the Spirit of God. Thus the Bible is the revelation of a supracultural God, communicated to culture-bound people, through writers living at specific points in history and in particular cultural milieux."

Because all men have basically the same spiritual needs, the message of the Bible speaks to all men in whatever culture they may live. It is not the message of Christianity that is under discussion but the outward practice.

Of course the principles of God's Word must never be violated to accommodate any culture. It is the culture that must change to conform to biblical principles. But this does not mean equating the Christian faith with Western cultural practices, or Japanese cultural practices. The Christian faith meets man where he is and effects change from within. When I speak of the Westernization of Christianity, I refer to the outward extrabiblical forms that tend to evolve around one's cultural patterns.

I am most definitely not prepared to accept the view that Christianity is merely an extension of Western colonialism, thus equating God's message to man with imperialism. I strongly object to such an inference. Those who held this view predicted that as Western colonialism faded from Asia and Africa so would the influence of Christianity. History has already proved them wrong. The fact is that Christianity has grown more rapidly since the retreat of European colonialism than it did during colonialism's heyday. These predictions obviously sprang from observations of the visible forms which Christianity often assumed during the days of colonialism. What is needed is a clear distinction in our minds of the difference between the message of God and the local expression of our faith in the Gospel.

Warren Webster has provided us with clear direction. He notes, "The Gospel is God's gracious provision of salvation through Jesus Christ to all men in every age and clime who submit themselves to Him in faith and trust. Christianity, on the other hand, is the human response to the Gospel. The Gospel is the power of God unto salvation—divine, pure, universal in its application. Christianity is the local expression of the Gospel as it takes root in the soul and in the soil of a given place. The Gospel message is universal. Christianity is often compounded with provincial customs, local tradition, and human fallibility."

In retrospect, it was at this point that the missionaries possibly made their greatest mistake. Coming as we did from the West, we brought both our Western culture and our Western style of worship. We seemed determined to make the Church in China as much like the church back home as we could. We tended to build the same-shaped churches, we installed the same form of church government, we affixed the same names to the door of the church and even taught the same hymns and hymn tunes.

I well remember, as a boy, hearing the Chinese Christians struggling valiantly but without much success to sing Frederick W. Faber's great hymn, "Faith of our Fathers Living Still." I knew that most of their fathers were Buddhists. Neither the words nor the music fit. Chinese is a tonal language. Western music destroys the Chinese tonal system, thus making the words totally incomprehensible to a Chinese listener unless he has the words visibly before him. As a consequence, even the sound of Christians worshiping was branded with the dreaded label of foreignism. We certainly did not intentionally make it difficult for the Chinese to accept Christianity, but I am afraid the effect was the same.

The Chinese people, with a culture much older than ours, and a natural suspicion of anything from the West, found it difficult to accept and become a part of the Christian community. Almost everything about our practice of the Christian faith was difficult for them to accept, in spite of the fact that Christ was born on the fringes of Asia, of a mother whose blood can be considered Oriental. The Oriental customs of Bible times are more easily understood by a Chinese than by a Westerner. Yet we insisted on exporting the Church in virtually the same form as it had developed in our Western culture.

To make it worse, we assumed the major share of the financial responsibility. The poverty prevalent throughout China had caused a deluge of sympathetic giving back home in the West. With this often sacrificially given money, the missionary became the source of much-needed finance in desperate times. The missionary always seemed, at least in the eye of the poverty-plagued Chinese, to be wealthy. And he was, in comparison with the average Chinese. All of this served to produce a weak and dependent Chinese Church that had not learned to lean on God's sufficiency.

The Westernization of Christianity also produced few real leaders in the Chinese Church. It was difficult for the Chinese to fit in and supply the kind of leadership the missionary represented. If the missionary was the kind of leadership Christianity demanded, then the West would have to continue to supply the leaders. It was a vicious circle. The Westerner decried the fact that he could not find leaders in the Chinese Church. The Chinese reckoned that he could never be like the Western missionary. The result was a stalemate.

When the Communists took control of China, they saw the Christian Church as a major obstacle to the spread of Marxism. The allegiance of the Chinese Christian was to a living God, and frequently to a Western missionary. Both these loyalties, from the Communist viewpoint, had to be broken. The strong link which the Chinese Church had with the Western world was most galling.

It is important to note that these non-Chinese links did not exist in the folk religions or even in Buddhism, for Buddhism had become a truly Chinese faith. The Sinicization of Indian Buddhism was virtually complete, whereas Christianity was still closely tied to Western culture and, in the Marxist mind, Western imperialism. Christianity, consequently, received special attention from the Communists. Strong emphasis was placed on severing Christianity's link with the West. This eventually resulted in the mass exodus of almost every foreign missionary in China by 1953.

The Christian faith meets
man where he is.

Given the dependence of many Chinese Christians on the Westerner, it is not difficult to understand why the Communists obviously believed that if the Western links could be severed the Christian Church in China would not be able to survive. To the Communists the solution of the problem of Christianity in China seemed simple enough.

Actually, what they considered a "solution" was an essential element in God's plan for China's Church. Few churches in history have been so totally cut off from outside influence as the Chinese Church—especially since 1965. Foreign influence has virtually been eliminated. The Chinese Church has thus become a truly Chinese Church. This was essential.

The dependence of the Chinese Church had to be broken. The time had come for the Chinese Church to learn God's complete sufficiency. What better training ground could God have provided for this lesson than the past years under Communism. Certainly no Western finances could be depended on. The government, on the other hand, was certainly not going to aid and abet the growth of Christianity if they could help it. Fellow Christians in China all were reduced to the poverty level, even if they once had been relatively wealthy. There was no one to look to now but God. Either God could supply their needs or He could not. His promise to "supply all your needs" (Phil. 4:19) was either reliable or it was not to be depended on. I would venture to say that the Christians of China now know more about God's total sufficiency than most of the Christians in the West. This lesson has been learned the hard way, and perhaps that's the only way it can be learned.

We have noted previously that the Westernization of the Chinese Church produced few strong leaders. The causes for this situation were many. One cause has already been mentioned, that of the Western missionary as the pattern of leadership in Christianity. How was such a person to be duplicated in China? The Chinese were an entirely different people with a completely disparate cultural background. Their sense of values was very divergent from that of the missionary. That's why I concluded that "if the missionary was the kind of leadership Christianity demanded then the West would have to continue to supply the leaders." The matter of ability is not the question. The Chinese had proved their leadership ability through long centuries of history. What is involved are the cultural nuances of the Christianity which the Western missionary represented.

The Chinese were well equipped to lead a distinctly Chinese Church, as Watchman Nee and others have amply demonstrated. The indigenous Chinese Churches had strong national leadership. What the Chinese were ill-prepared to do was to function in the shoes of the Western missionary. The solution to this problem was a two-step remolding of the Chinese Church.

The first step involved the removal of Western leadership. This was a traumatic experience for both. The missionary loved the people and felt that if he left China he would be unable to fulfill the call of God on his life. He had certainly proved conclusively that he would make virtually any necessary sacrifice to further the cause of Christ in China. It is doubtful, however, if anything short of the Communist revolution would have persuaded him to leave China. The Communists left him no choice.

The Chinese Christian, on the other hand, on his own virtually for the first time, felt somewhat abandoned and alone. The missionary had become his friend, his spiritual mentor, and his decision maker. Given these factors, and the inbred politeness of the Chinese people, it is also doubtful if he would have suggested that the missionary leave, at least for decades to come. Once again, it was a revolution that God used to sever the umbilical cord of dependence on the missionary. Now that the missionary had gone, leadership would have to come from within. The Chinese Church was left without a choice.

The second step necessary for the remolding of the Chinese Church was a little more complicated. The problem, to state it simply, was the Westernized form of Christianity that was brought to China. This form, though suitable to the West, did not fit into the cultural pattern of the Chinese social system. I am referring specifically to the family system. We have already noted that this system made conversion of the Chinese to either Christianity or Marxism difficult. The Chinese do not easily form themselves into units other than family units, nor do they normally function effectively outside of the family unit. The Chinese are a nation of families. Within that family unit, whether large or small, there is usually effective leadership.

It is an observable characteristic that most Chinese function best in family units. This is amply demonstrated in the world of industry. There are many Chinese millionaires throughout Asia but no General Motors or Sony Corporations among the Chinese. In other words, most of the wealthy Chinese head their own family businesses. Corporate success is rare outside the family. In this regard, they are virtually opposite from the Japanese, who seem to function most effectively in large corporate structures. We are now talking about leaders. Men with leadership ability in the Chinese community do not tend to form corporate structures outside the family. Very few exceptions can be found.

This is an important cultural characteristic that must be faced in the quest for leadership in the Chinese Church. The Western form of the Christian Church is more of a corporate structure. Family ties are not normally a pivotal factor in the Western Church. This would not be so in the Chinese Church. Centuries of life built around the family leadership concept have made too deep an imprint on the Chinese character to be easily ignored or erased. For the Chinese to provide strong leadership in the church, this family concept must be given proper consideration.

It is most interesting to observe how the Chinese Church has evolved under Communism. Two steps which the Maoists have taken were cunningly calculated to weaken the Chinese Church, but have actually served to strengthen it immeasurably. First of all, pastors and church leaders were separated from their congregations and sent off to labor camps or prisons. Secondly, all church buildings were either destroyed or appropriated for state purposes. Virtually no congregation in China had worshiped in a "church" building for more than a decade.

The effect of these two moves was to drive the Chinese Church into a pattern in which they function most effectively. In other words, the Communists have driven the Chinese Church from weakness to strength. Let's see how and why this is so:

By separating the pastors from their congregations, the Communists have forced the Chinese Church to seek leadership from within the congregation. The leaders which emerged were laymen or laywomen who, for the most part, had not been indoctrinated with the Western concepts of church leadership. The result has been that the Chinese Church has sought its own level, a level in which it could function most effectively. Thus, the Church in mainland China has formed itself into family units, where natural leadership would already exist.

The effect of denying Chinese Christians the use of their church buildings was precisely the same. The only alternative open to the Christian in China was to meet in the home. The risks involved in meeting would be greatly minimized if those meeting together were all members of the same family. Consequently, this was the pattern that began to develop, especially during and right after the Cultural Revolution, when the pressure on the Church was the greatest. This is not to say that only members of the family could attend. Others were always welcome, and even visitors from outside the Mainland occasionally worshiped with them. The family however, became the backbone of the home meeting. A member of the family with which the group meets usually is the spiritual leader. There are exceptions to this pattern, but they are just that—exceptions.

The form of the Chinese Church which emerged was an ideal form to fit into the Chinese culture. It is also strikingly close to the New Testament pattern. During the early centuries of Christianity the Church inevitably met in the home. Whether this was because it was the natural influence of the

Oriental world into which Christianity came or not is possibly debatable. The fact is, if one is to follow the New Testament pattern the Church would meet in the home and leadership would come from one of the members in whose home the fellowship meets. This is the pattern of the Church in most of China today.

In addition, we need to relate this development to the dramatic people movements that are being observed in various parts of the world. It has been recognized that conversions of a large segment of any given people are better accomplished through "group conversion." Conversion, of course, is and must be an individual experience. What is meant by "group conversion" is a whole group turning to Christ at one time. Perhaps we should adopt the present missiological term, "multi-individual" conversions. This usually occurs when a natural leader in that group finds Christ—the chief, the village elder, the tribal patriarch, etc. He then encourages all the others to accept Christ and a whole group experiences individual conversion. The closer the family or group unity, the more readily this will occur.

At this point, our Western culture is so different that it makes understanding difficult. Alan R. Tippett describes the "non-Western world of extended families, clans, tribes, castes and age-grades, where whole villages may represent precise ethnic entities, and where such groups may elect to turn from Animism to Christianity as total units at one precise point of time." The Westerner, to whom Christianization is, as Donald McGavran says, "an extremely individualistic process," finds it difficult to understand, much less accept, the concept of multi-individual conversions. A better understanding could be achieved by pondering this paragraph by Donald McGavran:

"To understand the psychology of the innumerable subsocieties which make up the non-Christian nations, it is essential that the leaders of the churches and missions strive

to see life from the point of view of a people to whom individual action is treachery. . . . The individual does not
think of himself as a self-sufficient unit but as part of the
group. His business deals, his children's marriages, his personal problems, and his difficulties he has with his wife are
properly settled by group thinking. Peoples become Christian as this group-mind is brought into life-giving relationship to Jesus as Lord."

This is certainly the case in the tight-knit Chinese social
system where the family, not the individual, is the dominant
decision maker.

Understandably, it was usually this family unit which
blocked the conversion of many in the missionary era in
China. Furthermore, if and when an individual did accept
Christ it was extremely difficult for him to function as a
Christian within a largely alien family setting. Seeking to
convert individuals to Christianity thus posed enormous
problems. These problems would be greatly minimized if
the Church functioned along family lines.

It is probable, then, that God has been preparing the
Church in the People's Republic for a massive "people
movement" or multi-individual revival that would sweep
millions into the Kingdom of God. I personally believe that
is precisely what the Holy Spirit has been doing in China.

"A cobweb is as good as the mightiest cable when there is
no strain upon it," wisely observed Henry Ward Beecher.
It's when strain is applied that strength is tested. Trials in
the life of the Christian have a twofold function. They not
only test but they strengthen the tested. Great trials seem to
be a necessary preparation for great duty. That is why, as
Beecher observed, "We are always in the forge or on the
anvil: by trials God is shaping us for higher things." The
fires of persecution and the hammer blows of atheistic

resentment have been preparing the Church in the PRC for greater things.

It is hardly necessary for me to point out that the Chinese Church has not achieved perfection. God is not through with the Chinese Church. It is still on the potter's wheel responding to the Master's molding. However, by what we can see, the Chinese Church for the most part closely resembles the original blueprint as drawn in the Book of Acts. The form is an authentic New Testament Church. The design on the outer surface is now authentically Chinese. This augurs well for the future in both time and eternity.

17

Through the Open Door

There is tremendous excitement in evangelical circles because of the fast-moving developments in China. Plans are being prayerfully formulated in the "board rooms" of some mission societies. Others, seeing the enormous promotional value of a China-related program, are rushing to join the China bandwagon. Stan Mooneyham described some of them in these words: "The evangelical opportunists, well meaning for the most part, fired by zeal but with little knowledge, will rush their crash programs into the market place to take advantage of the awakened Christian's interest in China." Leslie Lyall warned of the tragedy of letting "loose on a suspicious, even hostile, Chinese population a motley horde of ill-prepared, ill-equipped, disorganized and blundering, if enthusiastic, missionaries."

Because I am constantly being asked my advice and opinion on the subject of the return of missionaries to China, I want to take this opportunity to put some of my feelings and opinions on paper. In doing so, I realize that there is much more that needs to be said that cannot be covered in this extremely brief summary. I also realize that most groups guilty of the kind of thing described by Mooneyham and Lyall in the preceding paragraph will be unable to recognize themselves. They never look into the mirror.

It must also be said that the term *missionary* in relation to China needs some explanation. This term is so closely identified with the past that some may get the impression that I am speaking of the return of traditional missionaries to China. I am not. I am speaking of the opportunities to be a witness *to* China or *in* China, given the present-day realities. Thus the work and the image of the "missionary" might be quite different today. Yesterday is gone forever. This is a new day with a totally different situation both inside and outside of China. I use the term *missionary* only for want of a better term. The missionary to China today may be quite different from his predecessors.

May I address these thoughts to all my fellow workers in Christ around the world who are genuinely challenged and burdened for China. For the sake of brevity and clarity, my suggestions are grouped under six headings.

Keep the goal before you.

A missionary is a "sent one." But it is important to remember that an evangelical missionary's primary goal is to bring men and women into proper relationship to Jesus Christ, man's only Savior. This is what we are "sent" to do. Missionaries may be called on to do many things, but above all they have been called and sent to proclaim the lost condition of men without Christ (Rom. 3:19) and to proclaim, as well as demonstrate, the saving power of the Lord Jesus Christ (Rom. 10:12-13) made possible by God's eternal love (John 3:16).

Some of the initial "missionaries" going into China in the immediate future will probably be educators or medical personnel. On reaching China they will be so overwhelmed by the social needs that unless they are unusual people or are adequately programmed they will tend to lose sight of the real goal. The gospel they have been "sent" to proclaim will be lost in the busyness of alleviating obvious human need. This was frequently true in the missionary endeavors of the past in China. The means became the end. Around the world today this is still an unresolved major mission problem. Unfortunately, social work seldom produces spiritual harvest. China is still a poor country with endless human need. The human need could blind us to China's greatest need—a Savior—unless constant emphasis is placed on our redemptive goal. Donald McGavran says it well: "The lift due to mission aid (schools, agriculture, medicine, care) must in the minds of the people, Christian and non-Christian alike, neither displace the redemption due to the Holy Spirit or even bulk larger. No churchman wants it (social work) to seem more important, but unless lift is consciously balanced with UNUSUAL STRESS on redemption as the great good the wrong impression will be given." More important, the lesser goal may be accomplished but the major goal won't. This would be tragic. We must keep our eyes on the reason why we have "been sent."

Be aware of the potential for disaster.

Some of the information coming into my hands and reaching my ears concerning the programs that are currently being rushed for the evangelization of China are, in my opinion, clear-cut formulas for disaster. Leslie Lyall and Stan Mooneyham's warnings must be heeded. I see the massive mistakes of the past, all without exception, being repeated in some of these plans. They brought disaster in the past—they will lead to disaster again. In fact, we may be heading for even greater disaster than in the past because of two factors:

1. The strong anti-Communist bias of some evangelical Christians seems to take precedence over a burden for the eternal souls of the Chinese people. Anything to get back at the Communists is justified as long as it is done in the name of

"evangelism." The motive is wrong; therefore, the results will be wrong. The scope for potential disaster in these actions, which will inevitably conversely affect all other Christian efforts, is frightening, to say nothing of the suffering it may cause China's Christians. We simply have no right to heap additional suffering on them by our brash actions.

2. The power of modern mass communication could serve to compound the mistakes. Promotion is regarded by some groups to be of paramount importance. Consequently, some plans for China are being formulated for their promotional impact rather than for their true value. The potential for disaster in this is obvious. On the other hand, some very vital projects may be neglected simply because they do not have great promotional value. When programs are tied to promotion and publicity appeals, maintaining the proper biblical perspective is difficult. As a general rule the less publicity given to our ministries to China the better.

Cooperation may be preferable but hardly probable.

It is relatively simple to get a group of organizations interested in the evangelization of China together for a consultation. That consultation could conclude that cooperative efforts would save a lot of duplication and make for a more cautious and practical approach. However, the mindset of most Christian organizations will probably mean, unfortunately, that cooperative efforts will be few and far between. It is my conviction that where a possibility for cooperative effort exists, that possibility must be explored to the full. This brings to mind the statement, "There is no limit to what you can do for God if you don't care who gets the credit."

Preparation must be emphasized.

Whether on a cooperative or individual basis, it must be stressed that tomorrow's missionaries to China must be more adequately prepared than in the past. I would suggest that emphasis be placed on the following areas of preparation. Please keep in mind that these suggestions are based on the assumption that the missionary is already adequately prepared in biblical knowledge and in the Chinese language. Those are the starting points which cannot be reached overnight. Once the matters of theology and linguistics are adequately provided for, then the following areas should be emphasized:

1. There *must be* adequate study in the field of anthropology and sociology as they relate to China. Students of missionary work in China from Latourette to Glasser concur that these areas of study are vital in preparation for work with the Chinese. They have observed that this was the point at which the China missionaries of the past were most inadequately prepared. Given China's long history, its centuries of isolation, and its communal pattern of life, to know and understand culture is extremely important. In fact, it is more important than in most other cultures.

2. Confucianism and Taoism are still powerful influences in Chinese culture. The contemporary form of these philosophies-cum-religions must be studied. Every Chinese is one-half Taoist and one-half Confucianist. What does that mean?

3. Study must certainly be given to the influence of Communism on the Chinese mind over the past thirty years. Just how deep or how shallow are the mental grooves carved in the Chinese mind by the Mao era?

    Westerners who have resided in post-Mao China have unanimously spoken of the need for a Christian apologetic. That is to say, all wished they had been better prepared to give an adequate answer to the questing minds of China's ideologically indoctrinated youth.

4. Intensive study must be given to the Chinese Church as it emerges from the Mao Era. The form that has emerged at this time, though substantially different from the Church of

the missionary era, is the form of the Chinese Church that must be perpetuated in the years ahead. We must not be guilty of undoing the work of the Holy Spirit over the past thirty years. He has been molding His Church into a truly Chinese and a truly New Testament Church. It would be a crime to force the Chinese Church back into an ill-fitting Western mold. Will the denominations be willing to allow the Church in China to function along radically different lines than the Church in the West? I certainly hope so.

Missions must be colorblind.

A great debate is raging as to whether missionaries to China should be nationals or internationals, that is, Chinese or other nationalities. The current Four Modernization drive is clearly saying that it doesn't matter. Teng Hsiao-ping's (Deng Xiaoping's) most famous quotation is, "It doesn't matter if a cat is black or white, as long as it catches mice." Obviously it does matter. All things being equal, Chinese nationals would be most readily accepted.

Three groups of Asians can be singled out as the ones with the greatest immediate opportunities to assist in carrying the Gospel to earth's largest unevangelized mission field:

The Hong Kong Chinese are faced with the most immediate opportunity. Most Hong Kong Chinese still hold Chinese citizenship, and those who don't find their homeland welcomes them. Even escapees and those born in Hong Kong are welcome. This is all made abundantly clear by the warm reception these Chinese have enjoyed all through the period of the revolution. They have never been barred from entry into China, even during the Cultural Revolution. There have been times when they feared to go, but the door has always been basically open. In addition, most of them have relatives living in the Mainland which they can readily visit.

Now China has an even warmer welcome for them. An increasing number of Hong Kong Chinese are establishing business contacts in China. Some are even establishing joint-venture factories in China. More trains and more ferries are being added to accommodate them. The rail link between Hong Kong and Guangzhou (Canton) is now uninterrupted at the border. China is going all-out to organize large weekend tours for Hong Kong people. At Chinese New Year and Ching Ming Festival over 800,000 people stream across the Hong Kong border into China on a single weekend. Beijing (Peking) and neighboring Guangdong (Kwangtung) Province would like to see this happen more frequently. The primary reason is that the Hong Kong people take significant sums of money when they go to the Mainland.

The second group, the Overseas Chinese, are in a somewhat different category. They are thought to number over forty million. Generally speaking, they are well educated and have done very well in business in whatever country they have settled. China welcomes them for several reasons:

1. China never loses any citizens. Most Overseas Chinese still consider China to be home, or at least their ancestral home. The feeling of belonging is mutual.
2. They are usually very wealthy by China's standards. She would like to see more of their money spent in China both for tourism and investment.
3. They possess the kind of technical expertise China so desperately needs at this time. An increasing number of Overseas Chinese will be responding to China's call as they become convinced that China has really changed, or even that they can in some way aid their ancestral land.

The third group is made up of other Asians. At this point, we are talking mainly about the Japanese, although I look for

The Maoists have struck a severe blow at the Chinese family system. One result has been that the young people are more accoooible and less bound to the opinions and convictions of their family elders.

Massive literacy programs erupted throughout China.

Communist China's new Simplified Script and current word usage made the available Chinese Bible virtually obsolete and a new translation exclusively for China was vitally needed. In 1975 Asian Outreach met that need by publishing the New Testament.

others to be involved before long. The Japanese, with their economic strength, technical proficiency, and penchant for tourism, are becoming a significant factor in China's "Four Modernizations" drive. The accomplishments of Japan, an Asian country, are a beacon light towards which China is aiming. Many more Japanese will be traveling in and out of China in the immediate future.

Asian Christians are thus being presented with an enormous challenge. Many Asians will be wanting to satisfy their curiosity about China by tourism. Others will be eager to respond to the prospects of making money in the world's largest consumer market. What remains to be seen is how many Asian Christians will respond to the difficult challenge of taking the Gospel of Christ in the world's largest mission field.

Christians sometimes need to be reminded that what they can do for Christ they will be required to do. An opportunity is a divine commission. Will the Chinese Christians of Hong Kong be in the forefront of China ministry? The door is more open for them than for anyone else.

It is encouraging to report that there are a number of Hong Kong-based China-concerned groups that meet regularly for fellowship, sharing and prayer. These include Christian Communications, the Far East Broadcasting Company, Trans World Radio, The Chinese Church Research Center, and Asian Outreach. Other groups are working in close relationship. It is good to see coordinated efforts developing on the part of the local Chinese.

An increasing number of Westerners are living in China. The vanguard is composed of diplomats, technicians, journalists, businessmen, and teachers. The possibilities of witness for Christ, open to the Christians among them, are worth considering.

I am well aware that there are some Christian groups who are saying that these Westerners should not attempt overt evangelism but simply confine themselves to setting the example of Christian living. Christian example is good, but according to the Scriptures not good enough. What do you do with Ezekiel 33:8: "If thou dost not speak to warn the wicked (a person without Christ) from his way, that wicked man shall die in his iniquity but his blood will I require at thine hand"? God-given responsibility cannot be avoided or rationalized away. How do you ignore Christ's divine commission given to every one of His followers: "Go ye into all the world and preach the Gospel to every creature"?

All who have not lived in the People's Republic of China will be easily identifiable as foreigners, whatever the color of their skin. The question then becomes one of God's commission on individual lives and their preparedness to be used of God rather than one of the color of their skin.

Missionaries must be "supernaturalists."

It is the cry of Moses that must be burning in every missionary's soul: "If thy presence go not with me carry me not up hence." It will be the supernatural presence and power of God and that alone that will make an impact for eternity in China. Divine work cannot be accomplished apart from divine power.

Before looking at some of the specific ministries presently functioning, I would like to stress that any form of ministry to China is by nature a specialized ministry. This is a most important consideration.

Not only are we dealing with one of the oldest and most deeply cultured civilizations on earth, but we are dealing with a nation that has developed in self-imposed isolation over the past three decades. During those years China has experimented with the most massive and intensive effort to change an entire race of people. Nothing like it has ever been attempted before. What changes have or have not occurred during the period of isolation is a pertinent question.

There is absolutely no precedent to follow in developing many aspects of ministry to today's China. There are no faint footprints on the sands of time to provide us with even a sense of direction. This is a totally new challenge. This is why any form of ministry to China must be a specialized ministry. Nor will the required expertise be developed overnight. We need to beware of instant experts.

The fact is very few people, and even fewer Christians outside of China, have bothered to acquire the needed expertise in the language, the thought patterns, and the background of the people of Communist China. As Paul Kratochril, a Chinese-language expert, has written: "For better or worse, there is only one modern standard Chinese, and that is the norm emerging in the language community living in the territory of the People's Republic of China."

This lack of expertise applies not merely to Westerners but to the Chinese of the dispersion as well. Professor James H.Y. Tai has clearly explained the need for such expertise. He wrote, "On the simplest level, effective communication requires a knowledge of what constitutes Modern Standard Chinese in China to avoid misunderstanding or alienating the audience because the language used is unfamiliar, outdated, or otherwise inappropriate."

Up until 1949 China really had no national language. The closest one could come to a national language was a form of the Beijing (Peking) dialect known as Putonghua (Pu-tung-hua), or *common speech*. By far the majority of the Chinese people could not speak or even understand common speech. There were some three hundred dialects, often so different that one could not be understood by another. Consequently, a missionary attempting to communicate the Gospel faced this tremendous obstacle. It was difficult enough to learn a foreign language, especially Chinese, but which of the many dialects should one learn? Once he learned a specific dialect his ministry was largely restricted to the region where that dialect was spoken. The lack of a national language was a severe obstacle to the spread of the Gospel.

The Communists faced precisely this same problem when they attempted to spread the gospel of Marxism. The problem was a severe one. For instance, Chairman Mao was a native of Hunan province. He was forced to learn the Mandarin language; but he spoke with such a thick Hunanese accent that he could barely be understood on radio. The unification of a country virtually demands the unification of language. This was especially true for Mao and his cohorts. They believed that the mass media were the key to communizing a nation. The Maoists were convinced that sheer political agitation using the mass media, coupled with grassroots oral participation, could transform one-fourth of the human race. But in order to use the mass media effectively to achieve their set goals, a national language was an imperative. Premier Zhou Enlai (Chou En-lai) said in 1958, "The diversity in dialects has an unfavorable effect on the political, economic, and cultural life of our people. . . . Without a common speech, we shall, to a greater or lesser extent, meet with difficulties in our national construction." Consequently, great emphasis was placed on making the Beijing (Peking) dialect into the national language.

Mandarin, as it is called, was taught by every conceivable means, using every possible agency throughout the country. Vigorous efforts have been made to provide China with a national language for the first time in history. Today China does have an official national language. In spite of continuing regional opposition, a growing percentage of the Chinese people speak and understand Mandarin. This unification of language was a necessity for the spread of the gospel of Christ. It is my conviction that in this way God has used the Communists to prepare China for the spread of the gospel in God's own time.

The natural process of language evolution, normally slow, even glacial, has been greatly accelerated in The People's

Republic of China. Its isolation from other countries and the rapid social changes within the country accelerated the process. How far-reaching these changes are in the meaning of words may be more clearly understood by the following examples:

幫助 *Help*
Old meaning   Help a person, a positive act of kindness
New meaning   "May I help you by assisting to brainwash you?"

拉拉扯扯 *To pull and push* (Old Chinese slang)
Old meaning   Chatting, holding a friendly conversation
New meaning   Getting together to form secret groups (Negative)

檢討 *Review*
Old meaning   Discuss and review
New meaning   Now only used in reference to confessing crimes against the State.

Changes in the spoken language have a profound effect on all literature—including the Bible—printed before the "liberation." Take, for example, the simple word *good* represented by the Chinese characters 良善. Today that adjective *good* is never applied to a person in China unless he is politically acceptable and has the government-approved family background. At least this is how it is used in all literature.

The Bible contains the verse: "Why callest thou me good —there is none good but God" (Luke 18:19). The current usage of this term in the Chinese Bible would then create a completely false impression of God. It would virtually make God a Communist.

An even more serious problem which the missionaries faced was the problem of illiteracy. As late as 1949, the year of "liberation," only 20 percent of the Chinese people could read and write. It was very difficult to teach God's Word to a people who could not read the Bible. Missionaries, seeing this need, had placed great emphasis on literacy programs and education. Perhaps more emphasis should have been placed on literacy and less on higher education, but that is debatable. What is not debatable is the fact that the contributions made by missionaries to the literacy and educational programs in China were considerable. Progress was very slow because of the conditions in the country, the lack of governmental backing, and the nature of the language. Literature has generally been the major method of spreading the Gospel throughout the world. In China, literature would only have limited value until the rate of literacy could be dramatically increased. Illiteracy was a major obstacle for the Christian missionary.

The Communists faced precisely the same obstacle. They realized the importance of combating illiteracy to achieve their twin objectives, the inculcation of socialist principles, and the creation of an industrial society.

Drastic action was called for. Having governmental control, they tackled the problem in a way the missionary never could. Massive literacy programs erupted throughout China. In spite of all the pressures a Communist régime is capable of generating, progress was very slow. Nine years after the Communist takeover the literacy rate among peasants in the fourteen-to-forty age group was still only 30 percent in some areas. In 1964, China's scholar-politician Guo Moruo (Juo Mo-jo) said, "For more than ten years we have been trying to eradicate illiteracy among the people, but our motherland is still a nation with masses of illiterates and semiliterates."

Experts assigned by the Maoists to study the reason literacy programs were not more successful came to the conclusion that the language itself was too difficult (missionaries had come to this same conclusion years before). The Language Reform Committee of the Communist Party decided that the written language must be simplified. This was a massive task and it met with strong opposition from the intellectuals (language reform had been unsuccessfully attempted before). Under the Communists the reforms were forced. First a list of 1,100 characters was discarded from use. Then a gradual program of language reform, starting with the use of 355 simplified characters, was carried out. This number was gradually increased until about one-fourth of all the characters in use had been simplified.

As a result virtually a new form of the centuries-old Chinese written language had been created. The Chinese written language is one of the most complicated and complex on earth. A simple Chinese typewriter contains about 6,000 characters, each one significantly different. There is no alphabet from which to form words. It is an ideographic (i.e. idea-depicting language). Each character is a separate creation of strokes, lines, and dots, which may range from just one stroke to almost forty strokes in a single character.

Simplification had been suggested during several periods of Chinese history—even as late as President Chiang Kai-Shek's time. Each time it was strongly opposed by the scholar class, who jealously guarded their privileged position which, to a large degree, was made possible by the complexity of the written language. The written language was beyond the grasp of the common man, and the scholars wanted to keep it that way. The average peasant had neither the time nor the opportunity to master such a complicated written language. Consequently, the rate of illiteracy was extremely high in China.

Can you imagine doing all your business correspondence by hand? This is certainly the case in China. Even today, no method faster than penmanship has been devised in the

Chinese language, apart from some sophisticated computer systems under development. The Chinese typewriter, with some 6,000 characters, is actually considerably slower than penmanship. However, to whatever degree the Communists could simplify the written language, at least to that degree it would speed up both education and business. After all, both the Koreans and the Japanese, who once used the Chinese characters, have developed simpler written languages.

This, then, became a high-priority project in the Chinese Communist scheme. It was no simple process. First, many scholars had to be imprisoned or sent to labor camps so that the task could proceed unopposed. Even without opposition it was a difficult and complex task. The simplification process has not been a mere random change here and there but a systematic scholarly endeavor. The result is a written language that is significantly different and easier to learn.

To one who has been educated in the old form, anything written in the new simplified characters is difficult if not impossible to understand. By way of illustration, imagine there was a Chinese character containing three strokes that resembled the letter "H" (there is no such Chinese character). Now to simplify it we remove one stroke and the character becomes "H." That symbol by itself would have absolutely no meaning to the person who has not been educated to the new form of the character. Thus the Simplified Script or "Mao Script" as it has been popularly called is virtually a new form of the written language.

The table will give just a few representative examples of how the characters have been simplified. On an average, one out of every four characters in common use has been simplified. After studying the changes, ask yourself this question: if you were educated to the old form of the characters, would you be able to read the Simplified Script? Answer—only by association in a sentence would there be any possibility of your "guesstimating" the meaning of the Simplified Script.

Old	No. of Strokes	Simplified Script	No. of Strokes
廠	15	厂	2
蔔	15	卜	2
義	13	义	3
豐	18	丰	4

In 1974 Asian Outreach published a completely new translation of the New Testament in the Simplified Script. The name of the traditional New Testament is 新約全書. In the Simplified Script we have given it the name 当代喜讯. We have found that many Chinese, educated in the old script, cannot decipher the meaning of the bottom four characters. This, then, will give some idea of the nature of the significant changes in the written language.

Apart from the simplification process, there have been other pervasive changes in the written language. The standard Chinese Bible since 1919 has been the Union Mandarin Version (U.M.V.). This is still a fine translation and is used throughout the Chinese world. Even in China itself it is the most beloved translation of the older generation of Christians. However, since that translation was revised there have been a number of language changes. Here are a few examples:

1. Only five kinds of punctuations are used in the U.M.V. Today, the Chinese language has adopted the complete international punctuation system, using fourteen different punctuation marks.

2. The U.M.V. makes no distinction between the adjective and the adverb 的. The Chinese now have two separate characters to denote adjective and adverb: 的, 地.
3. The U.M.V. used the pronoun 他 for *he, him, she, her,* and *it.* In present-day language usage, each of these latter four pronouns has its own distinctive Chinese character: 他, 她, 它, 牠.

There has been another change that makes today's Chinese distinctive. Before the "liberation" (1949) all Chinese books opened completely reverse to books in the West. Now all books in China open precisely the same as books in the West.

Before the "liberation," all Chinese writing descended vertically from the top of the page to the bottom and from the right to left. Now writing and printing in China are horizontal, from the left-hand side of the page to the right-hand side, as it is in the West. These significant visual changes certainly brand all books produced in the preliberation style.

Because of all these and other changes within China we began work in 1968 on a New Translation of the Bible into the Chinese language. Our target audience was primarily the youth, educated in the new language form, with virtually no understanding of Christianity. This translation in the Simplified Script, published in January 1980, is called *Dang Dai Xi Xun (Dang Dai Xi Xin).*

A Bible that was understood only by the older generation, the scholars and those educated before 1955, just was not enough. The Bible must be in the language of the majority of the people, hence this new communicative translation produced by Asian Outreach.

There are, at this writing, a variety of current ministries to the PRC. I will discuss these ministries in general terms and refer to some of the Christian groups who are involved. At present current ministries are largely related to literature and radio.

Literature.   For several years now there has been a steady movement of Christian literature into China. This has primarily taken the form of Bibles. Undoubtedly this had to take first priority. If little or no literature is available to the Christians of China then the Word of God is certainly the most needed and welcome.

Getting the Scriptures into China has been the work of many individuals and groups, literally around the world. Some have been working to encourage Hong Kong and Overseas Chinese Christians to take Bibles with them when they visit relatives in China. Some have worked at various border-crossing points in Asia to get the Scripture into China. Some have put Bibles into the hands of Communist Chinese who have been working in Africa building railroads. Others have visited Communist Chinese ships calling at ports around the world and distributed Scriptures to as many members of the crew as they could. Others have contacted the Chinese in embassies and in the United Nations. It has been a worldwide effort by a relatively small number of Christians. Many of the Scriptures used in these efforts have been in the Simplified Script.

Christians going into China have also taken small quantities of other Christian literature. We do know that one of the most wanted pieces of Chinese Christian literature has been, and is, *Streams in the Desert*. This is traditionally the second Bible in every Chinese Christian home. Asian Outreach has produced, in conjunction with OMS International, a new Simplified Script edition of this classic daily devotional. Up to now, demand has exceeded supply.

A group of Hong Kong young people felt compelled by the Lord to make a missionary journey to China. Among their belongings they prayerfully placed several copies of the New Testament in the Simplified Script and several copies of *Streams in the Desert*. Reaching their destination, they carefully distributed their precious gifts to Christians whom they met.

The Chinese Christians, mostly young people who had recently found Christ, said to the visitors who were about to return to Hong Kong, "Thank you for bringing the New Testament and the *Streams in the Desert*. You see," explained the Chinese Christians, "we do have a few Bibles and a few New Testaments among us. Most of these belong to older Christians who have had them since before 'liberation,' but we have no books that help us new Christians to understand the Bible. These daily devotions are just what we need. It teaches us to take a Bible verse every day and apply that verse to our daily lives. In this way we not only learn the Bible but we learn how the Bible speaks to us every day."

It may be difficult for us to sympathize with these new Christians. We have access to so much teaching, so many books, so much help in understanding God's Word. For them, *Streams in the Desert* is virtually a Bible commentary. As of this writing, little significant Christian literature is available in China's present language form. Work is progressing, however, on a number of significant projects.

Preparation of other literature is a current ministry to China and a vital one. As the door to China widens, and the pressure on the Church eases, the demand for extrabiblical Christian literature has increased. For this to be effective it should be in the Simplified Script. It should also be produced with an awareness of present language forms in use in China.

It is not just a matter of reprinting what is already available in Chinese. It is a whole new form of literature that must be produced to meet the needs of everyone from new converts to spiritual leaders in China. We should also be producing more preevangelistic literature that will open hearts for the Gospel. We need specifically designed evangelistic literature which takes into account the Marxist impact of the immediate past and the underlying humanism of the Chinese people. Asian Outreach has produced several booklets to help meet this need.

The old China approach is no longer valid. Literature developed for the Overseas Chinese is not really relevant. Producing a full range of new Christian literature for China could well be one of the greatest challenges of our time. Literature is an expensive process and there is virtually no way to recover the investment. It is a ministry in the deepest sense of the word, given with no thought of remuneration.

At this point it must be made clear that all the Chinese literature of Asian Outreach is made available, without charge, to anyone going into the Mainland. We are also making these complete Bibles, New Testaments, and Scripture portions available to other Christian organizations who we feel have a valid means of delivery to our target audience. These offers must obviously be qualified by the statement "as God provides." We can give only as God's people provide.

Research.   Another ministry that could be listed as a present ministry is China Research. This research must be undertaken to help us understand the situation as it relates to the church in China. We must know contemporary communication methods in China. We must meet the educational standard. We must assess our own effectiveness. A significant amount of research is underway by several groups in Hong Kong and around the world. Asian Outreach began its research program in 1968. Several joint projects are also underway. The aim of all our research efforts is to strengthen the church in China.

Radio.   Radio is definitely a current ministry in China. It is, as indicated earlier, a ministry that is becoming increasingly effective. The two groups that have specialized in this ministry, and without whom there would be no radio to China, deserve broad support. They are the Far East Broadcasting Company and Trans World Radio. Both provide powerful transmission facilities and produce some of the programming. The balance of the programming is produced by groups who are skilled at communicating to the mainland China audience. Some of those known to be producing effective programs for China are Overseas Radio and Television, The Christian and Missionary Alliance, and Asian Outreach.

During times of severe governmental pressure, radio was the only source of encouragement and spiritual food for many of China's Christians who listened in secret. Now that restrictions have been minimized, and the atmosphere has become more liberal, significant quantities of mail are being received from China in response to the radio ministries.

Before leaving the subject of current ministries, let me say that these are not highly publicized ministries, nor should they be. The less we call attention to these ministries at the present time, the better from the standpoint of penetration. The most effective ministries have been working diligently and quietly for some years. They are not novices, but neither have they been highly publicized. The basic position of the People's Republic of China is still one of atheistic antagonism to the Christian Gospel, although there are signs of a thaw. What is being done by Christian groups to help the Christians of China is not illegal but is definitely not appreciated by the Government. We hope the attitude of the Beijing (Peking) regime will soon change as a result of the new initiatives. Until it does we must be circumspect. This is not to say that absolutely no publicity should be permitted. There is certainly a necessity to generate the prayer and considerable financial support needed to make these present ministries possible. We must weigh these elements carefully in any publicity.

It is also true that some elements in the leadership of the Three Self Movement resent our efforts, claiming that they must be the only ones providing for the Church in China. We understand the difficult position they are in. But the task is simply too immense to be accomplished without the sympathetic and sensitive involvement of the Church around the world. This is how God intends His work to be done. Many pastors in the Three Self Movement agree with this position and gladly welcome low-profile endeavors.

The thought of revival among one-quarter of the population of planet earth is staggering. It is my personal conviction that the Church of Jesus Christ must be deeply involved now in preparation for that great revival. This, of course, is in addition to what the Holy Spirit Himself is doing now to prepare the people and the Church of China for revival. God, in His sovereignty, has certainly been working in China.

The Church is one body. The Church in China is a part of the universal body of Christ. We must be involved and concerned. We must be available. When one portion of the body is in need then the balance of the body must be ready to respond to that need.

Reaching into China must be distinguished from the efforts of the Church inside China. Both efforts must proceed with great vigor. We must "spare not," as Isaiah the Prophet commands us. We must work in harmony with

China's living Church. We must not impose our concepts. We must listen and respond in such a way that China's Church is strengthened without becoming either dependent or diverted from its own responsibilities.

18

West Meets East Again

What about a quotation from the late Chairman Mao that did not appear in the now defunct Little Red Book? "You Americans can go on withholding recognition of our government for 100 years, but I doubt if you can withhold it on the 101st year. One day the United States will have to establish diplomatic relations with us. When the Americans come to China then, and look around, they will find it too late for regrets. They would not find any friends here."

As it turned out, the United States withheld recognition for only thirty years. In the interim, however, the United States did not suffer, but China did. As for the allegation that Americans would find no friends in China when they returned, Chairman Mao was wrong again. Perhaps we can excuse him because it was a statement made in frustration and anger back in 1956. The fact is, Americans and Chinese celebrated the restoration of diplomatic relations in solemn old Beijing (Peking) by singing "God Bless America" and "Home on the Range." So much for the quotations of Chairman Mao.

Not only the government of China but the common people on the street were obviously delighted with normalization. The news blared from loudspeakers around Beijing (Peking). All over the People's Republic people gathered around radios and what television sets there were to hear Chairman Hua make the announcement that would change the course of history. Foreigners who talked to Chinese on the streets quickly sensed the general popularity of the announcement. The Yankees were coming back to a warm welcome. In fact, one of the posters on the "Wall of Democracy" read, "LOVE AMERICA!"

In view of the restoration of full diplomatic relations between China and the U.S., I would like to take a closer look at what this could mean for world evangelism.

Although most Western countries already had diplomatic ties with Beijing (Peking), this rapprochement with the leader of the capitalist world is considered to be the single most significant event in China's recent history. It certainly is a significant event on the world missions scene.

Born of an American father and a Canadian mother and with lifetime ties with the people of China, I am well aware of America's involvement with China in the past. Perhaps my somewhat intimate knowledge of the China of yesterday and of today, and of the special qualities that make up the American people, qualify me to make some observations and perhaps even a few suggestions. What I have to say about Americans will also be relevant, to some degree, to all Westerners. Although this chapter highlights America's role, it really is concerned with the West's relationship with China. To the Chinese we are all foreigners.

The Chinese people as a whole have a deep-seated respect for Americans.

I personally experienced this almost uncanny respect not only as a boy growing up in old China but as a visitor to the New China. Despite thirty years of official animosity and anti-American propaganda, I found the respect was still there, even before the restoration of diplomatic relations. Conversing in Mandarin during a post-Mao visit to the Mainland, I was inevitably asked by people I met on the street what country I was from. With me was my wife Janet, a Canadian, and two Swedish Christian brothers. I would introduce them and tell what country they were from. When they heard that I was an American, it immediately triggered curiosity. This happened, incidentally, before normalization and while their government was still carrying on its anti-American campaign.

It was not merely interest the common people of China were expressing but an obvious respect. The difference is easy to detect. Deserved or not, the respect was there. It was as though the Chinese people had paid no attention whatever to Mao's thirty years of belligerent anti-American propaganda. In fact, judging by the jubilation in Beijing (Peking) at the resumption of diplomatic relations, you would think China had just defeated America. Mao had threatened to "bury the capitalists." Now the Chinese were joyously embracing them.

It is my opinion that Americans will become prime factors in China's modernization drive now that diplomatic relations have been normalized, not primarily because of America's famed, but not always appreciated, aggressive salesmanship, nor because America has much of the technical know-how that China seeks. I am referring instead to the unique place America holds in the minds of the Chinese people. I can't explain it, but I know it is there. After the normalization, I talked with an Australian girl who had been studying language in China. She said that after normalization she was often stopped on the street and embraced as an American. Naturally she didn't think it was one bit funny. Her country had recognized China years before. She personally had resided in China for several years in language study but had never received that kind of a welcome. She said she was disgusted with the way the Chinese were "fawning over all Americans, or anyone who looked like he might be an American."

No one is more aware than I of the fact that Americans don't deserve such respect. The record of our past dealings with China is definitely unenviable. We were very much a part of the colonialism that preceded, and to some degree triggered, the Communist revolution. We virtually abandoned China to the Communists. We have much to be ashamed of. Nevertheless, there does exist an exceptional bond between the Chinese and American people.

This feeling towards Americans, which borders on affection, was again made clear to me by a phone call received in our Hong Kong office. Hours earlier the world had been surprised by the announcement of the restoration of diplomatic ties with U.S. On the other end of the line was a Communist official, resident in Hong Kong, with whom my associate, David Wang, and I had brief contact several years ago. After introducing himself, he asked about our families. Then he said, "Isn't it wonderful we can now be real friends." The term he used for 'real' meant genuine. His voice was animated. His joy was obvious. "Isn't it wonderful we can now be *real* friends." There was a world of meaning behind that statement. Here was a Communist official overjoyed that once more we could be *genuine* friends. This was his way of saying, "We have always been friends, but now we can be friends openly and with government approval." He was obviously delighted.

The official extended to us a warm invitation to visit China and offered to assist us in any way he could. The big surprise was yet to come however. He closed off the phone conversation by wishing us "Merry Christmas." Mind boggling! This Christian term has long been taboo to the Communists. They avoid it in any way they can. The Communist

China Products stores in Hong Kong put up big signs to take advantage of Christmas shopping but the signs read, "Do your winter-festival shopping early." Now here was a Communist official wishing us "Merry Christmas!" I don't mind telling you it was a thrill to hear those two words.

There is no doubt that the Chinese people generally look on Americans with a degree of admiration and affection. This will be reflected in their attitude to all Westerners. Let's try harder to be worthy.

I see normalization as a positive step for the spread of the Gospel in China.

There are at least five reasons why the normalization of the U.S.-China relations will hasten the spread of the Gospel in China:

1. It will create a new openness on the part of the Chinese people to new concepts and ideas. This will inevitably make it easier to make Christ known.

2. Some of the Westerners who are going to be involved in China's modernization drive will be committed Christians. Their lives and their lips will speak for Christ.

3. Chinese students are studying in our universities in rapidly increasing numbers as China strives for modernization. It has been repeatedly demonstrated that students isolated from their cultural milieu are more easily won to Christ. These students returning to China as Christians will be in a position of influence in a developing country. Then, of course, some Westerners will be studying, and others teaching, in China. Currently China is searching for teachers of English. It is my hope that significant numbers of these teachers and students going to China will be Christians.

4. Now that diplomatic ties have been restored, Christians will no longer tend to look on China as a closed door. This will dramatically alter the attitude of Western Christians toward

China. A word of caution here. Americans tend to overreact. We need to understand the door is only slightly ajar.

5. The religious barrier Mao set up will have to come down if China is to continue good relations with the Western world. The possibility of Western missionaries returning to China is now no longer such a remote possibility. The only question is whether this would be advisable.

We must work harder this time at separating the Gospel of Christ from our Western culture.

Many of the mistakes of past efforts to evangelize China stem from failure to segregate Christianity from the culture of the missionary. We did not permit Christianity to blossom in the cultural soil of the hearers. Such a task is not easy. It requires intense, conscious effort. America is such a vast country that we tend to live in cultural isolation from the rest of the world. The too often accurate image of the Ugly American is one that we must try harder to obliterate. What we see in the mirror may not be what others see when they look at us. It's what others see that is important.

Perhaps the following paragraphs from an astute Chinese journalist will help. Mr. Chang Kuo-sin writes regularly for a Hong Kong English-language newspaper. He knows both Chinese and Americans well. Remember, this is a sympathetic Chinese writing:

"In seeking normalization of relations with the United States, even to the extent of humbling its Socialism to American Capitalism, Beijing's (Peking's) thoughts and hopes are on deriving benefits from American finance, American science, and American technology, to help in its Four Modernizations, importing them without at the same time having to import the less desirable or undesirable parts of the American system.

"What Beijing (Peking) has probably not fully realized or reckoned with is that as in the case of package tours, the

American system also comes in a package, the undesirable coming with the desirable, the vices coming with the virtues. In opening a whole new vista of potentialities, normalization has brought a whole new range of hazards.

"Restoration of friendship with the Americans cannot be done on a selective basis. It would be a mistake for Beijing (Peking) to think it could be a question of priorities. Beijing (Peking) has to take it or leave it, as it comes. Once the door is opened, it is opened to all Americans, and the Americans, known for their freewheeling and devil-may-care aggressiveness and expansiveness and never known to stand on ceremony, may come in droves strong enough to overwhelm any possible restraining Chinese reservations.

"The ugly Americans will be coming with the beautiful Americans, some willing to work acquiescently with the Chinese whatever they may think of the Chinese ideology, and some probably continuing to grow with contempt for the Communist system of government, but all with the innate American hatred of any form of authoritarian control."

The question is, "Can we Western Christians humble ourselves and become servants for Christ's sake?" This is what the apostle Paul was talking about in Romans. "Don't do anything that will cause criticism against yourself even though you know what you do is right. After all, the important thing for us as Christians is not what we eat or drink" (Rom. 14:16-17 LB). The apostle Paul is warning us against letting our customs—which in themselves may not be wrong —destroy someone for whom Christ died. It is our Christian graces that must be evident, not our Americanism or foreignness. One, we know, will attract; the other could possibly repel.

As we prayerfully approach China, we must not be soapbox orators shouting to a lost world. The Gospel must certainly be communicated differently than Coca Cola, Winston cigarettes, or even Singer sewing machines. We are not commercial purveyors of Christianity. We cannot allow ourselves to be loudmouthed hucksters. We are "witnesses of the things we have seen and we have heard." We have a "story to tell to the nations"—not a product of Madison Avenue to market to the nation of China. We must speak out of love from personal experience. What China has done for us must be the cutting edge, but let us not equate that with material prosperity. It is the salvation of our souls and the joy of the Lord in our lives that we need to communicate, not the high standard of living in the West.

The message we have for China is that Christ did for us what Chairman Mao failed to do for them. Christ has made us a new creation. Old things have passed away and all things have become new. The Chinese will soon discern between reality and pretense. The message of Jesus had relevance to the world of His day because He lived where they lived and spoke out of love to the area of their immediate need.

Let us approach China humbly and prayerfully. There may not be a third chance. The coming of Christ cannot be far away.

Let us guard against rash, ill-prepared efforts to evangelize China.

It is already evident that many Christian groups in America and the West are rushing to get on the China bandwagon. I shudder to think of "China Evangelism" becoming the new evangelical fad. China is a magic word that could generate more money even than starving children, and that's saying a lot. For this reason alone, some groups who until recently demonstrated little or no interest in earth's largest unevangelized mission field will now be wanting to immediately capitalize on China's new open door. I cannot conceive of any greater potential for tragedy.

I would advise extreme caution before becoming involved with any hastily conceived China thrust. There will no doubt be many such endeavors, but they could do more harm than good. This has already been the case with some.

Christians need to be good stewards of the money God has entrusted to them. Investigate! Don't be afraid to ask questions!

It should be obvious to any thinking person that thorough research and preparation must precede any significant endeavor to evangelize China. The possible pitfalls are numerous. The potential rewards for eternity are enormous. Let's not get involved with ill-prepared efforts on behalf of China. The souls of millions are at stake.

Imprudent actions on the part of perhaps well-meaning but ill-prepared and ill-advised groups, or even individuals, could cause the door to China to slam shut almost before it's fully open.

China's form of government is still dictatorship. We are dealing with a government with a strong Marxist orientation. China's expressed goal is still a socialist state. Christianity does not fit into their present plans. They certainly have the power to tighten the screws at any time. Furthermore, the political climate in China will not be entirely stable for sometime to come. China has known very few periods of stable government through its long history. The situation remains volatile. The extreme swings of recent years are an indication of what might happen again. Let us make sure, as much as is possible, that no rash moves on the part of Christian groups force the government's hand. The door is now ajar. Caution must be exercised lest we destroy a God-given, long-prayed-for opportunity.

Westerners will find it very difficult to relate to the way of life in China.

The gap between the Western way of life and that of China is a yawning chasm of stupendous dimensions. Let's not forget that we are the ones who must cross that canyon and adjust and relate to their way of life. We have not been commissioned by Christ to change their culture or interfere with their political system.

The pervasive atmosphere in China is one of secrecy and fear. Can we, who come from the cradle of liberty, relate to that? The contrast between the permissiveness of Western society and the highly controlled nature of Chinese society will be enormous. Are we prepared to see the values in a less permissive society? China is a poor country. Can we, who come from a society of exaggerated materialism, refrain from imposing our standards on a people who have learned contentment with far less? Can we understand that the Chinese people, for the sake of mere survival, have learned to say whatever was necessary to say? What they say may or may not be what they know or believe to be true. Survival hinged on saying what they were supposed to say. This will not change rapidly. This has been their way of life all through the Communist era.

The Church in China, too, has learned to function in an atmosphere of secrecy. Do not expect them to change overnight. Christians in China had to be secretive just to survive. Can we learn to function in harmony with their still highly controlled world? Will we, for the sake of publicity, be inclined to betray the confidence they may choose to place in us? Whatever the cost, Westerners in China must learn to

relate to the situation as it is. If the Christians of China can
survive and function under those difficult circumstances,
then as long as Western Christians are guests in their country we must understand and relate. It won't be easy.

Americans cannot be proud of the price our government
paid for rapprochement with China.

We gave in to all the demands that Beijing (Peking) made
in relation to Taiwan and its seventeen million people, who
had been our long-time allies. The abrogation of our treaty
with Taiwan adds yet another black page to our history
books. America's credibility is now in tatters.

As one bitter China expert put it, "By cravenly yielding to
Beijing's (Peking's) demand and failing to obtain Beijing's
(Peking's) explicit promise not to annex Taiwan by force,
President Carter has made the seventeen million people in
Taiwan hostage to the Chinese Communists. The harm
Carter caused to the freedom and rights of the Taiwanese
people makes his human-rights campaign a laughing stock."

The nation that had promised never to abandon South
Vietnam and Taiwan has now abandoned both. Expediency
has once again been allowed to prevail over morality. This
kind of thing has been happening with shocking regularity
in recent years. Have we, as a government, lost our moral
foundations? We have flagrantly broken the golden rule by
doing to Taiwan what we would not want anyone to do to
us. Let's not be surprised if the seeds we sow someday bear
fruit.

Taiwan and China will learn to live with each other.

To be fair and accurate, China refused to sign a guarantee
not to attack Taiwan because, as they pointed out, how
could they agree not to attack their own country or territory? Their refusal was not necessarily because at some
point they intend to attack Taiwan. This cannot be assumed.

The heat of passion generated by the Beijing (Peking)-Washington ties will eventually cool off. Even the head of Taiwan's Central News Agency, Mr. P. O. Tang, has stated that the goals of the Mainland in respect to modernization "correspond closely with those of Taiwan and only the method of reaching those goals differ."

More than one China observer, including this one, has suggested the possibility of some sort of autonomous status for Taiwan or even a Hong Kong-type role.

Weeks after normalization, Vice Premier Deng told Taiwan they could remain an autonomous part of China and keep their armed forces as long as the people of Taiwan wanted it that way. It will be difficult for Taiwan's leader, Chiang Ching-kuo, to accept reconciliation with his father's dreaded enemy. This may be the greatest stumbling block. Some have suggested Taiwan might look to the Soviet Union now that it has been virtually abandoned by the U.S. This looks extremely remote in spite of, or perhaps even because of, Chiang's twelve years of residence and study in the Soviet Union. Taiwan's hatred of Communism will not permit such a move no matter how attractive it might appear on the surface.

Taiwan, at the time of writing, is turning a deaf ear to all of Beijing's (Peking's) initiatives. Beijing (Peking) will have a hard time convincing Taiwan of its sincerity. In the meantime, Taiwan is a strong, largely self-sufficient nation. Her economy is considerably stronger than that of the PRC. Taiwan's air force and navy are decidedly superior. Although outnumbered eight to one, its troops have superior armament and the advantage of watery isolation. Even apart from the relative strength of the Armed Forces, I see the possibility of a military confrontation as being remote, unless Taiwan makes some rash move. Taiwan and Beijing (Peking) will eventually reach an understanding—perhaps sooner than most expect.

I would caution Westerners against too much euphoria.

It seems strange that I, of all people, should be issuing such a caution. I have been writing and preaching about the possibility of China reopening for twenty years. Actual preparations for this day have been underway for over twenty years in the organization I founded. I believed that China would reopen, both from my study of the Scriptures and from my study of the China scene. My faith has been rewarded!

The basis of my suggested caution is the historically difficult task of governing the massive nation of China. The great helmsman Mao, or any old helmsman, may turn the wheel, but the massive ship of state does not always respond to directions. History has demonstrated that China may be conquered but not easily controlled. It's not a foregone conclusion that the normalization of relations with the United States will lead to the kind of situation that Americans will be pleased with or even that Deng will relish. Progress will be slow. Deng may be a man in a hurry but that doesn't mean that everyone else in China is. Real progress may be agonizingly slow.

The road ahead has many rough places before the desire of the people is realized. The Chinese are above all a patient people—Americans are noted for their impatience. This alone will be cause for friction. Progress in China must be measured in years, not in days. The rapidity of change in the past months would tend to weaken that statement. Given the record of history, I still believe it is true.

The symbolic placard, "Yankee Come Back," has been hung by the Beijing (Peking) government and greeted with enthusiasm by many of the nation's people. This alone marks a significant watershed. What is past is past! Samuel Johnson wisely observed, "The future is purchased by the present." We must carefully weigh every move we Westerners make at the present time and in the future. The former General Motors' great Charles F. Kettering put it this way: "I expect to spend the rest of my life in the future, so I want to be reasonably sure of what kind of future it's going to be. This is my reason for planning." Americans and all Westerners by their actions and reactions today will play a significant role in China's future. At present the future of China evangelism is a shining white page. Let's not be guilty of staining that page because of carelessness or a lack of prayerful planning.

19

The Contemporary Challenge

The hearts of Christians around the world throb with the compulsion of the Great Commission. Visions of gigantic plans dance in the hearts and minds of those who contemplate the massive task of evangelization of China.

Christians worldwide are wondering how they can participate. Well-meaning but tragic plans are being devised by those too far removed from the situation to be realistic. It is time to ask, What is the contemporary challenge?

The spiritual harvest now being garnered in China has been in preparation for a considerable period of time. During the last two decades the Chinese Communists have overpoliticized Chinese society. The people are not only completely weary of it all but a strong backlash is also occurring. There is unquestionably a spiritual vacuum. Resistance to attempts at new political "struggles" will almost certainly be stubborn if not overt.

The attempt to reform the minds of Chinese society will, in the long run, backfire as men instinctively reach out for truth and God. This is clearly evident by the number of young people turning to Christ inside China. In his comprehensive study, *Religion in Chinese Society*, C. K. Yang, in an obvious understatement, pointed out that Communism would "probably be unable to cope with all social and personal crises that may arise." He predicted that if this were so then Communism would have to develop "permanent toleration of theistic religion." I believe this is happening in China.

Long ago Heinrich Heine saw the coming of Communism into world prominence. In 1842 he called it the dread antagonist that is "destined for a great if temporary role in the modern tragedy." Then he foresaw a theistic backlash setting in. He asked, "Will the religious doctrines of the past rise in all countries in desperate resistance—and will perhaps this attempt constitute the third act?" I believe it will.

Severe blows have been struck at China's non-Christian religions. How destructive these blows have been is not yet clear. A missionary in Hudson Taylor's time called them "fortresses erected by satanic art to impede the progress of Christianity." He looked forward in faith to the day when these fortresses would be overthrown. Although the religions, based on superstitions, do seem to be surfacing again it is highly unlikely that they will regain their former prominence.

So the stage was being set over the past thirty years. Now the curtain has gone up to reveal an unexpected scenario. The Chinese Church, without outside help, is experiencing a greater harvest than the missionary era could have even imagined. The Chinese Church has come of age. A new day has dawned for them as well as for us.

It is imperative that we almost completely reverse our traditional thinking. Many are still thinking in terms of taking the initiative and sending missionaries in—of being the spearhead of the evangelistic thrust. This approach ignores reality and must be abandoned. Stanley Mooneyham, facing up to the prospects for the evangelization of China, wrote of the Chinese Church, "It might be more appropriate to respectfully ask to sit at their feet than to stand in their pulpits." This calls for a 360-degree change in our present attitude.

Under no foreseeable circumstances should leadership in China evangelism be in the hands of any but the Chinese Church itself—and I mean by that, *the Church inside Mainland China.* The days of an imperialistic approach to China evangelism must be confined to the past. Even the Chinese Church outside the Mainland has become too foreign, in my opinion, to assume a role of leadership. China is now virtually an unknown "foreign" country to them. The participation of the Chinese Church outside the Mainland may be welcomed, but theirs must not be the key role. The leadership must come from within China's own living Church.

The most successful evangelism ever done in China has been done by the Chinese Christians themselves without even the slightest assistance from those of us in the West. This is now a fact. Undoubtedly it is difficult for us to adjust to this reality. We are so used to being at the forefront of evangelism. God, in His wisdom, has decided that in China, at least for the present and foreseeable future, it is the Chinese Christians that must assume the major share of this responsibility.

The evangelization of China in this generation has begun and the West is largely excluded from participation. Even the involvement of the Chinese of the Diaspora is limited. The mantle has fallen on China's tribulation-purged witnesses. It is highly improbable that any other witnesses from anywhere else on planet earth could be as effective as these homegrown evangels. The record of the last ten years underscores their divinely enabled effectiveness.

Certain features of evangelism in China need to be noted. I see several noteworthy aspects that have contributed and will contribute to its productivity.

The single most important factor in any spiritual ingathering is God's timing. It is possible to pinpoint some of the factors that prepared China for a spiritual awakening. It is also possible to delineate some of the factors God is using today. But God's timing overshadows all other considerations and efforts. This appears to be God's time for China.

A copy of the new Chinese Bible.

The Holy Spirit sovereignly moving on the hearts of men and women produces a hunger for God and conviction of sin. Without that divine factor there can be no spiritual harvest. Consequently, we must assume that God, in His sovereign wisdom, has determined that He will at this time pour out His Holy Spirit on earth's most populous nation. This may well be a significant part of God's end-time strategy. If that is true then the present spiritual harvest in China may be an indication that Christ's return is imminent.

This outpouring of the Holy Spirit is occurring while China is still largely isolated from the rest of the world. This is not accidental nor incidental. God knows what He is doing. This is His world. He is in complete charge. Our responsibility is to fit into God's plans.

Years of enforced isolation have, for the first time, guaranteed nearly perfect cultural identification for Chinese evangelistic endeavors. Too long evangelism in China carried a distinctly foreign flavor. This must not be permitted to reoccur, particularly in China where such importance has been and will be placed on things distinctly Chinese. The Gospel communicated by Chinese evangels in a Chinese setting is important to today's Chinese climate. This does not totally eliminate the need for, or the effectiveness of, a Christian witness by visitors from the West. Such a witness can be especially influential to one's own peer group. But Christianity must never again appear as a Western importation. Christianity came from the East to the West. It is this cultural identity that must be stressed particularly in China, given the unfortunate historical record of early endeavors. Only the Chinese themselves, isolated from the West, can do this.

There is one feature of Chinese evangelism that I long to see. This is the Chinese people accepting responsibility for carrying the Gospel outside the boundaries of their Jerusalem.

It is too early yet to detect whether the Chinese have broken out of the traditional mold which has stifled cross-cultural Chinese missionary endeavor in the past. It has never been known as a missionary church. A world vision has seldom emerged in the past. Their own family-oriented culture and the failure of most missionaries to proclaim the responsibilities of the Great Commission developed a church that was interested only in the conversion of the Han race. Evangelism directed to those outside their own race would be a very welcome development in China's Church. Admittedly this would be most difficult given the present situation. However, it is a development that would indicate the maturation of China's Church.

What we can be sure of is that China's Church will be a witnessing Church dedicated to sharing the gospel with their countrymen. The most massive evangelism effort ever undertaken in China is now underway. It is indigenous evangelism.

Personal evangelism is and will continue to be a principal method of evangelism. China's Church has developed effective personal witnessing under most difficult circumstances. It is also true that personal evangelism lends itself to the development of the family-oriented concept of Christian fellowships such as are common in China. This means of evangelism will not have to wait for a complete reversal of governmental policy and will continue to accelerate as opportunity affords. Most forms of mass evangelism are not available to them. Personal evangelism will remain the cornerstone of Chinese evangelism.

The Chinese must be one of the most print-conscious people on earth. The unprecedented massive use of the printed page during the Mao régime, and the high percentage of newly literate coupled with the traditional Chinese respect for literature, make this a reality. Those of us who have taken small quantities of Christian literature into China can

China's church will be a witnessing church, dedicated to sharing the gospel with their countrymen.

testify to an insatiable hunger for literature on the part of non-Christians as well as Christians.

The current shortage of Christian literature in China is regrettable. Relatively small quantities are once again being produced, some by the Three Self Movement who are able to obtain permission and some supplies from government stocks. Their Bibles and Bible Correspondence Courses that we have seen contain no extra-biblical material. We have also seen literature produced by other Christian groups, usually local churches that somehow have access to supplies and equipment. Often the quantity is quite small. Some literature is being produced and reproduced by small ditto-type reproduction one shoot at a time. Hand copied literature is still fairly common.

By far the most significant quantities have been produced by Christian groups outside of China whose supplies, equipment, and finance are more readily available. This is seen as a temporary measure until such time as there is sufficient freedom and opportunity to produce the massive quantities needed by China's rapidly expanding Christian community.

Virtually all Christian literature inside China was destroyed during the "ten terrible years." Christians must start all over again to produce everything from Scriptures to theological tomes. The demand for literature is being heard distinctly above the understandable protestations of the Three Self Movement that they are self-sufficient. For instance, supplies of Bibles in some cities are reaching an acceptable level, but the adjacent countryside receives little or no literature. The more remote the area, the more limited the supplies. Another complicating factor is the extremely rapid growth of the church in the rural areas. Their needs are equally acute.

Literature has definitely become a very significant factor in Chinese evangelism and in the witnessing of the new believers.

The Bible, not particular creeds or denominations, will be the major rallying point of the Church and the focus of its evangelism. A major characteristic of China's great pastors and evangelists even before 1949 was that they were Bible centered. They preached the *Word*. The fact that the Chinese Church has been denied the physical possession of the Bible for so long will serve only to increase their emphasis on the Bible. Having their Bibles taken from them will not only increase their appetite for God's Word but will also serve to emphasize the staying power and the keeping power of the Word of God. God's Word has become their most valued possession. The Bible will most certainly be the heart of all their evangelistic endeavors.

Older Christians who somehow preserved their Bibles from Red Guard destruction by plastering them in their mud walls, or burying them, or in some other way retaining them, value the Scriptures as few others can. The younger believers have experienced very great difficulty in obtaining a copy of the Scriptures, which emphasizes the intrinsic value of the Scriptures. Without question the Bible is the focal point for the vast majority of China's believers.

The Chinese have never been known as shallow thinkers. Decades of satanic attack, however, have forced Chinese Christians to probe even deeper to find firm foundations for their faith. Either they have found the foundation or they have been inundated by the raging storm. The houses built on sand have long since collapsed. It can therefore be predicted that theirs will be responsible evangelism striving to reach beyond emotions to the fountainhead of human emotion. A man must be led to the rock because storms are inevitable.

Suffering and persecution have created within the core of the Chinese Church qualities and depths that spring from no other source. For this reason Christians fleeing the Mainland frequently express their keen disappointment with the shallowness of the Church they have found outside.

The Chinese Church will speak to their world with profound conviction and understanding, no mere shouting from the housetops but a meaningful anointed confrontation with human hearts. Like the early Christians they will speak with authority.

Unquestionably a new day has dawned for China's Church. Out of the purging fires of relentless persecution is emerging a church that is vastly different from anything seen in China before. From what I know of that church, I believe that God is preparing a people who will gladly give their all to proclaim the Gospel of Christ We, their brethren, must equal their dedication and prepare ourselves to meaningfully answer their call for specific assistance.

Into the vacuum created by sterile Communism there has come a nationwide thirst for God and reality. The result is one of the great spiritual awakenings in China's history. We must stand behind China's Christians with the spiritual undergirding of prayer. We must recognize the cultural maturation of China's Church and not permit our culture to again infiltrate and thus deform a church that has, at great price, become truly indigenous. We must recognize that Satan will not easily surrender China's millions. Consequently theirs is a spiritual battle not with flesh and blood but with spiritual forces, unseen but potent. This is where we can be involved on a daily basis. The battle is now raging in the heavens. Warriors are urgently needed.

China's Church is far short of perfection. It is also critically short of pastors, teachers and Biblical literature. The present atmosphere of relative freedom may well be a greater challenge than the days of persecution. But what cannot be denied is that into the spiritual vacuum created by sterile Communism there has come a nationwide search for

God and reality. China is experiencing a spiritual awakening, an awakening unprecedented in China's intriguing
history. This is the contemporary challenge.

Spelling Guide

To make it easier for the reader to learn the new Pinyin spelling of Chinese names and places, we have listed the new spelling along with the old Wade-Giles system.

Wade-Giles	Pinyin	Wade-Giles	Pinyin
Amoy	Xiamen	Lee Han-wen	Li Hanwen
Anwei	Anhui	Li Lien-ying	Li Lianying
Canton	Guangzhou	Lin Piao	Lin Biao
Chai Lun	Cai Lun	Lin Tse-hsu	Lin Zexu
Chang-on	Changan	Li Po	Li Bai
Chekiang	Zhejiang	Liu Shao-chi	Liu Shaoqi
Chen Po-ta	Chen Boda	Mao Tse-tung	Mao Zedong
Cheung Ching	Zhang Qian	Nanking	Nanjing
Chiang Ch'ing	Jiang Qing	Ningpo	Ningbo
Ch'in	Qin	P'an Ku	Pan Gu
Ching Tien-ying	Jing Tianying	Peking	Beijing
Ch'ing	Qing	Pu-tung-hua	Putonghua
Chou	Zhou	Shantung	Shandong
Chou En-lai	Zhou Enlai	Shih	Shi
Chung Kuo	Zhong Guo	Shih Huang Ti	Shi Huang Di
Dang Dai Xi Xin	Dang Dai Xi Xun	Sinkiang	Xinjiang
Foochow	Fuzhou	Soochow	Suzhou
Fukien	Fujian	Sung	Song
Hangchow	Hangzhou	Sun Tzu	Sun-tzu
Hankow	Hankou	Sun Yat-sen	Sun Yi-xian
Han-tsu	Han Zu	Szechuan	Sichuan
Honan	Henan	T'ai-p'ing t'ien-kuo	Taiping Tianguo
Hui Shih	Hui Shi	Teng Hsiao-ping	Deng Xiaoping
Hung Hsiu-ch'üan	Hong Xiu Quan	Tientsin	Tianjin
I Ho Ch'uan	Yi He Quan	Ting	Ding
Juo Mo-jo	Guo Moruo	Tsinghua	Qinghua
Kansu	Gansu	Tsingtao	Qingdao
Kao-tsung	Gaozong	Tu Fu	Du Fu
Kiaochow	Jiaozhou	Tzu Hsi	Ci Xi
Kuomintang	Guomindang	Wang Ming-tao	Wang Mingdao
Kuo Mo-jo	Guo Mo-jo	Ye-su Chia-Ting	Yesu Jiating
Kwangsi	Guangxi	Yuan Shih-kai	Yuan Shi-Kai
Kwangtung	Guangdong	Yunan	Yunnan
Kwon Yu	Guan Yu		